Healing the
Trauma
of Abuse

a women's workbook

Mary Ellen Copeland, M.A., M.S.
Maxine Harris, Ph.D.

New Harbinger Publications, INC.

Publisher's Note

Distributed in Canada by Raincoast Books.

Copyright © 2000 by   Mary Ellen Copeland and Maxine Harris
New Harbinger Publications, Inc.
5674 Shattuck Avenue
Oakland, CA 94609

The drawings in topic 3, by nina Reimer, were originally published in *Our Bodies, Ourselves for the New Century* (Boston Women's Health Collective, New York: Simon and Schuster, 1999) and are reprinted wih permission of the Boston Women's Health Collective.

Cover design © by Lightbourne Images
Edited by Donna Long
Text design by Michele Waters

Library of Congress Card Catalog Number: 99-75294
ISBN 157224-199-3 Paperback

Printed in the United States of America

New Harbinger Publications' Web site address: www.newharbinger.com

05   04   03

10   9   8   7   6

To the courageous women at Community Connections who shared their stories

—M.H.

To Laurie Smith and Judy Young in honor of their persistence and bravery in addressing issues of trauma and abuse in their lives

—M.E.C.

Contents

Part 3 Creating Life Changes

Part 4 Closing Rituals

Before You Begin

This workbook is a practical, step-by-step guide through the recovery and healing process for women who have experienced sexual, emotional, or physical abuse in childhood and/or adulthood. The workbook is based on an approach to trauma recovery developed by Maxine Harris and clinicians at Community Connections, a private, not-for-profit mental health agency in Washington, D.C. The community of women who developed the model included some who had experienced trauma themselves. An instructional manual for clinicians, *Trauma Recovery and Empowerment: A Clinician's Guide for Working with Women in Groups* (New York: Free Press, 1998), lays out the model in detail and forms the basis for this workbook.

If you were traumatized either as a child or as an adult, you may not be aware of the effect that it is having on your life. Or you may be aware of the effects and not know what to do about them. Perhaps you've tried unsuccessfully to relieve the effects of the trauma.

Whether you can remember any abuse or not, if you answer yes to some of the following questions, taking the time to work through the exercises in this workbook may help you feel good about yourself, be the way you want to be, and do the things you want to do in your life.

1. Do you feel sad, depressed, and empty? Does accomplishing small tasks seem almost impossible? Is it very hard, even impossible, for you to manage your home and pursue a career? Do you feel as though you are totally incompetent—that you can never do anything right, that you are worthless and hopeless? Do you feel that life is not worth living?

2. Are you angry and easily provoked much of the time? Do you drive too fast, scream too loud, and drink too much? Do you rebel against rules and regulations? Do you commit crimes to get the things you feel you need and deserve? Do you sometimes have to commit crimes to protect yourself against further abuse? Do you sometimes feel like mistreating your children and others you love?

3. Have you been diagnosed as having a serious mental illness? Have you been treated with medications or even hospitalized—and still felt you weren't getting the help you needed?

4. Do you sometimes feel unconnected to your body? Do you have periods of time that you can't remember—hours or days? Do images of bad things that have happened to you in the past keep coming into your mind?

5. Do you always feel tense and alert—like you can never relax?

If some of these questions describe the way you feel or act most of time, you may want to continue reading.

How Can This Workbook Help You?

- This workbook will lead you on a healing journey that will:

- Teach you how the emotional, physical, and sexual abuse you experienced in the past is connected to the way you feel and act now.

- Help you understand that your current symptoms are ways of trying to cope with unbearable trauma.

- Introduce you to effective problem-solving strategies to replace old strategies that have been destructive.

- Help you develop skills in assertiveness, self-advocacy, self-management, and successful relationship building.

- Educate you about female sexuality and help you develop a positive view of yourself as a woman.

- Discover and connect you with past experiences, feelings, and insights.

- Give you the opportunity to experience a sense of adequacy and resolution as you face difficult issues from the past, learn to trust your own perceptions about reality, and understand the validity of these perceptions.

How Do I Know if I'm Ready?

The decision about whether you should do this work and when you should begin is up to you. No one else can make this decision for you. You must be in charge of your own healing process in every way.

You will know you are ready to do this work if:

- You really want to do it.

- You feel inside yourself (intuitively) that it is the right thing to do.

- You are tired of living with the effects of the trauma—low self-esteem, fear, panic attacks, flashbacks, dissociation, anxiety, depression, and/or unsuccessful relationships.

This may not be the right time to begin this work if:

- You are trying to get out of an abusive relationship.

- There are other big changes going on in your life, such as a divorce or a close relative with a terminal illness.

- You are trying to heal from a major illness or surgery.

- You are in an addiction-rehabilitation program.

I feel I am ready to begin working on recovering from the effects of trauma in my life.

_____ Yes

_____ No

If you answered Yes, read through the following guidelines before beginning this workbook.

Guidelines

1. You may have been living with the effects of traumatic or bad experiences in your life for a long time. Perhaps you feel you can never get past these effects. However, many people who have experienced trauma get over its bad effects and do what they want with their lives. Keep in mind that from time to time something may remind you of the trauma and some of the effects may return, but with the help of this book you will learn how to deal with these effects without having them turn into a bad situation or a crisis.

2. You are always the person in charge. The readings, exercises, and activities here are _suggestions_ for how you can recover from traumatic or bad experiences. It is always up to you to choose what you do. If doing something doesn't feel right to you, don't do it!

3. This is a workbook. It belongs to you personally and was designed to be written in, because the book itself and the things you write in it will become an important part of your healing journey. Writing in a book may be difficult for you at first, but hopefully you'll soon do so freely and easily.

   Because this is your book and no one else is going to look at it or read it unless you ask them to, there are some things you don't have to worry about: neatness, staying in the margins (you can write in the margins, on the cover, or _anywhere_ else you want to write!), spelling, grammar, punctuation, and word usage—if it sounds right to you it's right.

4. All of us learn in different ways—some of us through reading, others by hearing, feeling, writing, or doing. Some of us learn most easily when we are moving around, others when we are sitting quietly. Some of us like background music or noise when we are learning. Some prefer quiet. To respect different learning styles, this book provides choices about how to do many of the exercises and activities. In addition, you can use your creativity and adapt the exercises and activities to better match your learning style.

5. Set aside an hour each week to work on the readings, exercises, and activities in this book. You don't have to work for the full hour—do it for as long as it feels comfortable to you—but in general do not work for more than an hour because that can become overwhelming and can make you feel worse.

6. Don't try to do this work if you are very upset or feel very rushed. Wait until you feel better.

7. Before you begin to do the readings and exercises, and after you finish, spend some time involved in an activity you enjoy.

8. Take good care of yourself in every way while you are doing work on relieving the effects of trauma in your life. Eat well, exercise, spend time outdoors, and get plenty of rest. Spend as much time as possible with people you enjoy—people who make you feel good about yourself. Avoid people who have not treated you well.

9. If you feel upset by something you have read or something you have thought of while working on relieving the effects of trauma in your life, the best thing to do is to talk to an understanding, supportive person. If that isn't possible, stop work for the moment and engage in an activity you enjoy.

10. If you are addicted to alcohol or drugs, try to avoid using them as a way of dealing with issues that come up as you are working on relieving the effects of trauma. Call a friend or do something you enjoy instead. This book is designed to teach you healthy coping strategies for dealing with hard times.

11. If you are currently being abused in any way—physically, emotionally, or sexually, including forced contact that is uncomfortable or sexual—and you are not working with a counselor to correct this situation, contact your local mental health agency before deciding to work through your trauma with this book.

12. Do not expect to feel better right away. Recovery and healing take time, and it is not unusual to feel worse before you feel better. If you find yourself feeling worse, spend more time doing things that make you feel good—take a bubble bath, get a massage, relax with a good book, paint a picture, listen to music, play a game with a child—whatever it is that makes you feel really good.

Does all this sounds okay to you? When you feel ready, begin working on topic 1: Taking Stock and Getting Started.

Part 1

Empowerment

Topic 1

Taking Stock and Getting Started

This book is the beginning of a process—the process of reducing the effects of trauma in your life. This chapter focuses on getting yourself ready to do this work to help insure that your experience is effective and successful.

How Do I Use This Book?

This book is divided into four parts: Empowerment, Trauma Recovery, Creating Life Changes, and Closing Rituals. Each part has a number of topics for you to work on, one at a time. On some days you may only feel like reading one paragraph or doing one exercise. That's fine. You know what is best for you. Listen to how you feel and do this work accordingly. Do only as much as you feel is right for you on any day.

This book contains numerous writing exercises. If you don't feel like writing, share your responses with a supportive friend instead. Or, sit back in a comfortable chair, take some deep breaths, and then think about or visualize your answers.

This work may often make you feel sad and apprehensive. That's okay. These are feelings we all have to learn to live with. However, if you are becoming very fatigued, frightened, anxious, or obsessed with negative thoughts, put the book away until the next week and involve yourself in a fun, comforting, and soothing activity or talk to a friend.

If you feel yourself spacing out—you don't know where you are or what time it is—you may want to stop, get up, walk around, and rub your arms and legs. Make sure you feel like yourself and are in control before you begin again.

This book is designed to be used from front to back. You may want to jump around, perhaps doing topic 22 first, then topic 13, then on to topic 4, but this book is not meant to be used in that way. It is a process—a journey from beginning to end. Each new topic builds on information in the previous topics. Of course, if you come to a topic, section, exercise, or activity that doesn't feel right to you at this time, you may skip over it and go on to the subsequent item.

As discussed under guideline number 5 in the previous chapter, we recommended that you spend about one hour a week doing this work. Each topic takes most people about an hour. If you don't finish a particular topic in an hour, leave it and finish it the following week. You can work on the same topic for several weeks if you want to, but do not try to do more than one topic a week because it takes time to assimilate the information and skills you are learning and to practice them in your life. Make this work just a small part of what you are doing in your life, and spend the rest of your time doing things that feel good to you, taking care of yourself, and taking care of your responsibilities.

What Are My Goals for Doing This Work?

You are at a very important place in your life. Because you are interested in working on the effects of trauma or resolving some of the bad things that have happened in your life and you want to create some positive change in your life, it may help to define your goals. Some ideas from others include:

- letting go of anger,

- learning positive ways to cope with stress and hard times,

- developing personal strength,

- learning about my true self,

- regaining my self-esteem,

- becoming less eager to please and submit to the wishes of others, and

- feeling alive again.

Write down your personal goals for doing this work.

_____

_____

_____

_____

_____

As you proceed with this work, you may want to come back and review these goals. You may notice that you have made some progress in achieving your goals and want to write new ones, or you may notice that your goals have changed and that you want to add some new ones. Revise your goals at any time.

If your goals are not clear to you right now, come back to this section another time or skip it. You do not need to know your final destination in order to take your first step.

When and Where Will I Do This Work?

You may find it helpful to set aside special time to focus on this work. Choose a time of day when your surroundings are fairly quiet and you are least likely to be interrupted, such as when your children are in school or at night when everyone else is sleeping. Ask others to leave you alone unless there's an emergency, and turn off the phone. Don't answer the door. If you have to do this work in a noisy place, try playing some soothing background music to block out the sound.

Mark the time on a calendar or in your date book. You are making an appointment with yourself; give it the same respect you would give any other commitment.

I will do this work on this day at this time: _____

Remember, you can always change the time if and when you have to. Don't feel guilty if you need to skip a week, just get back to it as soon as you feel ready. Sometimes, just a few minutes of reading or working on an exercise is plenty.

Do you have a private place where you can do this work? Perhaps you're fortunate enough to have a room of your own, or perhaps you'll have to carve out a small working space for yourself in a corner of your living room or bedroom. Decorate that space with a candle, a favorite picture, a pretty stone, or some other treasure that makes you feel good before you begin to work.

You can also choose to work on a bench in the park or under a favorite tree. Maybe you have a favorite chair in a shelter or dormitory, workplace or library. Again, try carrying a special stone or memento that feels good to you and becomes associated with your healing and recovery.

In short, anyplace where there is privacy, a flat surface to write on, and a comfortable place to sit will do. Many women find that if they are working inside, it's nice to have a view of the outdoors. Sometimes a brief break to look out at the sky or the trees can calm you and allow you to keep working. You will want to avoid doing this work in places that have not been safe for you in the past or that don't feel good to you.

Depending on your chosen location, you may be able to leave the space set up so you can return to it each week and find it just the way you left it, or you may have to set it up each week. Readying the space can be a good way to prepare yourself for doing this work.

I will do this work in this location, and I will decorate the space in the following way:

_____

_____

Keeping Healthy and Happy While You Work

Throughout the course of this workbook, take care to do everything you can to keep yourself well. What kinds of things do you need to do, or not do, for yourself every day to keep yourself feeling well? Make a list in the spaces below. Some ideas from others include: eat breakfast, exercise, take a shower, avoid eating sugar, drink plenty of water, stay away from bars.

_____

_____

_____

_____

_____

_____

_____

You may want to copy this list and hang it on your refrigerator or near your calendar, or keep it in your date book. Check it regularly to make sure you are on track.

It's also a good idea to do one or several things you enjoy every day, *especially* when you are doing this work. Many women can't remember the last time they did something they truly enjoyed. Sometimes, women can't even remember what they enjoy doing! What do you really enjoy doing—are there things that make you forget your troubles and feel happy, even if only for a little while? Perhaps you can revisit something you enjoyed doing when you were young: arts and crafts such as jewelry making, bead stringing, or knitting; writing poetry or keeping a journal; drawing; painting; reading; walking; playing a musical instrument; or taking photographs.

What do you really enjoy doing?

_____

_____

_____

_____

_____

Stop and do one of these activities whenever the work in this book is upsetting to you. Some people like to do one of their favorite activities before they begin their weekly work, and the same activity or a different one after they're done.

It helps to set aside some of the things you need to do the things you enjoy in a handy place where they will not be disturbed by others. Then you can get to them quickly when you need to. You could keep them in a drawer, a box, a can, or a basket. You could decorate it or leave it the way it is. Make a place where you can keep the things you enjoy, and fill it with these things.

One woman shares the following: "I have a basket where I keep my journal, a good book, a small book of affirmations, some colored markers, drawing paper, several favorite tapes, and a bottle of lotion that smells good and makes me feel good. Whenever I feel overwhelmed or need a break from life, I check out my basket and I always find something to do that will relieve the stress."

I will keep the things I need to do the things I enjoy in the following place:

_____

It will include:

_____

_____

_____

_____

Friends and Supporters

Hopefully, you have one or several supportive persons whom you can talk to about this workbook—people who will sit and chat with you or share a fun activity with you. Like other people who have had trauma in their lives, however, you may feel that there is no one you can trust. If that's true for you and you don't have anyone you can put on your list now, that's okay. As you progress, you will learn ways to include supportive people in your life.

Try to think of the person or people in your life whom you like the best. These should be people who:

- have always treated you well;

- don't criticize, judge, or blame you;

- listen to what you have to say without giving advice;

- want to know what you are working on;

- listen when you let them know you are having a hard time;

- you enjoy being with or sharing fun activities with; and

- don't share personal information about you with others.

This list should not include anyone who has ever been emotionally, physically, or sexually abusive to you in any way.

Your friends and supporters could be much older or much younger than you are. For most women, a best friend is usually another woman, but it might be a man. It could be a family member, friend, or co-worker. It might be a social worker, case manager, counselor, or some other health care professional.

The following people can provide friendship and support while I am doing this work:

Name   **Phone Number**

_____   _____

_____   _____

_____   _____

_____   _____

_____   _____

Keep your relationship with these people healthy by being helpful and supportive of them when *they* need it, too. If they don't seem to need help and support, do something nice for them to let them know you appreciate their support.

Things to Remember Every Day

- Do all the things on your list of things you need to do to keep yourself healthy.

- Do one or several of the activities on your list of things you enjoy doing.

Topic 2

What It Means to Be a Woman

There are feelings and experiences that most women share. For example, we all go through puberty and menopause. In addition, we all get complicated and contradictory messages from our family, our culture, and society about what it means to be a woman. You may be told to be weak and then to be strong, to be less smart and then to do well in school, to look the best you can and then to stop paying so much attention to your appearance. Add a history of abuse and the picture becomes even murkier. Was I abused because I was a female? Is it therefore bad to be a woman? Lots of women report that they have no understanding of what it means to be woman. Consequently, they don't feel good about themselves.

Exploring the topic of what it means to be woman may help you resolve some of the complexity and contradiction around this issue. There is no one right answer, there are many—but only some of them are right for you. Hopefully, this chapter will help you discover things about your womanhood that you can acknowledge and treasure, and help you learn what it means to you to be a woman.

As you continue on this healing journey, you may want to return to the thoughts and feelings you discovered in this chapter.

Whom Do You Admire?

In thinking about your own feminine qualities, it helps to think of other women, especially women you admire. These people can be anyone—someone you know well, a prominent person you have never met, or even a historical figure such as Amelia Earhart or Harriet Tubman.

Mary Ellen shares the following about women she admires and who have served as role models in her life:

"The first women I admired were my grandmothers—both of them. One of them had five children and the other twelve. They worked hard from morning until night. They never thought of going out to dinner or catching a movie. They were very warm, compassionate women who seemed to know instinctively just what a little girl needed to feel safe and secure. I have fond memories of being held and cuddled. They were also both great pie makers. And I love to make pie (and eat it).

"As I grew up I developed a deep admiration for Eleanor Roosevelt. She seemed to break through all the stereotypes of what a woman should do and not do—and did whatever it was she wanted to do. She stood tall and spoke out. Hooray for Eleanor! I try to think of her whenever I feel limitations in my life. From her I learned there are no limits to what I can do. She influenced me to have dreams and goals, to believe I could be whatever it was I wanted to be.

"Then there is my daughter, Patti. At thirty-six, Patti has designed her life the way she wants it to be—and continues to refine it. She's definitely in charge. She has always felt comfortable living where she wants to live, spending time with the people of her choice, dressing the way she likes to dress, and doing the things she likes to do (that means sleeping outdoors in a tent in the summer). She didn't fall prey to living her life according to society's rules."

Think of one or several women whom you admire. Who are they?

_____

_____

_____

Think about one of these women for several minutes. Do whatever helps you to think—get up and walk around or lean back and relax with your eyes closed.

What was it about this woman, as a woman, that felt good to you?

_____

_____

_____

_____

Repeat this exercise for each of the women you thought of.

_____

_____

_____

_____

_____

_____

_____

_____

_____

If you can't think of a woman you admire, that's okay, too. Maxine draws a blank when she tries to think of a woman she admires. "I grew up with a family of women I loved, but no one ever seemed up on a pedestal. I can remember my mother encouraging me to look for the good things in myself."

Now, let's take a look at some of the thoughts, feelings, and sensations connected to being a woman. Make yourself comfortable. Sit back and relax, take a few deep breaths, then answer each of the following questions with the first word or phrase that comes into your mind. Try not to think about your answer, and don't censor it. If your answer does not make sense to you, that's okay. Just let it be what it is.

What do you think about being a woman?

_____

What do you feel about being a woman?

_____

What is the first sensation you feel when you think about being a woman?

_____

Are you surprised by your answers?

____ Yes

____ No

For now, don't worry about your answers. As you proceed with this work, you will get a clearer understanding of these answers and what they mean to you.

Gender Issues

Almost every woman has, at some time, wished she were a boy. As Mary Ellen explains, "I wished I was a boy when my brothers were playing ball and I was expected to stay in the house and play quietly with my paper dolls. I had a friend whose parents were always trying to coax her down out of a tree and convince her to do something more 'ladylike.' The word 'tomboy' has negative connotations for some of us and positive connotations for others."

Have you ever wished that you were a boy? If so, when was that?

_____

Why did you wish you were a boy?

_____

Do you still feel there are some advantages to being a male? If so, what are they?

_____

_____

_____

_____

Are you glad you are female? Why or why not?

_____

_____

_____

_____

_____

Family Issues

Your family of origin, those people you grew up with, often have a lot of influence over how you continue to feel about yourself. The messages you received from your family from the time you were born are hard to change when you get older.

One woman shared the following: "In my family of seven people it was expected that the two girls would take care of all the household chores after our mother was hospitalized (she was hospitalized for eight years). My brothers watched television and were off playing with their friends while my sister and I did the dishes, cleaned the house, and washed the clothes using an old wringer-type washing machine. We didn't have any time for play or to be involved in after-school activities. I didn't think about it too much then because it was just the way things were. When I think of it now it makes me angry."

Another woman told us, "In my family, I was the special one. I was put up on a pedestal. Everyone always thought I was so cute. I was dressed in lacy, frilly little outfits. I got whatever I wanted. My appearance—my cuteness—was everything. When my father's friends came over, I was told to kiss everyone on the cheek. My bothers were expected to play ball and get dirty and I was expected to play quietly with dolls. As an adult it has been hard for me to learn that my value is not based on being a cute little girl but on my positive and unique attributes. It's taken me years to learn to stand up for myself, to make my own decisions, and do what I want with my life."

Maxine remembers a story she heard growing up: "My father was so certain that his first child would be a son that he bet a friend a hundred dollars I would be a boy. Although my parents assured me they were delighted with a girl, I could not help feeling that I had somehow let them down. I have worked hard to be better than any son they might have had."

What messages did you get from your family about what it means to be a woman?

_____

_____

_____

_____

How did your family treat boys and girls differently?

_____

_____

_____

How do you think this has affected the way you feel about yourself as a woman?

_____

_____

_____

_____

Have you done anything to counteract erroneous messages you learned from your family about being a women?

_____

_____

_____

_____

Societal Issues

The way women are depicted in advertising, music, movies, and television can have a strong influence on how you feel about yourself as a woman. The television ad that shows the well-dressed, slim woman mopping a kitchen floor that is cleaner than any normal home carries with it a message that tries to say something about who women are, what they should look like, and what they should do. Many women who cannot meet these standards are left feeling that there is something wrong with them.

Ads for undergarments such as the Nobody's Perfect Bra give women a message that they are just not quite right, as do the proliferation of advertisements for products to create change in the natural ways we look and smell. Every women's magazine has an article on how to lose weight, along with one or several on "flattening your tummy" or "tightening your butt," and how many women have suffered through the agonies and aftermath of breast implants so that they would more closely meet society's ideal?

In movies, magazines, and newspapers, women are portrayed as sex objects and sexual commodities. Check out the pictures and lead stories in the magazines and newspapers as you leave the supermarket and register how they make you feel about yourself as a woman.

_____

_____

_____

Think about and, if you want to, describe a cultural or media incident that has made you feel bad about yourself or about the way women are viewed in our society.

_____

_____

_____

_____

Many women are actively working to insure that, in the future, women will be positively depicted in the media and throughout our culture. Meanwhile, you need to focus on liking yourself as you are, not the way someone else tries to make you think you should be.

Who Am I?

Now that you have thought about the concept of being a woman, and how that is related to other women in our lives, our family and our culture, think about who you are as a unique and special woman by doing the following exercises.

What roles do you have in life? Circle all that apply, and add any that are not in the list.

mother / grandmother / aunt / friend / partner / wife / lover / head of household / housekeeper / cook / wage earner / employee / employer / business owner / chauffeur / caretaker / buyer / manager / social director / confidant / supporter

_____

_____

_____

Many women report that when they look at their list they feel like a juggler trying to keep all the balls in the air at the same time. Just realizing how many roles they have give many women a greater appreciation of themselves in dealing with the complexity of life.

Remember, you are still a complete woman regardless of the number and nature of the roles you circled. Maxine does not have children and she used to wonder if she could be a "real woman" without being a mother. Now she realizes that being a "real woman" is not dependent on whether or not she chooses to have children.

How would you describe yourself? List adjectives such as "happy," "generous," "joyous," "caring," "warm," "creative," "inhibited," "sad," "quiet," "noisy," "introverted," and/or "extroverted."

_____

_____

_____

How would you describe yourself physically?

_____

_____

_____

_____

Try to remember that whatever you look like, you look great. Here's a visualization exercise that might help you think good thoughts about yourself physically. Sit back and relax. Take a few deep breaths. Then, take a few minutes to focus your attention on each part of your body. You can start with your toes and work up or begin with the top of your head and work down. As you focus on each part of your body, think about what it does for you and appreciate it.

Feeling Good about Yourself

Write down three or more things you have achieved in your life that you feel proud of. They don't have to be grand things; they can be as simple as, "I got an A on a test in high school," "I can make great spaghetti," or "I have a beautiful garden."

_____

_____

_____

_____

Get a pen and a sheet of colored paper. Spend ten minutes writing down everything good you can think of about yourself. Everything goes, as long as it's positive. If you have a hard time writing good things about yourself for ten minutes, you can repeat the same things over and over, or ask a supportive person to tell you some good things about yourself. When you are done, read what you have written. Then fold it up and put it under your pillow, on your bedside table, or in your pocket. Read it before you go to bed at night, when you first get up in the morning, and whenever you a have a free moment. Read it aloud whenever you can. Read it to a supportive friend.

Optional Activities

(All of the exercises in this book are optional in that you don't have to do them if they make you feel uncomfortable. When we use the term "optional," we mean that the activities we're about to list don't necessarily have to fit in to the weekly hour that you've set aside to work in this book. They can be done when and if you feel like it and if it is convenient for you.)

1. Set up a place to honor yourself—you may wish to call it an altar. It could be the top of a bureau or a box, a corner of a table or the whole table, or a shelf. Gather things

that are special to you and arrange them in a way that appeals to you. Your altar could include things such as shells; stones; pictures of yourself along with other people, places, and events that are special to you; knickknacks, jewelry, candles, or notes and cards. If you don't have a place to create an altar, keep these items in a special bag. It could even be a bag that you carry with you.

2. Make yourself a personal scrapbook. Include pictures of yourself at various times in your life, drawings, pictures cut out of magazines, and writings—either your own or special poems or sayings you enjoy. Take as much or as little time as you want to do this activity. When you have finished working on it, keep it in a special place and look at it regularly. Add new things to the scrapbook as you discover them.

3. Make a collage of yourself with the goal of expressing your uniqueness. Get a big piece of paper, some glue, scissors, and one or several magazines that you enjoy. Cut and paste a personal collage that expresses unique aspects of yourself.

4. Think back to when you had your first menstrual period. Share this story with a good friend, and ask her to share her story with you. As women, one thing we all have in common is menstruation, and sharing these sometimes funny or embarrassing stories can make us feel closer to each other.

5. Read any of the following books on female identity and images of womanhood.

    Faludi, Susan. *Backlash*. New York: Crown, 1991.

    Harris, Maxine. *Down from the Pedestal*. New York: Doubleday, 1994.

    Heilbrun, Carolyn. *Reinventing Womanhood*. New York: Norton, 1976.

    Hooks, Bell. *Ain't I A Woman: Black Women and Feminism*. Boston: South End Press, 1981.

    Ireland, Mardy. *Reconceiving Women*. New York: Guilford, 1993.

    Wolf, Naomi. *The Beauty Myth*. New York: Anchor, 1991.

Things to Remember Every Day

Copy the following rights on a piece of paper. Fold it up and carry it in your pocket or purse. Take it out and read it whenever you have a few moments to spare—riding on the subway, waiting for the bus or an appointment, before you go to bed, or while dinner is cooking.

- I have the right to be treated with dignity, compassion, and respect at all times.

- I have the right to make my own decisions about the course of my life.

- I have the right to have dreams—and to work toward making these dreams come true.

- I have the right to feel good about myself as a person and as a woman.

- I have the right to choose who will be my friends, whom I will spend time with, and whom I will confide in.

- I have the right to make mistakes.

- I have the right to change my mind. (Have you ever heard the saying, "If you haven't changed your mind lately, maybe you don't have one"?)
- I have the right to be happy.
- I have the right to ask for what I want.
- I have the right to follow my own values and standards.
- I have the right to express all of my feelings, both positive and negative.
- I have the right to say no.
- I have the right to determine my own priorities.
- I have the right not to be responsible for others' behavior, actions, feelings, or problems.
- I have the right to my own needs for personal space and time.
- I have the right to be in a nonabusive environment.
- I have the right to change and grow.
- I have the right to have my needs and wants respected by others.
- I have the right to be uniquely myself.

Topic 3

What Do You Know and How Do You Feel about Your Body?

You might assume that women who have been physically or sexually abused would know more than other women about their bodies and how they work. This is not generally true. Because sexual abuse exposes a person to sex in a harsh and unwelcome way, it teaches her nothing good about her body. She may even come to hate her body just because it was the object of the abuse. Women who have been abused often develop very negative feelings about their bodies and express feelings such as shame and disgust about their body parts and functions. The abuse experience also keeps women from learning things about themselves that they would usually learn at certain ages. For example, girls may tune out in school when sex education is discussed because it hurts too much to listen. Paula was a very bright student who wanted to be a doctor. She did fine in chemistry and math classes, but whenever the topic turned to the human body, she froze. She couldn't concentrate on the material because her memories and flashbacks kept intruding. Women like Paula often have very limited information about their bodies and how they work.

You probably learned a lot in school about the various systems of the body such as the digestive system and the nervous system, but the systems of the body specifically related to being a woman are often overlooked or addressed superficially because this is a loaded topic for both parents and school programs. But now that you are an adult and are in control of your own life, you may feel that it is safe for you to learn more about your body.

The following diagrams show (a) the names for the various parts of the body that are relevant to female sexuality (both sexual pleasure and reproduction) and (b) the lining of the uterus at the four stages of the menstrual cycle. Simple definitions of some of the words in these diagrams that may be unfamiliar to you are provided below.

Before you begin reviewing this information, say to yourself at least five times—out loud if possible—*My body is amazing and beautiful.* Large or small, fat or thin, your body is amazing and you are beautiful.

Here is a view of the vulva and clitoris area as if you were looking at it with a mirror held between your legs.

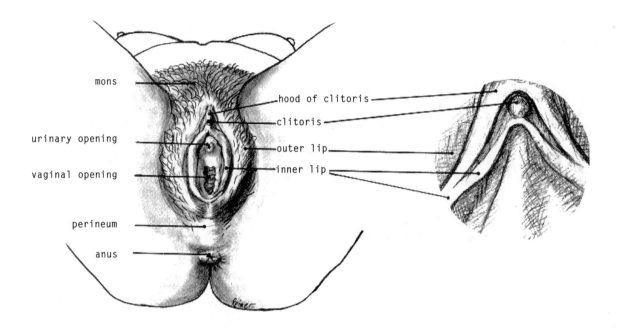

Here is a side view of the organs that are located in your lower abdomen, including the sexual organs.

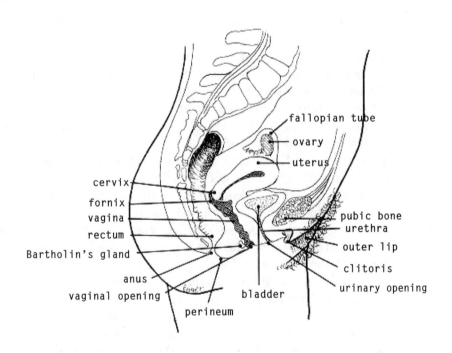

The following diagrams shows the endometrium (the lining of the uterus) as it changes during the four stages of the menstrual cycle (around twenty-eight days in most women). Through the first two phases, when an egg is released from the ovaries and as the lining prepares to nourish a fertilized egg, the endometrium thickens; in the latter phases, if a fertilized egg is not implanted, the lining shrinks and is discarded as menstrual flow.

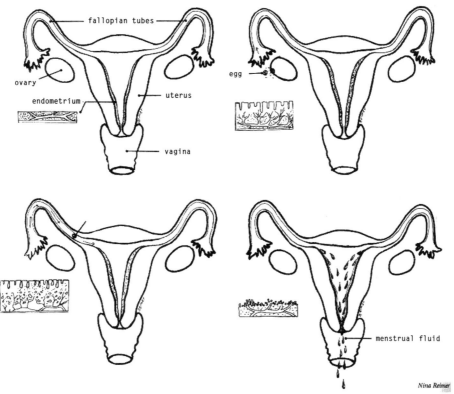

The endometrium at four stages of menstrual cycle: the end of menstration, ovulation, about five days after ovulation, and menstruation.

Bartholin's gland—small glands that you can feel on either side of the vaginal opening that may get infected and swollen from time to time. These glands release a tiny amount of fluid during sexual stimulation.

Cervix—the opening at the base of the uterus through which menstrual fluids and other secretions flow and that, at birth, expands to allow the infant to pass out of the uterus.

Clitoris—a small organ at the front of the pelvic area that is very sensitive to touch and that swells during sexual arousal.

Egg—the small group of cells that, if united with a male sperm in the fallopian tubes, descends to the uterus and matures into an embryo and an infant.

Endometrium—the lining of the uterus that grows and thickens right after an egg is released by the ovaries (to prepare for a possible pregnancy) and that shrinks and is shed as a menstrual period when pregnancy does not occur.

Fallopian tube—four-inch-long tubes through which eggs move on their way from the ovaries to the uterus.

Fornix—the upper end of the vagina.

Menstrual fluid—the discharge (four to six tablespoons of fluid) that comes out of the body when you have your period as the endometrium sheds its lining.

Mons—a triangular area of soft fatty tissue at the very bottom of your abdomen that is covered with pubic hair.

Ovaries—two small oval organs located on either side of the uterus that produce and release eggs so they can move into the fallopian tubes to be fertilized. The ovaries also produce sex hormones, including estrogen and progesterone.

Ovulation—the release of an egg from the ovaries that marks the beginning of the menstrual cycle.

Perineum—the outer area between the vaginal opening and the anus.

Pubic bone—the bone that surrounds the pelvic area.

Urethra—the tube through which urine flows from the bladder out of the body through the urinary opening.

Uterus—the organ in which the infant is nourished and grows between conception and birth.

Vagina—the birth canal that leads to the cervix.

If you have questions about your body and its function—things that you don't understand or want to know more about—write the questions down in the spaces below so you can look them up later in one of the books we've recommended.

_____

_____

_____

_____

_____

These body parts are commonly referred to by slang or vulgar terms that many women find demeaning. You may find that using the real names for these body parts helps you feel better about your body. If you feel uncomfortable, ashamed, and disgusted when people use slang words to describe parts of your body or other women's bodies, you can ask them to stop doing it—but only if you feel it is the right thing to do. You might say, "When you use those kinds of words in referring to parts of my body or parts of other women's bodies it makes me feel _____. I would like you to stop using those words in my presence." Although the other person may be embarrassed, usually they will apologize and promise to refrain from using those words in the future. If someone continues to use those words after you have asked them not to, you may choose to stay away from them. Remember, you have a right to be treated well by the people around you. Many of these slang words are angry, hostile terms and someone may use them with the intent of making you feel uneasy. You are not being a "prude" if you react negatively to these words. Your response is one hundred percent normal.

What kind of words would you like to use to refer to parts of your body and what words would you like others to use? Some women choose to use only anatomical or scientific words to refer to parts of their body. You might want to do the same, or you may choose to create words of your own—private, special words that feel good to you. What words do you want to use?

_____

_____

_____

Is there some action you would like to take now about how you or others refer to parts of your body? If so, what will you do?

_____

_____

_____

Feeling Better about Your Body

A woman in her sixties, when asked how she felt about her body, said, "I have always felt great about my body. I learned it from my mother. She felt good about her body and, without saying anything, passed on that feeling to me. I have always thought, through all the changes in my body and phases of my life, that my body is just fine."

Another woman told us that her mother has always emphasized to her how wonderful it is to be a woman and how very special and important our bodies are. She continues to feel very good about her body, despite pressure from the media and her peers who tried to tell her that lots of work is required to enhance a body to even make it okay.

Many women have very negative feelings about their own bodies. One woman reports, "When I was a child I was taunted and molested by a cousin. To make matters worse, my older brother was always making fun of my body. Consequently I grew up feeling that my body was bad and that there was something wrong with it. When I had a daughter, I tried to let her know that she was perfect just the way she was and that there was nothing wrong with having a female body."

What negative messages have others given you about your body?

_____

_____

_____

_____

What negative messages do you give yourself about your body?

_____

_____

_____

_____

_____

Such messages can affect the quality of your life. Never forget that you have the right to feel good about your body regardless of its size, shape, or color or the size, shape, or color of particular body parts. The following exercise can help you look at the way you have been thinking about your body to determine the effect these thoughts may be having on your life. Use this technique to address one negative thought at a time.

1. Determine the cost of the negative feeling. When I have the negative thought that I am _____ (for example, too fat, too thin, ugly, repulsive, misshapen) it makes me feel _____ (for example, bad about myself, sad, upset, angry, discouraged) and that keeps me from _____ (for example, buying myself nice clothes, having my picture taken, going outside).

2. Determine the benefit of the negative feeling. What do you get that is positive out of having this feeling? (For example, you can avoid having to be with other people.) Many people can't think of anything positive they get out of thinking or feeling negatively about their bodies. Coming to this realization can help you let go of negative thoughts and feelings about your body. If there is some benefit to the negative thought, think about other ways you might achieve that without having to trash yourself.

Next, you will need to learn how to turn negative thoughts about your body into positive ones. Refer to the list of negative thoughts about your body that you developed earlier, and choose just one or two to work on for now. You will develop positive statements about your body that you can use to counteract those negative messages and then reinforce the positive statements so that they replace the negative ones. The following guidelines will help you in developing these positive statements.

- Avoid using negative terms such as "ugly," "fat," "repulsive," or "homely." Instead, use only positive words such as "strong," "lovely," "warm," "comfortable," "powerful," or "beautiful."

- Substitute "it would be nice if" for "should."

- Use "I," "me," or your name in the positive rebuttal.

In the left-hand column, list your negative thoughts about your body. In the right-hand column, give a positive rebuttal. Two examples are provided to get you started.

I am fat. _____   _I look strong and powerful._ _____

My breasts are too big. _____   _My breasts are just right for me._ _____

_____	_____
_____	_____
_____	_____
_____	_____
_____	_____

Changing these negative thoughts takes time and persistence. If you use the following techniques consistently for four to six weeks, you will notice that you don't think these negative thoughts about yourself as much. If they recur at some other time, you can repeat these activities. Don't give up. You deserve to think good thoughts about your body!

1. Write the positive rebuttals on a piece of paper. Keep them in your pocket or some other convenient place. Read them over and over when you first wake in the morning. If possible, say them aloud. It's even more helpful if you say them aloud to a supportive person. Read them again before you go to bed at night. Read them or say them aloud to yourself or someone else any time you get a chance. Writing them out a few times whenever you get a chance also helps. You might also try taping them to your bathroom mirror and rereading them every time you look in the mirror. There are lots of creative ways to reinforce these positive rebuttals.

2. Every time you catch yourself thinking the negative thought about your body, replace it with the positive rebuttal.

Optional Activities

1. Explore your body in a gentle loving way. Look at your body parts. Tell them how much you love and appreciate them. Caress them gently in any way that feels comfortable to you. You might want to rub them with a soothing cream or lotion. Take as much time as you want.

2. Give your wonderful body a treat. Take a warm bath or shower and then rub your whole body with a favorite lotion. Even inexpensive baby oil will do. Dress in the most comfortable outfit you have (sloppy sweats or a robe) and relax.

3. Go to your favorite clothing store simply to try on anything you like—you don't have to buy anything. Then admire yourself in the mirror.

4. Look in the mirror every morning and say aloud, "I look great!" Then smile at yourself.

5. Learn more about your body by reading a good book on the topic. We especially like *The Black Women's Health Book,* edited by Evelyn White (Seattle: Seal Press, 1994).

Things to Remember Every Day

- My body is beautiful.
- My body is amazing.
- I look great.
- My body is perfect just the way it is.
- I am proud of my body.
- It's great to be a woman.

Preparation for the Next Topic

1. During the next week, notice how you feel in at least five different places such as the following:
   - walking on an isolated country road,
   - sitting in an open field or open area outdoors,
   - riding alone in an elevator,
   - sitting alone on a bench in the park,
   - being in the basement in your apartment building or home,
   - being in a room with no outdoor light,
   - being in a small room with only one exit,
   - being in a large open room,
   - being in a very noisy place,
   - being in a very quiet place,
   - being in a dark place,
   - walking down a dimly lit hallway,
   - walking in a wooded area, and
   - sitting in a room where you are unable to see the exit.

2. Notice how you feel in five situations involving proximity to other people, such as:
   - on a crowded sidewalk,
   - sitting on a bench in the park with a man or person you don't know,
   - sharing a seat on the bus with a person who seems unfriendly,
   - paying for a purchase at a department store that is not very busy,
   - standing in line to make a purchase,
   - sitting near a close friend or lover,
   - getting a hug from someone you have just met,
   - getting a hug from an acquaintance,
   - getting a hug from a close friend,
   - holding a baby,

- sitting near someone you don't know,
- being brushed against by a person you don't know,
- having someone stand very close to you when they are talking to you,
- having someone stop you to ask directions,
- having someone stop you to ask for money, and
- having someone whistle at you or make a comment or sexually suggestive gesture.

Topic 4

Physical Boundaries

As a child you began to learn about your physical boundaries. You identified those spaces that felt comfortable to you, feeling content in some places and discontent in others. You gradually began to identify those people you felt comfortable with, choosing to spend time with them, and staying away from people with whom you felt less safe and comfortable. If you found yourself in spaces or spending time with people who felt uncomfortable or unsafe to you, you clearly let others know by crying loudly until the situation was changed to your satisfaction. You responded to warm, gentle, loving touch positively while vigorously protesting any touch that didn't feel good to you. You learned from your experience, intuition, and from observing others whether or not they wanted you to come close to them. You also learned the limits of your own space—you became clear about where you stopped and where another person began. This is how you began to develop a notion of privacy and intimate space. The ability to choose and define your physical boundaries is a natural learning process, part of growing up. It helps you make decisions about what you need to do to keep yourself safe.

The process of learning and choosing your own physical boundaries can be interrupted or stopped if they are repeatedly violated. If you were abused or traumatized, people or things entered your space and violated your boundaries against your will. You may have lost the ability to discern what is safe and comfortable space for you and what your physical boundaries are. This loss can result in repeated abuse, trauma, and victimization. This topic will lead you through several exercises that will help you regain your ability to define your physical boundaries, helping you keep yourself comfortable and safe.

Exploring Space

At the end of the last topic, we asked you to notice how you felt in at least five places. One woman might feel uncomfortable when she is in a large, open room. Another might feel most comfortable and cozy in a small room with plenty of windows. You might be surprised to notice that you feel more comfortable sitting in the park than you do in your own living room.

Make a list of the places where you noticed how you felt and write how you felt in those places. Words you might use could include "comfortable," "safe," "secure," "cozy," "okay," "uneasy," "vulnerable," or "unsafe."

_____

_____

_____

_____

In doing this exercise, what did you learn about your physical boundaries?

_____

_____

_____

Were you surprised at some of the things you learned? If so, what were those things?

_____

_____

_____

How could you spend more time in places that feel good or safe to you?

_____

_____

_____

How could you spend less time in places that don't feel good to you or make you feel uneasy?

_____

_____

_____

If you must spend time in places that make you feel uncomfortable or uneasy, is there something you could change to make those places feel better to you? For instance, if you don't feel safe in your bedroom, could you rearrange the furniture or leave the door opened or closed to make the space feel better for you? If a workspace feels uncomfortable, could you request or arrange a change in furniture or equipment arrangement, a change in the ease of access by other employees, or a change in lighting?

_____

_____

_____

If there are places where you don't feel right but you'd like to try to make the space work for you, you can help yourself get over those feelings of uneasiness. Begin by spending short amounts of time in the space—you could start with one minute. When you notice you feel safe and comfortable for one minute, increase the time to one and a half or two minutes. Continue to increase the time you spend in the space until you feel comfortable and secure there all of the time. Only you can determine how often to go to the space, how long to spend there, and when you are comfortable being there. Another variation on this exercise is to have a person you really trust go with you and spend time with you in the space, decreasing the amount of time they are with you until you feel comfortable spending time there by yourself.

One woman noticed that she felt very uneasy when she went into the basement in her new home. Knowing that she couldn't always avoid going into the basement, she began spending time there working with her husband on household chores. She gradually decreased the amount of time he needed to be with her in the basement, spending increasing amounts of time by herself until she noticed that she no longer felt uneasy or afraid there.

Many women who were abused in a bedroom feel uneasy in any room where the sole activity is sleep. Debra turned her bedroom into a study with a chair and a pull-out sofa. She added a bookcase and a good reading lamp and turned her room into a place where she could feel safe and in control.

Boundaries Awareness

Here's an exercise to increase your awareness of space and how it feels to you.

Find a place where you can be alone for about ten minutes, and find a space within the place where you feel very safe and comfortable.

Is it near or further away from things?

_____

Can you clearly see all parts of the space from where you are?

_____

Can you see a way to leave the space from where you are?

_____

Can you look out at other areas close to this one from where you are or is the space closed in by walls or other things?

_____

Is the space filled with light or is it darker?

_____

Is it noisy or quiet?

_____

What else did you notice that is unique about this space?

_____

How do these things affect you?

_____

Spend several moments in another space within this place where you feel safe and comfortable, and respond to each of the questions again.

Move about. Is there anywhere within your place that does not feel safe or comfortable to you? If so, go to that space and answer each of the questions a third time.

You can repeat the exercise as many times as you wish, moving from space to space and noticing how you feel each time.

What did you learn from this exercise about where you like to be?

_____

_____

_____

Are there any changes you could make in your living space, or other spaces where you spend time, that would help you feel more comfortable and safe? How could you make these changes?

_____

_____

_____

Exploring Feelings When You Are Near Others

At the end of the last topic, we also asked you to notice how you felt in at least five circumstances where you were near other people. Paula noticed that she felt very comfortable sharing a seat on the bus with an older woman, but not at all comfortable when sharing the seat with a middle-aged man with light-colored hair and a dark beard. Jane felt anxious and unsafe when she was sitting in a large room crowded with people. However, when she was in a smaller room with several people she knew, she felt fine.

Make a list of the situations you chose and write how you felt in each of these situations.

_____

_____

_____

_____

_____

In doing this exercise, did you learn some things about your physical boundaries with other people? If so, what did you learn?

_____

_____

_____

Were you surprised at some of the things you noticed? If so, what surprised you?

_____

_____

_____

How could you spend more time with people and in situations that feel good or safe to you?

_____

_____

_____

Are there some ways you could spend less time with people in situations that don't feel good to you or make you feel uneasy?

_____

_____

_____

If someone violates or tries to violate your space, making you feel uncomfortable and unsafe, you can take action to change the situation. Depending on the situation and what you feel comfortable doing, you can:

1. Tell them how you feel—what is okay and not okay to you. For example, you might tell an uncle who is always trying to kiss you that you do not want to be kissed by him or that you do not want him to touch you at all. You can tell an acquaintance that you are uncomfortable being hugged by him or her.

2. Avoid people who are making you feel uncomfortable or unsafe. Stay away from places where they might be. For instance, if you don't like being around people who have been drinking, avoid places where alcohol is served. If a relative mistreated you in the past, avoid attending events where that person might be present. You might decide to no longer attend family reunions in order to avoid a cousin who harassed and molested you when you were a child. Or, you might stay out of parts of the city where you know illegal drugs are routinely sold. Avoidance is _not_ a cop-out! It is a totally acceptable way of keeping yourself safe.

3. If you are inadvertently in contact with someone who makes you feel uneasy or scared, leave the place as quickly as possible. Then share how you felt with a trusted friend or a counselor. If you have no one with whom you feel safe sharing the incident, write about it in your journal.

4. If someone violates your space or hurts you, and does not stop when you tell them to stop, do whatever you need to do to get away from them as quickly as possible while keeping yourself safe. Depending on the seriousness of the incident, contact your local women's crisis center, law enforcement officials, or mental health agency for support and assistance, and possibly to initiate legal action for further protection.

Exploring Feelings about Strangers

Ask a friend to accompany you to a place where there are many different strangers, such as a department store. Walk through this area and make note of the following questions.
Where did you feel most comfortable?

_____

Who was near you at this time?

_____

Where did you feel least comfortable?

_____

Who was near you at this time?

_____

Then ask the friend to wait for you while you walk through the area by yourself. (If you were unable to find a friend to help, you can begin the exercise here.) Again, answer each of the questions.

What did you learn about physical boundaries from this exercise?

_____

_____

_____

_____

Are there any changes you could make that would help you feel more comfortable and safe in these circumstances? How could you make these changes?

_____

_____

_____

_____

Touching or Being Touched

You also have the right and responsibility to not touch others or be touched in ways that are uncomfortable or hurtful to you. You have the right to say no to any uncomfortable touch. This may be very hard for you if you have been traumatized or abused. You may feel like you can't even tell the difference between wanted and unwanted touch.

The following exercise will help you learn to identify wanted and unwanted touch. Choose several of the following incidents related to touch (or, if none of the following have happened to you recently, any others you can think of) and note how the touch felt to you. For example, note how you felt when:

- A baby caressed your face.

- Your mother hugged you.

- A dog or cat rubbed against your legs.

- You gently rubbed your own face.

- You gently rubbed sensitive parts of your body.

- Someone else rubbed parts of your body.

- Your partner kissed you.

- Your partner touched you after a disagreement.

- A person walking on the street brushed against you.

- A person you did not know put his or her hand on your shoulder when you were conversing.

- A cashier inadvertently touched your hand.

Circumstance

_____

_____

How it felt

_____

_____

What I learned

_____

_____

Circumstance

_____

_____

How it felt

_____

_____

What I learned

_____

_____

Circumstance

_____

_____

How it felt

_____

_____

What I learned

_____

_____

Circumstance

_____

_____

How it felt

_____

_____

What I learned

_____

_____

Do you think you can avoid unwanted contact or touch, either now or in the future? Why or why not?

_____

_____

Of course, certain kinds of necessary medical testing and treatment may involve unwanted or uncomfortable touch. But even in such cases you can make decisions about what you will and will not have done to your body. You can ask for a particular person to administer the procedure or you can request a different procedure, anesthesia, or a pain-reducing medication. For instance, Marli was having a colonoscopy. The person who was to administer the procedure was a young man who reminded her of a man who had harassed her. She requested that a woman administer the procedure and her request was granted. She knew she had a right to refuse the test if a woman was not available, have it rescheduled on a day when a woman was available, or have the test administered at a different facility where a woman was available.

Many women find that visits to the gynecologist are especially troubling. In fact, a number of trauma survivors report that they avoid important tests such as Pap smears and mammograms because being touched makes them so frightened. If you are almost phobic about seeing a gynecologist, you are not alone.

There are some things you can do, however, to make your visit to the gynecologist easier. First, choose your doctor carefully. Would you feel better seeing a woman? A younger or an older physician? A friendly or an "all business" type? Get recommendations from friends before you make your appointment. Next, schedule an informational visit before you go in for an exam. Explain your history, briefly, and tell the physician what you will need in order to feel comfortable. If you sense any hesitation from him or her, choose another doctor. When you do go for your appointment, take a friend along to be present for as much of the appointment as you feel comfortable with. Finally, remember that you can stop the exam at any time if you are feeling too anxious.

Reading Body Language

Some people who have been traumatized have a hard time reading or interpreting body language. Others become even more aware of subtle clues. If you're in the latter category, you may not even be able to say what it is about the body language that gives you a message. What's important to remember is that it is not necessary to put the feelings into words in order take action based on your instincts. When Martha saw a man walking toward her on the street, she immediately began feeling uneasy. She acted on her feelings, turning around and walking quickly in the other direction in a very assertive manner. She went into a bank and waited until the man had passed by.

Sometimes the body language of people who have been traumatized does not accurately reflect what they want or don't want. You may want to think about this and practice making some changes in your body language to more accurately reflect what you really want and don't want. Practice the following, using body language only. If possible, ask a friend to interpret your body language to see if it accurately reflects what you are trying to say. Here are some scenarios for practice:

- You like someone.

- You care about someone.

- You want to get to know someone better.

- You want to talk to someone.

- You don't want to talk to someone.

- Someone is standing too close.

- You want someone to back off.

- You don't like someone.

- You don't want someone to touch you.

- You want someone to stop touching you.

Optional Activity

Whether you live alone or with others, you need and deserve a special place in the world that is just yours, a place where you feel comfortable and secure. It may be a small corner of a shared room, a room of your own, or a whole apartment or house. If you are traveling, your space may be the things you carry with you and use to make each new place where you stay feel comfortable. Now that you are more aware of your physical boundaries, are there some changes you can make in your special place to make it feel better to you? Consider some of the following ideas:

- Rearrange the furnishings.

- Reorganize your things.

- Cover furniture with pieces of cloth or scarves (things you have that you like or that you purchase at a thrift store or department store).

- Add furnishings that make the space feel better to you, such as pillows and throw rugs.

- Decorate with pictures, art, and objects you enjoy.

- Paint the walls, floor, and/or ceiling in colors that make you happy.

- Improve or replace (or have your landlord improve or replace) locks and other security devices.

You don't need to make these changes all at once; you can work on them gradually.

Things to Remember Every Day

- I have the right to define my own physical boundaries.

- I have the right to feel comfortable and safe.

- I can do what I need to do to keep myself comfortable and safe.

- I have the right to ask, expect, and insist that others respect my physical boundaries.

- I choose to spend my time in places and with people that make me feel comfortable and safe.

- I can protect myself from unwanted closeness and contact by saying no.

- I have the right to determine how and by whom I want to be touched.

Topic 5

Emotional Boundaries

As you explored the last topic, you may have discovered physical boundaries that you didn't know you had. Because you were traumatized, you may also have a hard time identifying your emotional boundaries: setting personal limits such as saying no and asking for what you want, need, and deserve for yourself.

When you were a child, you may not have been given choices. Perhaps you were made to do things and treated poorly. You were not given the opportunity to refuse to do these things. You learned that if you tried to refuse, the situation might worsen rather than improve and that you might cause yourself even more harm. If you took a risk and asked for what you needed for yourself, you may have been scolded, ridiculed, or even hurt. As a result, as you grew up you carried with you a fear of saying no and of asking for what you want, need, and deserve.

As a child, your control over your environment and the things that happened to you may have been very limited. If you were fortunate, the adults in your life cared about you and took good care of you. But when that didn't happen, you felt as though your life was out of your control—and at that time it was. That feeling of your life being out of your control can persist into adulthood, even when you are in charge of your life. You might need to remind yourself right now that you have the right to say no to anything you don't want to have happen to you, and a right to ask for what you need, want, and deserve for yourself. Write the following on a piece of paper:

I have the right to say no to anything I don't want to have happen to me, and a right to ask for what I need, want, and deserve for myself.

Read the statement over and over to yourself, out loud if possible. If you can, read it to a friend. Keep the piece of paper in the front of this book, and read it often.

If you are still living in a situation in which you feel that others have all the control, these words might seem like an impossible dream. Don't despair. Thousands of women just like you have seen the dream of taking control come true.

Learning to Say No

Do you ever find that you want to say no but are afraid that the results of saying it would be unsafe? Do you feel you can't say no to such things as:

- uncomfortable or intimate touch,

- sex,

- doing favors, such as lending money

- medical procedures,

- abuse and/or harassment,

- controlling behaviors by others,

- spending time with people who treat you badly,

- alcohol or drugs,

- going places you don't want to go, or

- doing things you don't want to do?

Below, list the things you may have a hard time saying no to.

_____

_____

_____

_____

_____

When you first realize that you can say no, it feels very different and very new. Although Marty, a twenty-eight-year-old social worker who was molested as a child, has had a hard time in her life saying no, she recalls an incident that she feels was a milestone in her life. She was at a college fraternity party. The same man kept asking her to dance over and over. Each time she danced with him, she felt more and more uncomfortable as he made more suggestive advances. When he asked her to go to his room, she did something that was unusual for her—she said no. He called her a tease, but eventually walked off and asked someone else to dance. She felt a bit shaken but relieved.

Describe a time that you said no that you feel good about.

_____

_____

_____

_____

_____

Describe circumstances in which you did not do things you wanted or needed to do for yourself, or let others push you around, because you were afraid of what might happen if you refused.

_____

_____

_____

_____

_____

What could have happened if you had said no?

_____

_____

_____

What would have been better—saying no, or having the other thing happen?

_____

_____

How could you take control and say no without getting hurt or having some other negative consequence?

_____

_____

_____

_____

You may have discovered some ways of taking some action to get the results you want without directly telling the other person no.

Kelly's husband wanted to control her life. If she did something her husband did not want her to do, he would fly into a rage, a situation that made Kelly feel very afraid. Rather than tell her husband what she was going to do, such as spend some time with her grandchildren, have a cup of tea with a friend, or apply for a different job, Kelly lied. Lying and plotting ways to keep her husband from finding out what she was doing became a very uncomfortable way of life for her.

Describe some other ways that Kelly might have used to get what she wanted, needed, and deserved without having to lie.

_____

_____

_____

_____

Jane was anxious to end her relationship with her boyfriend, but was very apprehensive about telling him she no longer wanted to see him. When he called to arrange times for them to get together, she made up excuses such as telling him she had to work late or that she had gotten a stomach virus.

Describe some other ways that Jane might have used to get what she wanted, needed, and deserved without making up excuses.

_____

_____

_____

_____

Describe any strategies that you have used to keep yourself from having to say no.

_____

_____

_____

_____

_____

While these strategies may be helpful at the moment, they continue to leave the other person with some control over your life. What are you afraid would happen if you just said no?

_____

_____

_____

The next time you notice you are about to take some action to avoid having to say no, how could you handle the situation differently? Could you say no? Why or why not?

_____

_____

_____

_____

The following is a very empowering exercise. Practice saying no to someone you have (or have had) a hard time saying it to. While staring intently at a picture of that person (or a picture you drew of that person), say no, out loud if possible, over and over again. You might want to ask a friend to be with you when you are doing this. Repeat this exercise whenever you feel as though you are having a hard time saying no.

Marion, a woman in her midfifties who was abused as a child, has two school-age granddaughters. Although she loves the girls dearly and spends a lot of her free time with them, she found herself becoming very annoyed and irritated by the ease with which they said no and demanded that their needs be met. In looking closely at the situation, Marion realized that her irritation came from her own inability to say no, and to ask for what she needs and deserves for herself. She now respects, appreciates, and is even thankful for her granddaughters' ability to do so. She is hopeful that it will protect them from being poorly treated, and that it will insure that their lives will be the way they want them to be.

Some women who are currently living with violent partners may be in serious danger if they stand up for themselves. Are you one of these women? If your partner has hit, kicked, pushed, or slapped you or has even threatened to do so to you, your children, your other family members, your friends, or your pets, then you should take the following steps before trying to assert yourself.

1. Tell someone you trust about your situation.

2. Seek advice, support, or services from a shelter for battered women.

3. Contact a domestic violence hotline or clinic.

4. Make a safety plan that includes a place to go, money, and people who will support you.

The goal of this book is for you to grow and get more of what you want in life, but you cannot grow if you are not safe.

Making Personal Choices

While some of the choices you have as an adult may by limited by financial circumstances or other disabilities (some of which can, with persistence, be changed), as an adult you have the right to make choices about your life, including both large and minor decisions such as:

- who you will live with;

- who you will be intimate with;

- who you will marry;

- whether or not you will have children;

- who your friends will be;

- where you will live;

- where you will work;

- the kind of education, work, or career you will pursue;

- the kind of clothes you will wear;

- how you will style your hair;

- how you will spend your time;

- what you will eat;

- how you will care for yourself;

- what you will do with your leisure time; and

- what your hobbies and special interests will be.

What are the choices that you, as an adult, can make about your life?

_____

_____

_____

_____

If someone else is making these choices for you, you can set boundaries in your relationships with others and make changes in your life so that you are in charge. In some cases you may want to permanently separate yourself from that person—such as an unsupportive spouse whom you no longer love. In other cases you may reduce the time you spend with people or set clear limits about what is okay and what is not in your time together. This is not easy work. It takes courage and persistence, and you'll need to work on small steps to reach bigger goals. (You may consult with a supportive friend or a counselor as you make these changes, but the final decision should be up to you.)

What are the changes you need to make so that you are in charge of your life?

_____

_____

_____

_____

In creating this change and setting personal boundaries, "I" statements—statements that describe how you feel without accusing the other person—can help insure that interactions with others will be positive. For example, if your partner has been telling you that you cannot change jobs, you can merely say, "I am going to change jobs." If he wants to engage you in a discussion about why you need to keep this job, just return to your "I" statement, saying, "I am going to change jobs." You can give some further explanation, such as, "This job is too hard on my back" or "The hours are too long," but all you really need to say is, "I am going to change jobs."

When you are using "I" statements, avoid saying anything negative about the other person, such as, "You are being unsupportive" or "You don't understand the situation," as this can make the situation more difficult. Keep the discussion focused on you.

For example, perhaps you want to tell your mother that you are going back to finish college. You know that your mother doesn't approve of this idea and will try to convince you that you are not smart enough to do it. When your mother begins giving you all the reasons why you shouldn't go back to college, you can stay in control of the situation by ignoring her comments and repeating, "I am going back to college," until your mother simply stops trying.

Following are some examples of "I" statements:

- I am ending this relationship.

- I am buying myself a new pair of slacks.

- I want the house to be quiet from nine at night until seven in the morning.

- I will not hug you.

- I will not wash the floor.

- I am taking a course at the community college.

- I am getting safe housing for my family.

- I will talk to my friend on the phone for as long as I want.

Make a list of "I" statements you may want to use:

_____

_____

_____

_____

_____

_____

_____

Taking Action

If you are not accustomed to making decisions for yourself or taking positive action in your own behalf, this exercise will give you some practice. You will choose something you want to do, something that others have made decisions for you about in the past. Start with a minor change such as buying yourself something you've wanted or moving a piece of furniture, and work up to major life changes such as leaving a relationship, changing jobs, or moving to a new place as you feel more confident. This exercise may seem overly simplified, but when you are creating change in your life, it helps to begin with an easy first step to bolster your self-confidence with a success. As you continue to work in this book, you will find that you are ready to make some bigger changes.

1. The first step is deciding what it is you want. Examples of minor changes include going for a walk every afternoon after work, getting help preparing dinner, taking time to visit with a friend, or fixing your hair a new way.

   I want to

   _____

   _____

2. Is there anything you need to know in order to do this? For instance, if you want to go for a walk every day, you will want to think about how long you will be walking, how far that will take you, and one or several routes you might follow.

   In order to do this I need answers to the following questions:

   _____

   _____

_____

_____

_____

3. Plan your strategy.

   When will you do it?

   _____

   _____

   How will you do it? (When you are first doing something new it helps to think about all the details involved.)

   _____

   _____

   _____

   Is there anyone you need to tell about your plan? If so, how and when will you tell them?

   _____

   _____

4. Get support. When you are doing something new or doing something a different way, it helps to tell one or several friends or family members. You may even want them to do the new thing with you. This person should always be on your side, someone whom you feel comfortable with and trust.

   I will tell _____ what I am going to do and why this is an important step for me.

5. Do whatever it is you decided to do. Do it at a time that feels right to you. When you have done it, give yourself a big pat on the back. Relax and think about what a good thing you have done for yourself.

   Was this exercise helpful for you? Why or why not?

   _____

   _____

   _____

_____

_____

One woman reflected on how difficult it was for her the first time she decided to buy a new outfit without asking anyone's permission. In her marriage, before she could go shopping, she had to ask her husband's permission. He usually made up some excuse to prevent her, such as "This isn't a good time," "You don't really need a new outfit," "It probably wouldn't look good on you," or "We can't afford it." Now, when she notices that she no longer likes the way her wardrobe looks, she checks the sales and heads to one of her favorite stores. She no longer needs to think about it or plan a strategy. But the first time she did it, she had to plan it very carefully and share what she was planning to do with a friend to get support. You may or may not be ready to make changes now; do it when it feels right to you.

Develop a list of things you want, need, or deserve.

_____

_____

_____

_____

_____

_____

Who is the person (or people) keeping you from getting what you need?

_____

_____

_____

What assertive action could you take to get what it is you need and want for yourself?

_____

_____

_____

When Karen and her new spouse merged their households, Karen found herself mothering seven teenagers, including her twenty-year-old son and his pregnant girlfriend. This son and his girlfriend became increasingly verbally abusive toward Karen, expecting her to drive them wherever they wanted to go, creating chaos with the other teens, and refusing to clean up after themselves. Karen found herself needing to escape and stay with a friend for several days. She was reluctant to tell them to move because they kept accusing her of being a bad mother. Finally, she did it. With the support of her spouse, she told them to leave immediately.

Optional Activities

1. Practice saying no and notice how it feels.

   When I say no it feels:

   _____

   _____

   _____

2. Practice using "I" statements to get what you need, want, and deserve for yourself.

   Do you find "I" statements effective?

   _____

   _____

   _____

3. Decide to do something nice for yourself and then do it. Examples could include taking yourself to lunch, buying yourself a pair of socks, taking a fifteen-minute break to watch the clouds go by, or calling a special friend just to say hi.

Things to Remember Every Day

- I have the right to say no.
- I have the right to make choices about my life and how I will live it.
- I do things when they feel right to me.
- I know what I need, want, and deserve.
- I take action to make my life the way I want it.

Topic 6

Self-Esteem

Most people experience feelings of low self-esteem from time to time. This is normal. However, if you were abused or traumatized when you were a child, low self-esteem may be your constant companion. The person or people who hurt you may have told you things about yourself that were not true—that you deserve to be hurt, you are not worth anything, you are bad or ugly, or that you never do anything right. They may have even tried to convince you that the abuse was your fault, that you deserved it.

You may know logically that the things these people said to you were wrong, but, in spite of having that knowledge, you may have carried these erroneous messages about yourself with you into adulthood, perpetuating the low self-esteem brought on by the abuse. You did not deserve to be hurt. You are a good, valuable, beautiful person. You do many things well. The abuse was not your fault and you did not deserve it. Feeling bad about yourself can keep you from doing the things you want to do and living the life you want to live. You have a right to feel good about yourself, so in this chapter you will work on raising your self-esteem.

Self-Esteem Building

To do this exercise you'll need a blank piece of paper. Set a timer for ten minutes or note the time on a clock. Write your name across the top of the paper, then write everything positive and good you can think of about yourself. Include special attributes, talents, and achievements. You can use single words or sentences, whichever you prefer. You can write the same things over and over if you want to emphasize them. Don't worry about spelling, grammar, or organization. Write down whatever comes to mind but avoid making any negative statements or using any negative words. One woman wrote the following:

"I am a warm, loving, and compassionate person. I am a very good person. I like to be kind to people. Many people like me. I love taking care of small children. When I am with them I feel like I am doing something really good for myself and for the child or children I am playing with. I am also a very hard worker. People can count on me. I always do what I say I will and I do it very well. When my mother was sick I went to her house and scrubbed it from top to bottom. She was very pleased. I like to think of nice things to do for others. I empathize with others. When they are having a hard time I try to do things for them to help them feel better. I am smart. In school I was very good at math. I could figure out the problems quickly. I help my kids with their math homework. I encourage others to do the best they can. People say I have a nice smile and a nice laugh."

When the ten minutes are up, read the paper to yourself. You may feel sad when you do so because it is a new, different, and positive way of thinking about yourself—a way that contradicts some of the negative thoughts you may have had about yourself. Read the paper several times, then put it in a convenient place—your pocket, purse, wallet, or the table beside your bed. Read it over to yourself several times a day to keep reminding yourself of how great you are!

Invalidating the Source

In learning to feel better about yourself, it helps to identify the person or people that gave you the erroneous messages about yourself in the first place and to make an accurate assessment of their qualifications to determine how you should feel about yourself .

Who gave you erroneous messages about yourself? List everyone: parents, siblings, grandparents, uncles, aunts, cousins, family friends, neighbors, other children, teachers, or clergy.

_____

_____

_____

_____

_____

_____

Review the list. Next, write down one or several reasons why that person was not qualified to determine how you should feel about yourself. For example: Uncle Bill—not qualified to judge me because he forced me to do things to him I did not want to do, and was mean to his own kids. Aunt Sally—drinks a lot of alcohol, uses illegal drugs, and said nasty things to her kids all the time.

_____

_____

_____

_____

_____

_____

_____

Based on these assessments, you probably don't want these people deciding how you should feel about yourself. However, letting go of the effect these people have on your thoughts is often very difficult. The following may help.

Write the names of all of these people on a sheet of paper. Then choose to do one of the following:

- Cut the paper into tiny pieces and throw them away.

- Rip the paper up and stuff it in a dumpster.

- Color all over it with a black marker and put it in an incinerator.

Make this into a "letting go" ceremony. Many women feel much freer when they do this exercise. They feel as though they have gotten rid of the person or people who made them feel bad about themselves—and along with that go the bad feelings. If you notice yourself thinking about these people or the bad things they said to you or did to you at some point in the future, repeat this exercise.

More Practice with Positive Thoughts

In topic 3 you learned to change negative thoughts about your body to positive ones. This exercise is similar to the one you did then. This time, you will make a list of negative thoughts you have about yourself and develop positive responses to teach one. Again, use the following guidelines in developing your positive statements.

- Avoid using negative terms such as "bad," " blame," "shame," or "guilty." Instead, use only positive words such as "friendly," "warm," "compassionate," "competent," or "responsible."

- Substitute "it would be nice if" for "should."

- Use "I," "me," or your name in the positive rebuttal.

Two examples are provided to get you started. With practice and persistence, you will find that you will think positive thoughts about yourself more and more often.

I never do anything right.   _I do lots of things well._

I'll never be worth anything.   _I am a valuable person._

_____   _____

_____   _____

_____   _____

_____   _____

_____   _____

_____   _____

As before, write the positive responses on a piece of paper and keep it in your pocket or some other convenient place to read over and over, several times a day. Every time you catch yourself thinking the negative thought about yourself, replace it with the positive response.

Taking Good Care of Yourself

Low self-esteem may make you feel as though you don't need to take good care of yourself. However, you deserve to take good care of yourself, and if you work at it, you will find that you will feel better about yourself.

Following are some ideas of things you can do right now. You may be doing some of them already, but there will be others that you need to work on. You will find that you will continue to learn new and better ways to take care of yourself over time, and as you incorporate these changes into your life, your self-esteem will continue to improve.

1. Diet

   A healthy daily diet would be: five or six servings of vegetables and fruit; six servings of whole-grain foods such as bread, pasta, cereal, and rice; and two servings of protein-containing foods such as meat, eggs, beans, and nuts. Eating healthy food is a gift you can give yourself. If too much junk food is an issue for you, try to remember that the calories you get from it are almost completely empty. They give you very few of the nutrients you need to feel well and consequently boost your self-esteem, and by filling up on such food you miss the opportunity to do something really good for yourself.

   _____ This is not an issue for me. I eat very well.

   _____ I need to try to eat less junk food and more healthful food. I am going to begin by:

   _____

   _____

   _____

2. Exercise

Moving your body helps you feel better and improves your self-esteem. Arrange a time every day or as often as possible when you can get some exercise, preferably outdoors. There are many different things you could do: walk, run, ride a bicycle, play a sport, climb up and down stairs several times, put on a tape and dance to the music—anything that feels good to you. If you have a health problem that may restrict your ability to exercise, check with your doctor before beginning or changing your exercise habits.

_____ This is not an issue for me. I already exercise regularly.

_____ I am going to begin exercising. I am going to:

_____

_____

I will begin on this day:

_____

3. Do something you enjoy. In topic 1, you made a list of things you enjoy doing. Go back and review that list, and take the time every day to do at least one item.

_____ This is not a problem for me. I do things I enjoy every day.

_____ I am committed to doing something I enjoy. I have decided to:

_____

_____

In order to do the things you enjoy, you may need to gather together some equipment or supplies such as a sewing machine, a Scrabble game, art supplies, or books.

I am going to collect the following items:

_____

_____

_____

_____

4. Get good health care for yourself. Has it been a long time since you last had a physical examination? Do you have a chronic or acute health problem that needs atten-

tion? When was the last time you went to the dentist or had a Pap smear? You deserve good health care. If you have a good insurance plan, this won't be a problem. If you don't, or if your access to health care is limited, see what is available in your community that is free or has sliding scale fees you could afford. Call your local hospital to check on available options. Accessing good health care can be hard, but it is worth making the effort and getting what you need and deserve for yourself.

_____ This is not a problem for me.

_____ I need a physical examination. I will call and arrange it on this day:

_____

_____ I have a health condition that needs attention. I am going to:

_____

_____

_____

5. If you have low self-esteem, you may neglect personal hygiene tasks that would make you feel better about yourself—things such as a regular shower or bath, washing and styling your hair, trimming your nails, brushing and flossing your teeth, changing your clothes, or even getting dressed (you may feel so badly about yourself some days that you never get out of your night clothes).

_____ This is not a problem for me.

_____ I need to do the following to improve my personal hygiene:

_____

_____

_____

I am going to begin doing these things on this day at this time:

_____

6. Are there any other things you are going to start doing to take better care of yourself? If so, list them here:

_____

_____

_____

Activities to Raise Self-Esteem

1. Make a list of your ten greatest achievements. For example:

   I survived.
   I raised a wonderful child.
   I learned to read.

   _____

   _____

   _____

   _____

   _____

   _____

   _____

   _____

   _____

   Read this list often.

2. Make a list of ten ways you can treat yourself that don't include food and that don't cost anything. For example:

   Take a walk in woods.
   Window shop.
   Watch children playing on a playground.
   Study a beautiful flower.
   Chat with a friend.

   _____

   _____

   _____

   _____

_____

_____

_____

_____

_____

_____

Give yourself one or several of these treats every day.

3. Laughing makes you feel good about yourself. Make a list of five things that make you laugh.

_____

_____

_____

_____

Do something that makes you laugh at least once every day.

Optional Activities

1. Make an appreciation paper. At the top of a sheet of paper, write Things I Like About [Your Name]. Have friends, acquaintances, and family members write a statement about how or why they appreciate you. When you read it, just accept it! Read this paper over and over. Keep it in a place where you will see it often.

2. Do a mutual complimenting exercise with a friend. Set aside ten minutes, and sit in two chairs facing each other. For the first five minutes tell the other person everything you like about them and list as many of their special attributes as you can think of. For the second five minutes, your friend will do the same for you.

3. In working on topic 1, you set up a special place to do this work, and you were encouraged to decorate that space with special mementos. Add to that space objects that remind you of what a wonderful, special person you are. Look at these objects whenever you need to bolster your self-esteem.

Things to Remember Every Day

- I deserve to feel good about myself.

- I deserve to take good care of myself. That includes eating right, getting plenty of exercise, doing things I enjoy, getting good health care, and attending to my personal hygiene needs.

- I choose to spend my time with people who are nice to me and make me feel good about myself.

- I am a good person and I deserve to be alive.

Topic 7

Self-Soothing

As part of growing up, you discovered ways to make yourself feel better when you had been hurt or when you were feeling bad. Some of the these ways may have been very helpful—like petting a kitten or playing with a favorite doll. Others may have helped you feel better at first, but later worsened your situation—like drinking alcohol or smoking cigarettes. You may still be using some of these techniques to comfort and soothe yourself. As you explore this topic, you will become more aware of those ways of helping yourself feel better that are neither good nor safe, and ways that you can use to help yourself feel better that really work for you.

Jane is a forty-year-old lawyer. As an adolescent she experienced a lot of anxiety that she feels was the result of ongoing emotional abuse from her father. She began drinking to ease the anxiety and make it easier for her to go out with other teens. She also began smoking at that time because it helped her fit in. She is still dealing with the consequences: she has been in treatment twice for alcohol addiction. With continued vigilance she feels she finally has that problem under control, but smoking is a real hardship for her. She is hoping that it will be easier for her to break this habit as she learns other ways to feel good.

Following is a list of self-soothing techniques that many people use, along with the possible negative consequences of using these techniques. There is space for you to add additional activities with negative consequences that you are aware of.

Negative self-soothing technique	Possible consequences
drinking alcohol	losing self-control and control of the situation being taken advantage of addiction with continued use
using street drugs	getting arrested, jail time addiction associating with dangerous people brain damage or death losing self-control and control of the situation being taken advantage of

Negative self-soothing technique	Possible consequences
overeating	weight gain poor body image poor health
compulsive activity	being unable to do the things you want to do annoying or irritating others
dissociation	memory loss loss of control failure to learn and process new information
self-cutting	scars infection pain embarrassment
smoking	dangerous to health expensive smelly inconvenient

List other ways that you have tried to help yourself feel better that had negative consequences.

_____

_____

_____

_____

If you are using any of these negative techniques now and would like to stop, one or several of the following options might be helpful to you. Circle the ones you are going to try.

inpatient treatment program / outpatient treatment program / support group / counseling / group therapy / peer counseling / self-help books / support from family members and friends / medical care / other kinds of health care

Other options you are going to pursue:

_____

_____

_____

How and when do you plan to take this action?

_____

_____

_____

Ways to Help Yourself Feel Better

There are many things that happen every day that can cause you to feel ill, uncomfortable, upset, anxious, or irritated. You will want to do things to help yourself feel better as quickly as possible, without using any of the techniques that have negative consequences. What have you done in the past to help yourself feel better that did not have any negative consequences?

_____

_____

_____

_____

These are important techniques to keep in mind when you are looking for ways to help yourself feel better, so a bit later in this chapter we'll ask you to write them again on a separate sheet of paper. First, are there any other ideas you might be able to brainstorm? The following list might give you additional ideas. Give one or more of them a try—it helps to know many different ways of making yourself feel better. Read through the list and check off the ideas that appeal to you.

1. Do something fun or creative. Ideas include
   - crafts;
   - needlework;
   - painting, drawing;
   - woodworking;
   - make a sculpture;
   - reading fiction, comics, mystery novels, or inspirational writings;
   - doing crossword or jigsaw puzzles;
   - playing a game;
   - taking some photographs;
   - going fishing;
   - going to a movie or other community event; or
   - gardening.

2. Get some exercise.

3. Write.
   One therapist we know works with groups of people on developing journaling skills. She says, "There are many ways to use a journal in self-care. You can keep lists, record dreams, respond to questions, and explore your feelings. All ways are correct. Some of you may think that you won't be able to keep a journal because you don't write well enough. Please know that you keep a journal *just for you* and that you will do just fine."

4. Use your spiritual resources.
   These resources will of course vary from person to person. For some this means praying, going to church, or reaching out to a member of the clergy. For others it is meditating or reading affirmations and other kinds of inspirational materials. It may include rituals and ceremonies —whatever feels right to you. Spiritual work does not necessarily occur within the bounds of an organized religion.

5. Do something routine.
   When you don't feel well, it helps to do something routine, such as taking a shower, making yourself a sandwich, calling a friend or family member, cleaning the house, walking the dog, and so on.

6. Wear something that makes you feel good.

7. Get some little things done.
   Accomplishing something will usually help you feel better, even if it is a very small thing. Are there any easy things you've been meaning to do for a while, such as cleaning out a drawer, putting photos in an album, dusting a bookcase, or sending someone a card or letter?

8. Learn something new.
   Think about a topic that you are interested in but have never explored. Look for information about it in a book or on the Internet, or find out if you can take a class. Or, look at something in a new way. Read a favorite saying, poem, or piece of scripture, and see if you can find new meaning in it.

9. Be present in the moment.
   This is often referred to as mindfulness. Many of us spend so much time focusing on the future or thinking about the past that we miss out on fully experiencing what is going on in the present. Making a conscious effort to focus your attention on what you are doing right now and what is happening around you can help you feel better. For example, stop what you are doing and take a long close look at a flower, a leaf, a plant, the sky, a work of art, a souvenir from an adventure, or a picture of a loved one. Notice how much better you feel after doing this.

10. Play with children or with a pet.
    You may find that playing with small children and pets will help you feel better. Romping in the grass with a dog, petting a kitten, reading a story to a child, rocking a baby, and similar activities have a calming effect.

11. Practice relaxation techniques.
    Try listening to a relaxation tape (CDs featuring sounds from nature such as waterfalls, bird calls, and whales are widely available) or do a relaxation exercise. There are three relaxation exercises (Breathing Awareness, Being Present in the Moment,

and Guided Imagery) toward the end of this chapter. Try each of them to discover which ones you prefer, and practice them daily.

12. Get a massage.
    Have a massage by a skilled professional, or ask your spouse or a good friend to do it. Many spas offer both massage and access to a Jacuzzi or hot tub, which are both relaxing and healing.

13. Give your olfactory senses a treat.
    Many people have discovered fragrances that help them feel good. Sometimes a bouquet of fragrant flowers such as lilacs or the smell of a freshly baked loaf of bread will help you feel better. Many health food stores have an aromatherapy section with tester vials so you can determine the ones that are right for you. They come in a variety of forms, including room scenters, perfume oils, lotions, body oil blends, bath products, hair products, and foot care.

14. Listen to music.
    Listening to music may enhance your sense of well-being. The key is to think about how the music you listen to helps you. Are you listening to music for a specific purpose? Maybe you find that soft instrumental and flute music can be very relaxing and a way of managing stress. Before you turn on the player, ask yourself what type of music you like, how it affects your mood, and what you want to do right now. Keep in mind that the kind of instrument that predominates the music you select may affect the way you feel. Below, list the kinds of music you enjoy and how they make you feel.

Kind of music	How it makes me feel

Maxine relates the following: "When I was a girl, teachers told me I was tone deaf and would never be able to enjoy music. For years I avoided listening to any music. A few years ago, I was riding in a cab and the driver had on a tape of classical music. I was about to ask him to turn it off, when I realized how soothing the music was. By the end of the ride, the stress of the day was almost gone. I thanked the driver for the wonderful gift he had given me."

Making your own music is also a good way to relieve tension, particularly drumming. Perhaps you have an instrument that you enjoy playing—the piano, a guitar, or the saxophone—or that you used to play and might like to take up again.

15. Sing
    Sing to yourself. Sing at the top of your lungs. Sing when you are driving your car. Sing when you are in the shower. Sing the favorite songs you remember from your childhood.

Which of these fifteen activities would you like to try? On a separate sheet of paper, list all of your new ideas as well as the ones you have successfully used in the past that you wrote down earlier in the chapter. Hang the list in a prominent place as a reminder for those times when you need to comfort yourself, or a special treat to yourself.

Focusing Exercise

This technique allows you to remove a problem from your life by focusing on it. While sometimes we feel soothed because we distract ourselves with comforting activities, other times we feel soothed because something noxious and troubling is identified, understood, and dealt with. The focusing sequence uses a series of well-defined questions or steps to help you focus on the actual issue, the one of most importance at a given time. This may be different from what you think is the issue or the problem. Sometimes we mistake what is really bothering us. For example, we may think we are stressed about what's happening at work when in fact our anxiety is coming from worry over the health of a loved one.

Once the key issue is identified, focusing helps make the connection with the feelings generated by that issue. When the feelings are explored, the result is an understanding at a new level that translates into a positive change in feeling.

As with any new technique that will help you feel better, the more you practice, the easier and more effective it becomes. You may find that focusing at least once a day addresses issues that are troubling and keeps them from becoming overwhelming. You can also try focusing on something really good that has happened so you can linger for a time with those good feelings.

Following is the basic procedure. These instructions can be refined any way you choose to meet your individual needs. Have a person you trust, and with whom you feel safe, slowly read the instructions to you, giving you time between each step to follow the instructions in your mind and body. You do not have to say anything to the reader—your responses are your own. If you would prefer, record the instructions, again allowing time for your thoughts, and play it to yourself whenever you want to do a focusing exercise. You may choose to write your responses to each step as you go along. We use focusing so much that we have memorized the instructions.

1. Get ready by settling down in a comfortable space and asking yourself, "How do I feel inside my body right now?" Search around inside your body to notice any feelings of uneasiness or discomfort and focus your attention on these feelings for a few moments.

2. Ask yourself, "What's between me and feeling fine?" Don't answer; let the feeling that comes in your body do the answering. As each concern comes up, make a mental note of it but set it aside for a moment and ask yourself, "Except for these things, am I fine?"

3. Review the list. See which problem stands out, which seems to be begging for your attention. It may be different from the one you thought was most important.

4. Ask yourself if it's okay to focus on the problem. If the answer is yes, notice what you sense in your body when you recall the whole of that problem. (If the answer is no, choose another problem that stands out and leave the other alone for the time being.)

5. Sense the whole feeling of the problem. Really feel it in your body for several minutes—focus on it.

6. Let a word, phrase, or image that matches the feeling of this problem come into your mind.

7. Go back and forth between the word, phrase, or image and the feeling in your body. Do they really match? If they don't, find another word, phrase, or image that does feel like a match. When they match, go back and forth several times between the word, phrase, or image and the feeling in your body. If the feeling in your body changes, follow it with your attention—notice it. Be with the whole of that feeling for several moments.

8. If you want, ask yourself the following questions about the problem to help yourself get a change in the way you feel:
   - How does the worst of this feel in my body?
   - What needs to happen inside me for this whole thing to change?
   - What would feel like a small step forward with all this?
   - What would feel like a breath of fresh air in this whole thing?
   - How would it feel inside if this were all okay?
   - What needs to change inside me for this to feel better?

9. Be with the feelings that came up for a few moments. Then ask yourself, "Am I ready to stop or should I do another round of focusing?" If you are going to stop, relax for a few minutes and notice how your feelings have changed before you resume your regular activities.

Breathing Awareness

Lie down on the floor with your legs flat or bent at the knees, your arms at your sides palms up, and your eyes closed. Breathe through your nose if you can. Focus on your breathing. Place your hand on the place that seems to rise and fall the most as you breathe. If this place is on your chest, you need to practice breathing more deeply so that your abdomen rises and falls most noticeably. When you are nervous or anxious you tend to breathe short, shallow breaths in the upper chest. Now place both hands on your abdomen and notice how your abdomen rises and falls with each breath. Notice if your chest is moving in harmony with your abdomen. Continue to do this for several minutes. Get up slowly. This is something you can do during a break at work. If you can't lie down you can do it sitting in a chair.

Being Present in the Moment

Most of the stress in our lives comes from thinking about the past or worrying about the future. Instead, experiment with placing all of your attention in the present moment, so that there is no room to feel anything else. When other thoughts intrude, just turn your awareness back to the present. It is not necessary to be alone in a special place to focus all your attention on the moment. Try doing it when you are feeling irritated, waiting in a line, stopped at a street light, stuck in traffic, or just feeling overwhelmed or worried. Notice how this exercise makes you feel.

Guided Imagery

Guided imagery refers to using your imagination to direct your focus in a way that is relaxing and healing.

1. Get in a very comfortable sitting or lying position. Make sure you will not be interrupted by the phone, doorbells, or the needs of others.

2. Stare at a spot above your head on the ceiling. Breathe in to a count of eight, hold it for a count of four, and let it out for a count of eight. Do that two more times.

3. Now close your eyes but keep them in the same position they were in when you were staring at the spot on the ceiling. Breathe in to a count of eight, hold for a count of four, and breathe out for a count of eight.

4. Now focus on your toes. Let them completely relax. Now move the relaxation slowly up your legs, through your heels and calves to your knees. Let the warm feeling of relaxation move up your thighs. Feel your whole lower body relaxing. Let the relaxation move very slowly through your buttocks, lower abdomen, and lower back. Now feel it moving, very slowly, up your spine and through your abdomen. Feel the warm relaxation flowing into your chest and upper back.

5. Let this relaxation flow from your shoulders, down your arms, through your elbows and wrists, and out through your hands and fingers. Now let the relaxation go slowly through your throat and up your neck, letting it all soften and relax. Let it now move up into your face. Feel the relaxation fill your jaw, cheek muscles, and around your eyes. Let it move up into your forehead. Now let your whole scalp relax and feel warm and comfortable. Your body is now completely relaxed with the warm feeling of relaxation filling every muscle and cell of your body.

6. Now picture yourself walking in the sand on the beach on a sunny day. As you stroll along you feel the warmth of the sun on your back. You lay down on the sand. The sand cradles you and feels warm and comfortable on your back. The sun warms your body. You hear the waves crashing against the shore in a steady rhythm. The sound of seagulls calling overhead adds to your feeling of blissful contentment.

7. As you lay here, you realize that you are perfectly and completely relaxed. You feel safe and at peace with the world. You know you have the power to relax yourself completely at any time you need to. You know that by completely relaxing, you are giving your body the opportunity to stabilize itself, and that when you wake up you will feel calm, relaxed, and able to get on with your tasks for the day.

    Now, slowly wiggle your fingers and toes. Gradually open your eyes and resume your activities.

Things to Remember Every Day

- I can help myself feel better.

- There are many good things I can do to help myself feel better.

- I am in control of my life.

Topic 8

Intimacy and Trust

Most children begin life thinking that adults—their parents, other relatives, family friends, and even strangers and older children—will protect them and keep them safe. When you were abused, that trust was violated. As a result you may have lost your ability to trust anyone and may have a hard time developing close relationships or even knowing what a close or intimate relationship is.

As you explore this topic you will learn to identify those relationships in your life that are intimate and trusting and those that are not, and how to create change in close relationships.

What Is an Intimate and Trusting Relationship?

Intimacy can be described as emotional closeness, caring, affection, friendship, or a strong connection or bond with another person. However, many women who have been abused think that intimacy is the same as being sexually involved with someone. This is not true. You can be intimate and trusting with a close friend, and you can be sexual with someone with whom you are not intimate and whom you do not trust at all.

An intimate relationship is always mutual or reciprocal. Both of the people in the relationship care deeply about each other, share openly with each other, and take equal responsibility for seeing that the relationship feels good. If the intimate relationship is with someone you live with, this may mean sharing household chores and responsibilities and providing some care for each other when needed. It means talking and listening to each other.

Trust and intimacy go hand in hand in relationships. If you have a trusting relationship, you have confidence in the other person and that person has confidence in you. You each have a sense of how the other person will respond, and feel comfortable that the response will be validating and affirming. Of course, intimate and trusting relationships don't feel good all the time. It is normal to be grumpy, out of sorts, or even angry and irritable sometimes. This does not mean the relationship is no longer intimate or that you can no longer trust the other person, it just means that it is a difficult time that will probably pass quickly. If it doesn't pass soon, you and the other person can talk about what you each need to do to make the relationship feel right again. (In having such a discussion, use the "I" statements described in topic 6.

Identifying Relationships That Are Intimate and Trusting

Make a list of the people with whom you interact regularly. They can be family members, friends, co-workers, or health care professionals.

_____

_____

_____

_____

_____

_____

_____

Beginning with the first name on your list, ask yourself the following questions about your relationship with each person on your list. Consider each question carefully. If your answer to the question is yes, write the number of the question after the person's name.

1. Do we treat each other well?

2. Are we loving, deeply caring, supportive, and respectful of each other?

3. Do we avoid criticizing, judging, or blaming each other?

4. Do we listen carefully to each other?

5. Can we talk to each other about our lives: difficult times, personal issues, hopes, dreams, and goals?

6. Do we share fun and interesting activities with each other?

7. Do we avoid sharing personal information about each other with others?

8. Are we forgiving of each other?

9. Do we accept each other as we are and avoid trying to change each other?

10. Do I feel safe when I am with this person?

11. Do we have mutual understanding and empathy for each other?

12. Is this a loving relationship?

13. Does the other person ever emotionally or physically hurt me, force me to do things against my will, or threaten me, my family members, my friends, or my pets?

14. Does the relationship involve lack of respect, dishonesty, betrayal, deceit, shaming, or blaming?

15. Do I do all the giving in the relationship and get little or nothing in return?

16. Is the other person critical and/or judgmental of me? Am I ever teased, ridiculed, or put down?

17. Are there certain subjects I cannot discuss with this person?

18. Does this person try to control me?

Go back and review each person's name on your list. If anybody has a "no" for items 1 through 12 or a "yes" for items 13 through 18, you need to consider that your relationship with that person is not intimate and trusting. If you've determined that you have relationships with people in your life that you would like to improve or change, the rest of this chapter can help you.

Improving a Close Relationship

Try telling the other person directly that you would like to improve the relationship, and then state your reason using an "I" statement. What will you tell him or her?

_____

_____

Madge has always wanted to be close to her sister Alice. However, she finds this difficult because Alice makes fun of Madge's weight problem in front of others and is very critical of her. Madge could say to Alice, "I would like to be in a close relationship with you, but I can't feel close because you make fun of my weight in front of others and you are critical of my choice of careers and my housekeeping style." Then it's up to Alice whether or not to change. If she does, the relationship may get closer. If she doesn't, Madge can choose to spend more time with people who are affirming and supportive and less time with Alice.

If you feel ready to do this now, how and when will you do it?

_____

_____

_____

If you are in a relationship that is not intimate and trusting and you wish it could be but you do not feel it is safe to talk to the other person about it, you may want to discuss this relationship with a counselor, a person who works at a crisis center, or a close friend to figure out what to do. You may decide for yourself that you want to limit the amount of time you spend with that person.

I plan to address this situation by:

_____

_____

_____

_____

_____

There are many issues that can get in the way of intimacy in a relationship. Substance abuse—the misuse of alcohol or drugs—is one of the most common. If a person is abusing substances they are often unreliable and lose the ability to be intimate. They may behave in ways that are hurtful or make you feel unsafe. Illness, stress, overwork, and fear can also affect the ability to stay strongly connected with another person.

Jill's partner Ann is in a very high-pressure corporate job. Her company was involved in restructuring and Ann was under a lot of stress. She began staying at work late, and when she came home she was often tired and very irritable. She stopped doing her share of the household tasks and refused to go out with friends or even go for a walk with Jill. Jill began feeling more and more separated from Ann and began thinking of leaving the relationship. First, she shared her concerns with her counselor. With the counselor's guidance and with the use of "I" statements to express how she felt, Jill discussed the situation with Ann. Now they are having regular meetings and are working together to resolve the issues troubling them.

List things that you feel would make it difficult to remain in intimate connection with another person.

_____

_____

_____

_____

_____

Each situation is different, and you will have to use the communication skills and other strategies you have learned in this book (such as "I" statements, saying no, being clear about your physical and emotional boundaries, and talking with supportive people) or have learned through the course of your life to decide what to do and what action to take each time a difficult situation comes up.

List some skills and strategies that you feel would help you deal with difficult situations in relationships.

_____

_____

_____

_____

_____

Is there some way you can tell if a relationship you are about to begin will be intimate and trusting?

Sally, a forty-two-year-old teacher, had been in six relationships with men that she thought were going to be intimate and trusting. After she had been with each of these men for a time, they became abusive—threatening her and trying to control her life. She found that she was becoming more and more reluctant to even go out on a date. She decided to develop for herself a list of red flags—clues that would help her see that a relationship would not be good _before_ she got so involved and it became more difficult or even unsafe to leave the relationship.

Sally's Red Flags

- He wants to know where I am, who I am with, and what I am doing.

- He badmouths my friends and family.

- He criticizes me or the way I do things in a way that feels like putting me down.

- He talks about himself a lot but does not listen to me.

- He abuses drugs or alcohol.

- He does not want to be seen with me in public places.

- He wants me to spend all of my time with him.

- He wants me to take care of him.

What would you put on your list of red flags that would let you know that you need to back away from a new relationship with a potential partner or a friend?

_____

_____

_____

_____

Use this list as a guide when you are considering a new relationship.

Describing an Intimate and Trusting Relationship

Many women who have been abused find it difficult to think of any good relationships at all. They often feel as though they are surrounded by people who don't understand them and treat them badly. It helps to think back carefully and come up with *someone* in your life with whom you had a good relationship.

Martha is a fifty-five-year-old social worker who has a hard time making and keeping friends. She feels that her inability to trust others causes her to back away when others start getting close. In other words, she sabotages relationships before they have a chance to get started. It helped her to think of the close relationship she shared with her grandmother when she was growing up. Her grandmother lived just down the block from where she lived, and Martha usually stopped there on her way home from school. Her grandmother always had a snack waiting for her such as home-baked cookies and hot chocolate. She listened intently while Martha shared the happenings of the day as well as her deepest feelings and secrets. Her grandmother told her stories of what it was like to grow up during the Depression when there was so little money. They played games, read books, and were silly together. Now, when Martha finds herself sabotaging a new relationship, she remembers her grandmother. She remembers that there are good people she can trust. This memory sometimes helps her have the courage to risk a new relationship.

Write about a person in your life with whom you enjoyed an intimate and trusting relationship. It could be a family member, friend, teacher, or employer.

_____

_____

_____

_____

_____

_____

_____

_____

Optional Activities

1. Draw a colorful picture or make a collage that shows how it feels when you are in a relationship with another person that feels good to you.

2. Spend at least ten minutes talking to a friend with whom you have an intimate and trusting relationship.

Things to Remember Every Day

- I deserve to have intimate, trusting relationships with others.

- I know that an intimate trusting relationship is mutual and safe.

- I decide who I want to be close to and with whom I want to have sex.

- I make plans and take action to deal with difficult circumstances in my life.

Topic 9

Female Sexuality

When you were young, your information on female sexuality may have come from so many different sources that it was difficult to figure out what was right and what was wrong. Your parents, the media, church, school, friends, and, later on, your partners may have all given different messages regarding what you should and should not feel and what you should and should not do. To make matters worse, if your first sexual experiences were under the control of someone else, you may feel that sex is taboo and that your own responses are bad or wrong.

This chapter will try to dispel some of the many myths around female sexuality, help you see your sexual responses as normal, help you to accept your body and its sexuality as a good thing, and help you decide for yourself how you feel about your sexuality. Changing the way you feel about your sexuality is a long process—it may go on for most or all of your life.

Molly is fifty-five and has worked as an emergency room nurse for most of her adult life, taking a few years off to raise her children. She remembers that as a young girl she was taught that if she touched herself "down there" for any reason other than to wash herself, it meant something was wrong with her. In church school she learned that touching the genital area was a sin and she should not even *want* to do it. When she was in nursing school, she heard other students discussing masturbation, and it was then she discovered that she could find pleasure in touching her own body. She has gradually learned other ways to enjoy her sexuality, such as taking a warm bubble bath in a candlelit room and looking at herself nude in front of a full-length mirror. Sometimes she even does a dance in the nude, enjoying the feeling of moving her body without the weight of clothing.

Changing the Way You Think about Sexuality

In learning about your sexuality you may have learned a lot of myths that may or may not be true. The following exercise gives you an opportunity to think about some of these myths and decide how you feel about them. If you wish, you can read our statement about the myth either before or after writing your own statement.

Myth: It's not okay for women to feel sexual or experience sexual pleasure.

New way of thinking: Women have a right to feel sexual and to experience sexual pleasure. Sexuality can be fun and can make you feel revitalized and energetic, passionate and healthy.

How do you feel?

_____

_____

_____

Myth: If you are too old, fat, or have a disability, you aren't sexual.

New way of thinking: Everyone is sexual. Women can enjoy their sexuality all their lives if they want to. While sexual feelings change as you age, women report that they continue to feel sexual or to enjoy sex even when they are quite elderly. Being overweight doesn't have anything to do with sexuality, and women with disabilities and chronic or acute diseases can also be sexual and enjoy sex. The book *Our Bodies, Ourselves for the New Century* (Boston Women's Health Collective, New York: Simon and Schuster, 1998) has a section on sexuality and disability that is well worth reading.

How do you feel?

_____

_____

_____

Myth: Being sexual means having intercourse with a partner.

New way of thinking: There are many ways to enjoy being sexual without having intercourse or even being with a partner: wearing something that makes you feel really sexy, such as a blouse that nicely outlines your breasts; thinking about past, future, or possible sexual experiences; or cuddling, hugging, and kissing.

How do you feel?

_____

_____

_____

Myth: If you think about doing something "kinky," like having group sex, it means you really want to do it—and it is bad to think these thoughts.

New way of thinking: Many women report that they fantasize about sexual things they would never really want to do. There is nothing wrong with it.

How do you feel?

Myth: Your genitals should never have any smell.

New way of thinking: There are normal bodily secretions that come from both female and male sexual organs. These secretions have distinctive odors that are perfectly normal.

How do you feel?

Myth: If you don't feel really sexy most of the time, you are not normal.

New way of thinking: Everyone feels more sexual sometimes and less sexual other times. It is easier to feel sexual when you are feeling well, are relaxed and well rested, are in a private space, and, perhaps, with a person with whom you have a close personal relationship. Drugs, alcohol, and certain medications can also reduce sexual feelings. If you notice you feel less sexual after you begin taking a medication, ask your doctor if he's aware that it could have such side effects, or look the medication up in a reference book such as *Consumer Drug Digest*. (Remember, if you don't like the side effect of a medication, you have the right not to take that medication or to ask the doctor to change you to a different one.)

How do you feel?

Myth: Masturbation or touching your breasts or genitals to give yourself pleasure is not okay.

New way of thinking: It's your body. It is normal to touch and rub your own body to give yourself pleasure.

How do you feel?

_____

_____

Myth: Female genitals are ugly and should not be looked at.

New way of thinking: It's up to you to decide whether you like the way your genitals look. Many women do—in fact, many enjoy looking at their genitals in a mirror.

How do you feel?

_____

_____

_____

Myth: Women of certain racial, cultural, and ethnic backgrounds are more sexual than other women.

New way of thinking: There is no proof of this. There is diversity among all women in their expression of sexuality.

How do you feel?

_____

_____

_____

Reading the above myths may have reminded you of others that you've heard over the years. Are there any myths and attitudes concerning your sexuality that you would like to clarify for yourself? If so, complete the following section. Again, don't be afraid to consult resources such as a book, a counselor, a health care professional or crisis worker, or other women with whom you feel comfortable.

Myth, issue, or attitude:

_____

Did I learn this from a reliable source of information on this topic?

_____

How do I really feel about this? What do I want to do about it?

_____

Does it hurt me or anyone else to feel this way?

_____

Do I need more information about this? How do I plan to get it?

_____

Myth, issue, or attitude:

_____

Did I learn this from a reliable source of information on this topic?

_____

How do I really feel about this? What do I want to do about it?

_____

Does it hurt me or anyone else to feel this way?

_____

Do I need more information about this? How do I plan to get it?

_____

Myth, issue, or attitude:

_____

Did I learn this from a reliable source of information on this topic?

_____

How do I really feel about this? What do I want to do about it?

_____

Does it hurt me or anyone else to feel this way?

_____

Do I need more information about this? How do I plan to get it?

_____

Feeling Sexual

Being sexually abused can keep you from feeling sexual feelings. You may associate sex with abuse, which can make your own sexual feelings seem dangerous. Or you may have learned to turn off your sexual feelings. You kept yourself safe by feeling nothing at all—a coping mechanism that helped you get through very difficult times. However, now that you are an adult, you will want to enjoy sexual feelings. They can still be aroused, even if you don't ever remember having felt them! The following exercise will help you identify those circumstances in which you feel most sexual. Use your answers here as a guide to awakening or increasing your sexuality.

1. Look through a popular magazine such as *People, Vanity Fair,* or *Outside.* Do you notice any subtle sexual feelings when you look at certain pictures? Write down the kinds of pictures that arouse some sexual feelings.

   _____

   _____

   _____

2. Look through your clothes and/or try on clothes in your favorite store.

   Which kind of clothes make you feel more sexual?

   _____

   _____

   How would you describe those clothes? What colors are they?

   _____

   _____

   How do the clothes that make you feel more sexual differ from the clothes that don't arouse any sexual feelings?

   _____

   _____

3. Look at yourself in the mirror. Experiment with different facial expressions. Which are more sexual? Which are less sexual?

   _____

   _____

   Do you feel more sexual if you wear makeup? If so, what kind?

   _____

   _____

If your hair is long enough, play with it—wrap it around your head, push it away from your face, pull some of it down over your forehead, and so on. When do you feel most sexual?

_____

_____

4. In front of a full-length mirror, if possible, experiment with the ways you stand and walk. Which ways of standing and walking make you feel most sexual?

_____

_____

5. Think about the things you do and the places you go. When do you feel most sexual?

_____

_____

When do you feel the least sexual?

_____

_____

Body Stimulation

You may have been taught that the only parts of the body that are involved in feeling sexual are the breasts and the genital area. This exercise will help you discover other parts of your body that have sexual feeling, too. If it feels comfortable to you, do this exercise partially clothed or unclothed. Using the tips of your fingers, rub every part of your body that you feel comfortable touching. Do it very slowly, using gentle circular motions, short, light strokes or whatever feels good to you. Vary the touch to please yourself.

Which areas made you feel most sexual?

_____

_____

_____

_____

_____

Did you learn anything new about your body by doing this exercise?

_____

_____

_____

Optional Activities

1. Talk with a trusted woman friend or a group of women about sexuality. Sharing with others will help you heal, feel affirmed and validated, reassess your beliefs, learn to be assertive about your needs, and feel connected with others. Topics that might be discussed include:
   * the first time you felt sexual,
   * your first menstrual period,
   * what makes you feel sexy, and
   * your first sexual experience.

2. Notice times during the day when you feel sexual. Write about them in your journal.

Things to Remember Every Day

* I am sexy.

* I have the right to feel and be sexual.

* Being sexual feels good.

* I enjoy my sexuality.

* I am changing the way I feel about my sexuality.

* I decide how I feel about issues related to my sexuality.

* My body looks and is great! It is fine just the way it is!

Topic 10

Sex with a Partner

Women who have been traumatized tend to respond to sex in one of three ways: oversexualizing all relationships and/or being indiscriminately sexual, shutting down sexual feelings and totally avoiding sexual encounters, or having sex with a loved partner but not fully enjoying it or, in some cases, not enjoying it at all. If you respond to sex in any of these ways, you may be missing some or all of the pleasure of enjoying a sexually intimate relationship with a partner. Sex can connect you with another person in a very special and delightful way. Everyone deserves to have good sexual experiences with a loving partner. This topic will help you find ways to address the issues that may be keeping you from having a good sexual relationship. You will not be able to complete all of the exercises that are suggested in this topic in your one-hour session—especially those that you would do with a partner or prospective partner—so you may want to return to this topic again and again. Skip over any sections or exercises that you feel would not be helpful to you.

As you begin to work on this topic, remember that when you have sex with a partner, you put yourself in a very vulnerable position. The end result of sexual contact can be wonderful, with both of you going on to enjoy future sexual contact and an increasingly intimate relationship. However, a sexual encounter can also lead to hurt and rejection. Like so many of the good things in life, it is a risk. To avoid this risk would be to limit one aspect of your life. However, you can reduce the risk of hurtful encounters if you proceed slowly and cautiously, listening closely to your intuition and avoiding sexual contact when it doesn't feel right or when you are not ready.

Becoming Sexually Active

If you have responded to sexual abuse by avoiding sex and you're ready to change that, you need to proceed slowly, taking very small steps. This is ongoing work and only you can decide when you are ready to get sexually involved with another person. Moving too quickly, or getting into a sexual relationship with an inappropriate person, could be more damaging than helpful. Here are some things to do and think about that should help you:

1. Refer back to the section Feeling Sexual from topic 9. Spend some additional time on each of the activities in that section, and continue to do them in your spare time until you feel comfortable with the information you have learned about your sexuality. Write about your findings in your journal.

2. Repeat the Body Stimulation exercise from topic 9 again and again. Each time you do it you will become more aware of and comfortable with touching those parts of your body that give you sexual pleasure.

3. Talk to someone whom you trust and feel comfortable with about this issue—a counselor or therapist, a crisis center worker, a close friend, or a woman or several members of a support group for women who have been sexually abused. Don't expect the other person to change or "fix" you. You don't need to be fixed or changed by someone else. You are experiencing normal reactions to bad things that happened to you. Talking will help you understand your feelings and will help you decide what you want to do about them. Ask the person who is listening to just be supportive—tell them that suggestions or advice, criticism, judging, or telling you about similar circumstances in their life would not be helpful. If the other person is a friend, you could divide the time in half so each of you have time to talk. You may need to talk to someone else many times about this issue.

I am going to talk to this person at this time:

_____

4. Think about the kinds of potential partners who are most attractive to you, who you find most interesting, or with whom you are most comfortable.

What gender would you prefer—male, female, or doesn't matter?

_____

Would this person be older or younger than you, or does age not matter?

_____

What would this person look like? Would looks really matter to you?

_____

What interests would this person have?

_____

_____

How would this person act?

_____

_____

What kinds of behavior from another person would tell you that you did not want to get further involved with him or her?

_____

_____

_____

Describe an ideal sexual partner.

_____

_____

_____

_____

_____

_____

5. Some women meet potential partners through support groups, special-interest groups or clubs, church, educational courses or workshops, social events, dating services, or bars. Where could you meet the kind of person you described above? Where would you feel comfortable going or what would you feel comfortable doing to meet him or her?

_____

_____

_____

6. Once you have met someone with whom you would like to become more intimate, it is generally wise to proceed very slowly. Having sex right away often doesn't feel good, and one-night stands can be especially problematic. Quick encounters connect you with a person before you know they are safe or deserving of your trust. Suggested steps in getting to know another person would be:

   • Get together casually several times in a public place—have lunch, coffee, go for a short walk, or attend a community program that is of mutual interest.

   • Begin dating casually—go to the movies, out to dinner, or whatever you prefer, and perhaps end the date with a hug and kiss.

- Spend time together at each other's homes watching television, playing a game, talking, or being with the other person's family.
- When you are both ready to be more intimate, do only what feels comfortable to both of you. Two ways of easing into a sexual relationship are the warm hug and body explorations:

Warm hug: Begin by standing several feet in front of your partner. Look into each other's eyes for several moments. Then walk toward each other and embrace, with your hands flat and firm on the other person's back. Hold your bodies closely together for several moments, pressing softly against each other from cheeks to knees. Step back and look into each other's eyes again. Do this at least several times when you are together.

Body explorations: Sit cross-legged on the floor or in some other comfortable position, facing your partner. Gently and softly take turns rubbing parts of each other's body wherever it feels comfortable to them. Avoid sensitive areas if either of you is hesitant.

When either of you suggests sexual activity, you may want to tell the other person you have had a difficult experience and need to proceed very slowly. A good potential partner will honor your wishes and not press you to proceed faster than you want to. This does not mean that you need to go into the details of your trauma history. You only need to say that you have had some bad experiences and now you need to feel safe and in control in order to explore a sexual relationship. As your relationship with this partner deepens, you may feel that you want to share more about your past history.

7. As you work on these issues, writing your thoughts and feelings will help you focus on and reinforce what you are learning. If you want to make sure no one else reads what you write, find a safe place to store your writings or destroy them. The purpose is in the writing, and not necessarily in having it available to reread later or to show to someone else.

Accurately Reading the Actions of Others

Women who have been sexually abused sometimes oversexualize relationships—they incorrectly sense sexual overtones and interest in contact with others even if the contact is very brief or inconsequential. Perhaps you fall into this category and you make sexual overtures based on this perceived interest. When the other person realizes you are making sexual overtures, he or she may either take advantage of the opportunity or back off.

Dana is a twenty-eight-year-old who works in the accounting department of a large supermarket chain. In her work she interacts with many different men and women throughout the day. She discovered that rather than thinking of a smile, a pat on the back, or a thank-you as a friendly gesture, she thought it meant the other person wanted to have sexual contact. Her responses were often inappropriate, which got her into some very difficult situations. She began flirting and making provocative comments to casual colleagues. She assumed that most of the single men and a few of the married men with whom she worked wanted to have sex with her. She even had one-night stands with a few of her co-workers. All this has made the workplace very uncomfortable for her, to the point where she is thinking of changing jobs. She wishes she could stop getting into these situations, but she has trouble reading a friendly gesture as such and mistakes kindness for seduction.

If this is a problem for you, you may want to rethink your thought patterns so that they more accurately reflect the message the other person is trying to give you. The following exercise will help you to do that.

Reality Checking

In this exercise you will begin learning to read the body language, words, and actions of others in a different way. For instance, you may have thought an ordinary smile meant that the other person found you sexually attractive. In reality, it may have been just a friendly gesture on the part of the other person to let you know they saw you. Think of things others have done and how you interpreted these gestures. Could you have interpreted them in a different way that was probably what the person really meant? Consider the following example:

Action or signal from other person:

Attractive male co-worker tells me I did a great job on a recent project!

Your interpretation:

He wants to have an affair with me!

A more accurate assessment of what the person probably meant:

He probably meant that he felt I did a really good job.

Think of actions or signals from other people that you feel you have misinterpreted in the past.

Action or signal from other person:

_____

_____

First thing that comes to my mind:

_____

_____

A more accurate assessment of what the person probably meant:

_____

_____

Action or signal from other person:

_____

_____

First thing that comes to my mind:

_____

_____

A more accurate assessment of what the person probably meant:

_____

_____

Action or signal from other person:

_____

_____

First thing that comes to my mind:

_____

_____

A more accurate assessment of what the person probably meant:

_____

_____

After you have completed this exercise, you will want to keep it in mind as you interact with others each day, doing reality checks on what their actions could really mean.

Personal List of Rules

Like Dana, you may want to have fewer brief sexual encounters and work on getting into an intimate long-term sexual relationship. To do this, it may be helpful to develop for yourself a set of personal guidelines or rules that will keep you out of brief sexual encounters and allow you to get more intimately involved with a person whom you know well and might want as a possible prospective partner.

Some rules you might consider are:

1. I won't have sex with anyone until I have gone out with them at least (you set the number) times.

2. I will stop spending time in bars (or name some other or more specific places) to look for possible partners.

3. I will not have sex with anyone who is in a relationship with someone else.

4. I will not go to the other person's home or have them come to my home until we have gotten together at least (you set the number) of times.

5. I will not have sex with anyone who tries to convince me to have sex with them before I feel ready.

6. I will not have sex with anyone who tries to convince me that things I know about sex are false.

7. In order to have sex with me, the other person must treat me with dignity, compassion, and respect at all times.

8. I will only consider sexual contact with a person who is not having sex with anyone else (that means I have to trust that what the other person is telling me is true).

Which of these rules would you include on your list and what other rules or guidelines would be helpful to you?

_____

_____

_____

_____

_____

Before You Have Sex

In order to keep yourself safe, there are several issues that need to be taken into consideration and decisions that have to be made before you get sexually involved with another person.

1. What do you plan to do about birth control? Keep in mind that birth control is the responsibility of both partners, so this is something you may wish to speak to your prospective partner about. Also, be aware of false information you may hear about pregnancy: It is not true that you can't get pregnant during, just prior to, or just after your menstrual period. Although women tend to ovulate midway between menstrual cycles, women do get pregnant throughout their cycle. Nor is it true that the withdrawal method is effective against pregnancy—small amounts of semen are left in the vagina even if he pulls out in time. (Actually, you can get pregnant if any semen is deposited in the genital area.) Finally, it is not true that douching immedi-

ately following intercourse will prevent pregnancy. Sperm are very vigorous and douching does not necessarily remove all of them.

Some women report that men who don't want to use birth control try to convince them that some of these erroneous beliefs are true. As a woman, you need to trust yourself, know that these beliefs are wrong, and take action accordingly. Are you sure you want to have sex with someone who would try to convince you of something that was not true?

2. What will you do to prevent AIDS and other sexually transmitted diseases? Everyone is at risk, even if you see yourself as being in a "low-risk" category. You have a responsibility to yourself and to a prospective sexual partner to be tested for AIDS and other diseases before becoming sexually involved. Free testing is available in most areas—contact your local AIDS organization, hospital, or other health care organization to get information.

3. Before a sexual relationship begins, both people need to agree that this is what they want to do. Both people have a right to say no to sex now *or* later. Always remember that no one has the right to force any kind of sexual activity upon you if it makes you uncomfortable.

List any other issues you want to consider before getting sexually involved with another person.

_____

_____

_____

_____

_____

Dealing with Frightening Memories

Sometimes sex may bring up frightening memories of bad things that happened to you in the past. It helps if your partner knows about your abuse history and knows about your potential for reliving these memories during sex, because he or she can then help you—you can ask to be held lovingly until you feel better. Take a break and remind yourself that you are not in the past, that this is the present and you are now in control of the situation.

If your memories during sex are too troubling, you should tell your partner that you will need to abstain until you feel safer. It is important for you to feel in control of your body and of your sexual activity.

If you are having intrusive memories, it's probably because some part of the sex act is triggering them. With your partner's help, try to figure out what it might be—kissing, having your breasts touched, being penetrated, or some other particular sexual contact may be causing the problem. If you can isolate the trigger, you can substitute behaviors that do not remind you of the past.

If you find that everything about sex causes you to remember the abuse, then you and your partner might want to see a counselor or trauma specialist together to help you. Remember, there are many ways to be close without being sexual. A loving partner will wait until sex feels right to you.

Fantasizing or Dissociating During Sex

You may find that, due to traumatic sexual experiences in the past, you automatically cope or "get through" sex by thinking about some other situation or feeling unconnected from your body. Many women find this habit to be very frustrating. They want to enjoy being with their present partner and to appreciate the intimacy they are sharing. To "be present" more and more when you are sexually involved, practice *being present in the moment*. That means focusing all your attention on what is happening right at that moment. You can begin to practice it while doing other things: when you are washing the dishes, focus only on scraping off the leftovers, putting the dish in the water, rubbing the plate with a sponge, feeling the warm soapy water on your hands, and so on, instead of thinking of something you have done in the past or something you are worried about. Practice this over and over again each day with different chores and errands. As you do, you will notice that you feel more relaxed and that you are enjoying life more. When you feel ready, try being present in the moment during sex, focusing your attention on the touch, the feelings, and on your partner. This is a skill that takes practice and improves over time. Looking into your partner's face and eyes may help you stay connected to and aware of your present partner.

Optional Activities

1. Think of the best sexual relationship you have ever had. What did you like about it?

_____

_____

_____

_____

_____

2. What are the pros and cons of getting into a sexual relationship?

_____

_____

_____

_____

_____

Things to Remember Every Day

- I am a very special and valuable person. My value is not related to whether or not I am willing to have sex.

- If I am in a relationship, I decide with my partner whether or not I will have sex. I don't need to have sex just because the person I am with wants me to. I don't need to do anything sexual that I don't want to do.

- I have the right to change my mind and the right to stop having sex after I've started. I have the right to decide what sexual activities I will do and for how long. This may be frustrating for the other person, but they need to respect my feelings and decisions.

- I don't need to have an orgasm to show my sexual partner what a good lover he or she is.

- Sex is more fun if I am in an equal role with my partner.

- All sexual contact—not just intercourse—is sex.

Topic 11

Transition from Empowerment to Trauma Recovery

In the first ten topics you worked on exercises to help you regain a true sense of your value and power as a woman, to learn to take good care of yourself, and to make some personal decisions about your life. This topic will serve as a bridge between your earlier work and the next part of the book: trauma recovery.

Celebrate Your Accomplishment

Before you begin work on the next part of this book, you deserve congratulations! You have just completed the first ten topics in your healing journey. This is a very remarkable achievement. To celebrate this feat, make a plan to do something very special for yourself in the coming week. Here are some ideas for a celebration.

- Ask someone you live with to take over your household responsibilities for a day.

- Ask someone to serve you breakfast in bed.

- If you can afford it, buy yourself a treat such as something special to wear, a tape or CD, a new journal, or a bouquet of flowers.

- Take yourself out for a special lunch.

- Go to the movies or to a concert.

- Spend some extra time with a special friend and tell that person about your accomplishment.

- Draw a picture of the "new" you.

To celebrate completion of the first ten topics in this book, I plan to:

_____

_____

Describe any advance planning or preparations you need to make:

_____

_____

Reviewing Your Goals

In topic 1, you wrote your personal goals for doing this work. Review them now . . . do you think you have made some progress? If so, how?

_____

_____

_____

_____

_____

_____

_____

Would you change any of these goals? If so, how?

_____

_____

_____

_____

_____

Would you eliminate any of these goals? If so, why?

_____

_____

_____

_____

_____

Would you add any new goals? If so, what would they be and why would you add them?

_____

_____

_____

_____

Identifying and Addressing Your Challenges

As you progressed through the first ten topics, some of the information and exercises may have been very easy for you while others may have been much more difficult and challenging. Now is a good time to go back and repeat an exercise or two in those topics you found most challenging. Which three of the last ten topics posed the greatest difficulty for you? After you've picked three, review those chapters and choose one or two exercises from each that you will repeat.

Activities or exercises I will do again:

_____

_____

_____

_____

_____

After you've completed round two of those exercises you selected, compare your new responses to your previous responses. How have they changed?

_____

_____

_____

_____

_____

_____

_____

_____

Optional Activity

Repeat other exercises of your choice in the preceding topics.

Things to Remember Every Day

- I am doing a great job on all of this.
- I am growing and changing.
- I feel good about myself.
- I am a unique and special person who deserves the very best that life has to offer.

Part 2

Trauma Recovery

Topic 12

Understanding Trauma

In this topic, you will learn about trauma and the feelings associated with it, and how you have learned to cope with trauma in your life. This is difficult work, and may bring up some strong emotions for you. You may not want to complete the whole chapter all at once. To help ease you into (and out of) this work, we'd like to first introduce you to a simple ritual. Each time you begin and end your work, use this ritual to keep yourself focused in the present and to remind yourself of the positive aspects of your life.

Beginning and Ending Ritual

Use this simple activity any time you are working on difficult issues. Some women like to complete this activity just prior to talking with a counselor, writing in a journal, visiting with a family member, doing some artwork related to trauma, or repeating an exercise from this book. First, write down four good things that happened to you in the last two days. They don't have to be big things—just things that made an impression on you and that were enjoyable. For instance, my list for the last two days is:

1. I saw a cute baby and she smiled at me.

2. I had a nice visit with an old friend.

3. I finished reading a heartwarming novel.

4. The sweater I put on this morning felt warm and cozy.

At the end of the session, write down two things you are looking forward to—one that is within the next few days and one in the more distant future. For example, my list would be:

1. Coming right up: buying a new kind of bread I really like at the grocery store.

2. In the future: spring—warm weather, flowers, and birds.

The purpose of this ritual is to help you stay connected with the good things in your life while you are doing this work and also to put a frame around your work so it becomes a small part of your life with a beginning and an end, not your whole life.

To begin work on this topic, write four good things that happened to you in the last two days:

_____

_____

_____

_____

Categorizing Your Traumas

Everyone experiences minor traumas—things that are temporarily upsetting and that may make us anxious and upset. Such things include:

- not getting an anticipated check on time,

- the car breaking down,

- missing an appointment,

- a friend being rude to you, or

- getting a cold.

Most of the time you probably get over these small traumas quickly. Below, list some minor traumas that you have experienced recently:

_____

_____

_____

From time to time everyone experiences trauma that is harder to deal with and more upsetting: seeing a beloved pet hit by a car, losing a friend to a devastating illness, having your house broken into, getting divorced, or being a victim of a robbery. These experiences may cause an increase in anxiety and fears, insomnia, depression, nightmares, and flashbacks. As time goes on, the impact of these traumas tends to decrease until finally, while the person may still think of such traumas from time to time, day-to-day activities are not significantly affected.

List any of these kinds of traumas you have experienced in your life.

_____

_____

_____

_____

Unfortunately, people also experience trauma that is so horrific that it may seem almost impossible to overcome—trauma that is so awful that the symptoms persist and often overwhelm the person's life. Examples of these kinds of trauma include child abuse, sexual abuse, physical abuse, emotional abuse, being a victim of a violent crime, losing one or several close family members, or living through a war. Sometimes right after the trauma occurs, and sometimes much later, people who experience these kinds of trauma develop severe and persistent symptoms such as depression, anxiety, rage, nightmares, flashbacks, and feeling out of touch with reality. They may turn to alcohol, illegal drugs, promiscuous sex, or self-harming behaviors to try to ease the pain.

Little notice was taken of the effects of trauma, or the relationship between traumatic experiences and these kinds of symptoms, until after World War II and, more recently, the Vietnam War. In fact, people who experienced severe war trauma were (and still are) often told that they had a mental illness. After World War II, some soldiers and survivors of the Nazi concentration camps displayed serious and persistent symptoms that demanded attention. Similarly, during the Vietnam War, veterans returned from the battlefield with symptoms so serious and so obviously related to their war experiences that the effects of trauma could not be ignored. In recent years, the effects of other kinds of horrific trauma have also been recognized—yet much of the literature about trauma still reflects what we learned from soldiers, especially prisoners of war, and holocaust survivors.

We now know that relieving the effects of trauma on a person's life takes very specialized treatment along with lots of persistence and courage. Activities such as the ones in this book can help you regain a sense of your power, validate your experiences, help you regain your sense of self so you can enjoy life, and relearn how to connect with others in meaningful ways.

What kinds of severe trauma have you experienced?

_____

_____

_____

_____

_____

Factors That Affect Recovery and Healing

Every person responds to trauma in his or her life differently. There is no set period of time for recovery. The factors that seem to affect how long it takes to get over the effects of trauma in one's life—or at least reduce these effects so they are not controlling the person's life—include:

- personality type;

- the environment you grew up in—was it hectic and chaotic, or calm and peaceful;

- your current living circumstances;

- your general health;

- substance abuse or addictions;

- the length of your exposure to the trauma;

- the number of traumas you have experienced—even minor traumas; and

- the severity of the trauma.

No one else can determine how a trauma could or should affect someone else; do not feel that your trauma was "too small" to have had such a powerful impact.

One woman told us that she grew up in a hectic and chaotic household—small traumas were happening all the time, such as burned dinners, people yelling at each other, lots of people moving in and out. Some traumas that were harder to deal with were also happening simultaneously—she lost her favorite pet and she was involved in a serious car accident. These factors all combined to make it harder for her to deal with a serious sexual assault when she was a teen.

What factors in your life do you feel affect your healing journey?

_____

_____

_____

_____

Sharing Feelings and Experiences

List five words that you often use to describe how you feel.

_____

_____

For many people, talking about the trauma helps—it's part of the healing process. You may be uncomfortable or not used to talking about it, but the inability to talk about feelings and the hard things that happen to us in our lives can make the healing process more difficult. In many families, people don't talk about trauma at all. There are a couple of reasons for this. First, family members may feel it is best to forget the bad things that have happened.

When Charlene was a little girl, her friend was killed in a very bad accident while she was playing with Charlene. Charlene's family felt it was best for her not to talk about the accident and they tried to get her to focus her attention on other things so she would forget. Charlene never forgot. As an adult she spent many years in counseling to relieve the effects of this trauma.

Many schools now offer children special programs and services when there has been a tragedy in the community to give students the opportunity to talk about the trauma and begin to heal.

A second reason for silence in families is that the family members don't want other people to find out about bad things that are happening, especially if it involves abuse. It becomes a family secret—a secret that protects the abuser and allows the abuse to go on. Family members may even be threatened to keep them from telling others what is happening, or there may be an unspoken rule in the family not to talk to anyone about certain things.

How did your family talk about feelings and other experiences?

_____

_____

_____

_____

It helps to think about the words associated with these experiences so you can think more clearly about them, write about them, and tell supportive people what happened to you.

In this exercise, you will write some words that could be used to describe feelings related to trauma. To help you think more clearly about the feelings associated with the word, think of a color that matches that feeling you are describing. (You can use the same color over and over if that feels right to you.) For example, "angry—bright red," "isolated—dark gray."

_____

_____

_____

_____

_____

_____

_____

Now make a list of ten "feeling" words that describe the trauma you experienced.

_____

_____

_____

How did it feel to write and think about these words?

_____

_____

_____

_____

_____

_____

Coping with Trauma

When you were traumatized, especially if you were traumatized repeatedly, you figured out some ways to cope with the trauma so you could get by and still go to school, do your homework, find some peace and quiet for yourself, play, and so on without feeling the pain so much. This took a lot of strength and creativity.

One woman found some special places in the woods near her home. She called these places "camps" and spent a lot of time there reading books, playing with her dolls, daydreaming, and watching the clouds through the treetops. She felt safe and comfortable there because nobody could find her.

Describe some ways that you learned to cope with abuse in your life.

_____

_____

_____

_____

_____

Repeat several times, out loud if possible, "I am a strong and creative person. I used these attributes to help me get through the hard times in my life."

Ending Ritual

Describe something you are looking forward to that will happen soon.

_____

_____

Describe something you are looking forward to that is happening in the more distant future.

_____

_____

Optional Activities

1. Glance at the headlines in your local paper. How do you think the people in these stories might have been affected by what happened to them? Do you think these things will be easy or hard for them to "get over"?

2. Begin talking about trauma. Briefly talk to someone you trust about your trauma—a sentence or two would be fine.

   How did that feel?

   _____

   _____

   _____

Things to Remember Every Day

- I can talk about feelings related to trauma if I wish. Talking to others about bad things that have happened to me helps me heal.

- I am a strong and creative person—I was able to develop some ways to cope with trauma that helped me at that time. I am proud of my strength and creativity.

Topic 13

The Body Remembers
What the Mind Forgets

Beginning Ritual

To begin work on this topic, write four good things that happened to you in the last two days:

_____

_____

_____

_____

Body Memories

Usually, when we are asked about a memory most of us assume that we must search for a story of some sort. We might try to conjure up a visual image of something that happened or a place where we spent time. Thoughts, words, and images do constitute our memories, but not entirely. We also remember things in other ways, such as through sound, smell, and taste. Sometimes the smell will be all we remember—the context is lost but the smell remains.

Our bodies also have memories. A feeling, an ache, an itch—these are physical sensations, but they can also be memories. Just as our intellects remember in words, our bodies' memories are stored in sensations. That pain in your back may be because you got too much exercise, or it may be a memory of something that happened a long time ago. In some cases, there will be other memories that accompany the pain, but in other cases the pain itself will be the only memory you have.

When you were traumatized, your body responded to this severe stress by trying to protect itself. It secreted hormones and other substances that may have given you some of the strength it took to endure what you went through. But with severe and repeated trauma, the body forgets how to shut this release off. You may feel tense, irritable, anxious, and nervous all or most of the time. When this goes on for a long period of time, you develop chronic tension and pain in various parts of your body—sometimes in the part of your body that was most affected by the trauma. You may have so much pain that you try to ignore it. You may feel that you are really out of touch with your body and how it feels, or perhaps the discomfort and pain is so persistent that it keeps you from doing the things you want to do. With consistent use of some of the relaxation and stress-reduction exercises in this topic, you will notice that your body starts feeling better and better.

Patsy, a thirty-year-old stockbroker, felt that her body was always very tense and tight. She assumed this was normal. However, when she started getting aches and pains in her neck, shoulders, and lower back, she sought help. She began getting massages from a physical therapist, and noticed that each time she received one, her body felt more loose, flexible, and comfortable. The physical therapist explained to her the connection between the tension in her body and the trauma she experienced as a child. She now uses stress-reduction exercises she learned from the physical therapist to continue to release the tension she has held in her body for so many years.

This topic contains several exercises that, if used regularly, will gradually help you relieve the tension in your body. Most people notice they feel much better each time they do a relaxation and stress-reduction exercise. Occasionally people report that while engaging in a relaxation exercise they suddenly feel overwhelmed by very uncomfortable feelings in their bodies. If this happens to you, open your eyes right away and stare at something that you really like to look at (a book, a plant, a pet, and so on) for several moments until the uncomfortable feelings go away. If this happens to you often, you could keep handy a collection of pictures or cards from friends to look at. Keep your collection near or in the place where you do these exercises so you can look at them when these feelings come up, and when you feel better you can either return to the exercise or leave the work until another time. (Don't forget to do your closing ritual before leaving your work for the day!)

Repeat the exercises in this chapter that feel good to you as often as possible—make them an important part of your life.

Body Scan

Read this exercise before you do it and then do it from memory—trying to read it as you are doing it will be too distracting.

Relax comfortably in a chair or lie down—whichever feels better to you. Loosen any tight clothing. Take three deep breaths. Notice how your body feels in the space it is in. Notice how your body feels as it comes in contact with the chair, or the floor or ground. Notice how your clothes feel on your body. Now pretend you have a searchlight. Use that searchlight to search inside your body to find places that feel relaxed. Spend a few moments focusing on each of these places. Next, use the searchlight to find places where your body feels tense or uncomfortable. Spend a few moments focusing on each of these places.

Where in your body did you feel comfortable and relaxed?

_____

_____

_____

Where did you feel tense?

_____

_____

_____

Why do you think you feel tense and uncomfortable in this part of your body? Do you feel it has to do with something that is going on now, such as stress at work or carrying a heavy object, or do you think it has to do with something that happened in your past?

_____

_____

_____

You may have had this tension or discomfort in your body for many years. It may have affected the way you sit, stand, and walk.

One woman noticed that she had a lot of tension in the upper part of her chest. Sometimes the pain became quite sharp and debilitating and she actually needed to hunch over to relieve it. Medical testing didn't show any problem. She remembered that the pain in her chest began when she was very young, when she felt afraid of the older boys in her neighborhood who frightened and hurt her.

You may not know why these places in your body feel the way they do. Fortunately, it is not necessary to know where the tension came from in order to release it.

Now that you have identified the places in your body that need help, try the exercises that follow. With practice, your body will begin to change the way it responds to the things that happen (and happened) to you.

Tension Releasing

Again, read the exercise before you begin, then put the book aside. This should take about five minutes. Play soft music in the background if you wish.

Choose one of the problem areas of your body to focus on. Explore that part of your body in detail with your mind. Ask yourself, "What are the sensations in this part of my body? How does it move?" Let this part of your body relax completely. Using your mind, imagine softness and warm light flowing into this part of your body.

How did you feel before you did this exercise?

_____

_____

How did you feel after you did this exercise?

_____

_____

Repeat this exercise as often as possible, focusing one at a time on each part of your body that is tense and uncomfortable. Do this exercise whenever you have a few free moments—before you go to sleep at night, if you awaken and have a hard time getting back to sleep, when you are taking a short break from your work.

Progressive Relaxation

Through teaching you to systematically tense and then relax muscle groups of your body, this exercise will help you learn to relax various parts of your body and help you understand how relaxation feels. Again, read the exercise before you begin, then put the book aside and do it from recall. Or, you might want to make a tape recording of this exercise—reading it into the microphone with soft music in the background. Be sure you leave yourself plenty of time on the tape to tense and relax your muscles. You could also have a good friend or counselor read it to you.

Always do this exercise in a quiet space where you will not be disturbed. You can do it either lying on your back or sitting in a chair, as long as you are comfortable.

Close your eyes. Clench your right fist as tightly as you can. Be aware of the tension as you do so. Keep it clenched for a moment. Now relax. Feel the looseness in your right hand and compare it to the tension you felt previously. Tense your right fist again, then relax it. Again, notice the difference.

Now clench your left fist as tightly as you can. Be aware of the tension as you do so. Keep it clenched for a moment. Now relax. Feel the looseness in your left hand and compare it to the tension you felt previously. Tense your left fist again, relax it, and again notice the difference.

Bend your elbows and tense your biceps as hard as you can. Notice the feeling of tightness. Relax and straighten out your arms. Let the relaxation flow through your arms and compare it to the tightness you felt previously. Tense and relax your biceps again.

Wrinkle your forehead as tightly as you can. Now relax it and let it smooth out. Feel your forehead and scalp becoming relaxed. Now frown and notice the tension spreading through your forehead again. Relax and allow your forehead to become smooth.

Close your eyes now and squint them very tightly. Feel the tension. Now relax your eyes. Tense and relax your eyes again. Now let them remain gently closed.

Now clench your jaw. Bite hard and feel the tension through your jaw. Now relax your jaw. Your lips will be slightly parted. Notice the difference. Clench and relax again.

Press your tongue against the roof of your mouth. Now relax. Do this again.

Press and purse your lips together. Now relax them. Repeat this.

Feel the relaxation throughout your forehead, scalp, eyes, jaw, tongue, and lips.

Hold your head back as far as it can comfortably go and observe the tightness in your neck. Roll it to the right and notice how the tension moves and changes. Roll your head to the left and notice how the tension moves and changes. Now straighten your head and bring it forward, pressing your chin against your chest. Notice the tension in your throat and the back of your neck. Now relax and allow your shoulders to return to a comfortable position. Allow yourself to feel more and more relaxed. Now shrug your shoulders and hunch your head down between your shoulders. Relax your shoulders. Allow them to drop back and feel the relaxation moving through your neck, throat, and shoulders; feel the lovely, very deep relaxation.

Give your whole body a chance to relax. Feel how comfortable and heavy it is.

Now breathe in and fill your lungs completely. Hold your breath and notice the tension. Now let your breath out and let your chest become loose. Continue relaxing, breathing gently in and out. Repeat this breathing several times and notice the tension draining out of your body.

Tighten your stomach and hold the tightness. Feel the tension. Now relax your stomach. Now place your hand on your stomach. Breathe deeply into your stomach, pushing your hand up. Hold for a moment and then relax. Now arch your back without straining, keeping the rest of your body as relaxed as possible. Notice the tension in your lower back. Now relax deeper and deeper.

Tighten your buttocks and thighs. Flex your thighs by pressing your heels down as hard as you can. Now relax and notice the difference. Do this again. Now curl your toes down, making your calves tense. Notice the tension. Now relax. Bend your toes toward your face, creating tension in your shins. Relax and notice the difference.

Feel the heaviness throughout your lower body as the relaxation gets deeper and deeper. Relax your feet, ankles, calves, shins, knees, thighs, and buttocks. Now let the relaxation spread to your stomach, lower back, and chest. Let go more and more. Experience deeper and deeper relaxation in your shoulders, arms, and hands, deeper and deeper. Notice the feeling of looseness and relaxation in your neck, jaws, and all your facial muscles. Now just relax and be aware of how your whole body feels before you return to your work in this book.

How did you feel before you did this exercise?

_____

_____

How did you feel after you did this exercise?

_____

_____

Here are some other ways that will help you release feelings and relax your body or specific parts of your body.

- If you can afford it, have a regular massage with a certified massage therapist.

- Take a warm bath as often as possible. If you wish, scent the water with lavender oil or some other scent that you find calming and relaxing.

- Gently rub parts of your body. If it feels comfortable, ask a friend or your partner to do this for you.

- Learn yoga. There are many good books that will teach you how to stretch and relax your body.

- Drink a cup of soothing herbal tea such as chamomile.

- Eat dairy foods, turkey, and leafy green and yellow vegetables—they contain calcium and will help you relax.

- Avoid foods that contain caffeine—coffee, black tea, soda, and chocolate—as they will make you feel more anxious.

- Avoid using alcohol or drugs to help you feel more relaxed and comfortable. While it may help briefly, it will make things much worse in the long run.

Dealing with Unusual Feelings, Sensations, and Responses

You also may have noticed that you have unusual feelings, sensations, and responses to certain events. For instance, if you see a car of a certain make and color, you may feel a sense of fear and dread. If a person you love speaks to you in a certain way, you may recoil in horror though what they said was perfectly acceptable. This is another example of the body remembering what the mind has forgotten. Your body is responding to situations, circumstances, and events that happened in the past. It is responding in ways that are no longer necessary and that interfere with your life, sometimes making you and others feel bad.

Describe some times when you have noticed unusual feelings, sensations, and responses to certain everyday events.

_____

_____

_____

_____

As you become aware of these situations, you can respond in ways that will help you feel better quickly and help you respond appropriately to the actions of others. Try getting in the habit of responding to these feelings in one or more of the following ways.

- Stop what you are doing. Breathe in slowly and deeply, paying close attention to your breath. Let the breath out very slowly, again paying close attention. Do this three or four more times. Notice the feeling of relaxation in your body after you do this.

- Do a reality check. Ask yourself the following questions:

  1. What is really going on here? Is this response helping or is it making the situation worse?

2. Are my feelings or is my response really appropriate to the situation, or is it based on something I learned in the past that is no longer applicable?

- Count to ten, or even a hundred.

- Take time out and do something you really enjoy—read a chapter in a good book, play with your dog, listen to a musical piece you like, or draw a picture.

- Talk to a friend about what happened.

List other ways you have discovered to respond to unusual feelings, sensations, and certain events.

_____

_____

_____

_____

_____

Ending Ritual

Describe something you are looking forward to that is happening soon.

_____

_____

Describe something you are looking forward to that will happen in the more distant future.

_____

_____

Optional Activity

Get a book on relaxation and stress-reduction techniques. Practice the exercises that are described, and make tape recordings of those that you find to be particularly helpful. For three titles that we especially like, see the Relaxation and Stress Reduction section of the Resources list at the back of this book.

Things to Remember Every Day

- I can teach my body new ways of responding to feelings, sensations, and events in my life.

- I am in charge of my responses.

Topic 14

What Is Physical Abuse?

Beginning Ritual

To begin work on this topic, write four good things that happened to you in the last two days:

_____

_____

_____

_____

Recovering from Physical Abuse

One of the essential components of recovering from the effects of all kinds of trauma is validation of what happened to you—you need someone you respect and trust to hear the story of what happened to you and say to you something such as, "That was horrible. That should not have happened to you. I understand why you are having such a hard time dealing with it." Unfortunately, many women report that when they've told another person about the abuse, they heard such things as, "Oh, that was nothing," "Everybody gets hurt at some time or other," "You asked for it," or, "You should just forgive and forget."

These statements are invalidating and not helpful. They make you doubt the validity of what happened to you, and make you feel that there is something wrong with you instead of that there is something wrong with the person who hurt you. The truth is, someone did something very bad to you. Of course you are having a very hard time with the effects of that.

If you heard invalidating things when you reported the abuse, what was said and who said it?

_____

_____

_____

_____

You may have become very confused when you were treated in this manner. Perhaps you are now unclear about what abuse is and whether or not you were actually abused. This chapter will help validate for you that what happened to you *was serious* and that the person or people who hurt you were wrong.

Who Is Responsible?

When one person physically hurts another, the person who is being hurt is never responsible. No one deserves to be hurt.

As a child, you have little choice about such things as whom you live with and where you go to school. In general, the adults who are supposed to look out for you and your best interests decide these things for you. However, sometimes these adults don't look out for your best interests, abuse you, or fail to protect you from abuse. As an adult you may find that you continue to have key people in your life who don't treat you well or who abuse you. The experience of being abused may cause you to make bad decisions about whom you should or should not be with.

Describe the attributes of people whom you would like to involve in your life.

_____

_____

_____

_____

If you insisted on spending all of your time with people who have these attributes, is there anyone in your life now with whom you would no longer spend time? If so, who are they?

_____

_____

_____

_____

How and when could you make a change and eliminate these people from your life?

_____

_____

_____

_____

Where have you met people who were nice to you?

_____

_____

How could you become more closely connected to nice people?

_____

_____

_____

_____

Confronting Your Abuser

Some women feel that it would be helpful to their healing process to confront the person who abused them—either in person, on the phone, or by letter—to let the abuser know how the abuse has affected them and perhaps ask for an apology. You do not have to do this in order to heal from the effects of abuse. In fact, it might be a very poor idea—even unsafe.

How do you feel about confronting your abuser?

_____

_____

_____

_____

_____

If you feel it would be helpful, how would it be helpful?

_____

_____

_____

_____

How could it be harmful?

_____

_____

_____

_____

One woman we spoke with often thought about confronting the man who had physically abused her when she was a child. She thought about how she would like to let him know how badly this kind of abuse affects children. However, after she considered it carefully, she felt that seeing him might trigger flashbacks, and that by "stirring him up" she might put herself or others at risk of further harm. She decided she could achieve the same results by writing him a letter and not sending it, and by sharing her feelings about these bad experiences with understanding friends. She also decided that, as a way of getting back at her abuser, she would join a committee at her children's school to explore ways the community could work together to protect children from abuse.

What are some ways that do not include confrontation that would allow you to address issues and feelings that have to do with your abuser?

_____

_____

_____

_____

Regaining Control

When you were physically abused, a person or people took over control of your life for a short time—or perhaps for months or years. Ongoing threats of more physical abuse may have kept you under their control. You may have had no control over your own life—no ability to make choices for yourself or to do the things you needed to do to take care of yourself. You may be so accustomed to being controlled by others that, as an adult, you feel that you still have no control or sense of your own power. There are many things that you can do to regain a sense of control and power:

- Take action to make your life the way you want it to be.

  Write two simple things you could do to make your life the way you want it to be.

  _____

  _____

- Take good care of yourself. Do the things you know you need to do to get well and stay well.
- Spend time with people who treat you well and respect you as a person.

What else can you do to regain control over your life?

_____

_____

_____

_____

_____

Telling Your Story

Again, telling someone else what happened to you, having your story be believed, and having its seriousness validated is part of the healing process. The best way to do this is to tell another person or people (such as in a support group). However, you may not feel ready to do that. Or you may feel that you do not have people in your life whose responses you could trust. The first place you can safely share your story of physical abuse may be here in this book (after all, we, the authors of this book, validate the seriousness of what happened to you and its effect on your life). You can write it on this page in the space provided or, if you're more comfortable doing so, on a separate sheet of paper that you will dispose of when you're done. The value of this exercise is in getting the experience outside of yourself, not in having something to reread at a later time, although you can do that if you want to. Write as much or as little as you want to.

My Story of Physical Abuse

by _____

_____

_____

_____

_____

_____

_____

_____

_____

Using a separate piece of paper, a pencil, pen, colored markers or paints, make a picture that illustrates your feelings when you were telling your story.

What Impact Has the Abuse Had on Your Life?

You have learned that physical abuse can lead to feelings of disempowerment and lack of control over your life. It can cause you to spend time with people who do not treat you well and to accept bad treatment that should not be tolerated. In what other ways do you think physical abuse has affected your life?

One woman felt that her physical abuse has caused her to be very fearful about interacting with any men who are tall and have long dark hair—men who look something like her abuser. To address this fear, she decided to do a reality check. She asked herself, does the height, color, and length of hair have anything to do with whether or not a person is an abuser? She decided it did not. Then, every time she saw a man who reminded her of her abuser, she said to herself several times, "Height, color, and length of hair do not affect a person's character."

Effect of physical abuse on my life:

_____

_____

_____

_____

_____

_____

How I could get over these effects?

_____

_____

_____

_____

_____

_____

Ending Ritual

Describe something you are looking forward to that is happening soon.

_____

_____

Describe something you are looking forward to that will happen in the more distant future.

_____

_____

Optional Activities

1. Tell your story of physical abuse to a person or people you trust. You can begin by just telling them a sentence or two—just enough to let them know something happened to you. You can tell them more at other times. Doing it slowly will help you feel more comfortable and trusting.

2. Attend an activity in your community where you might have an opportunity to meet nice people.

3. Spend some time playing with a small child, and treat that child the way you wish you had been treated when you were a child. If this is not possible, or if you do not feel comfortable with children, find a doll or a stuffed animal to hold gently and lovingly.

4. Do a few of the things you identified in the last section of this topic that you determined might help you get over some of the effects of your abuse.

   I will:

   _____

   _____

   _____

Things to Remember Every Day

- I am in charge of my life.

- The abuse that happened to me was very serious. Experiencing serious effects from the abuse is understandable.

- The person or people who abused me were wrong.

- I am a good person who did not deserve to be abused. No one deserves abuse.

- I do not need to forgive my abuser or abusers.

- I have the right to be treated well and to spend my life with people who treat me well.

Topic 15

What Is Sexual Abuse?

Beginning Ritual

To begin work on this topic, write four good things that happened to you in the last two days:

_____

_____

_____

_____

Many people, when asked about sexual abuse, may think only of rape. You may have found some sexual incidents very troubling to you, but were told by others that "it was nothing," or it wasn't really sexual abuse. The following may help clarify the way you feel about sexual abuse and validate the significance of your experiences.

Myth: It's not sexual abuse if you weren't physically forced.

Another way of thinking: There are many ways, in addition to physical force, that abusers take advantage of the person or people they are abusing. They include manipulation; coercion; threats; choosing vulnerable subjects such as the sick, inebriated, disabled, or young; and seeking to make their victims vulnerable by giving them drugs or alcohol.

Your thoughts about this issue:

_____

_____

_____

_____

Myth: It's not sexual abuse if you weren't touched.

Another way of thinking: It is sexual abuse if someone forces you to look at or touch their sexual organs, forces you to show them parts of your body, forces you to perform sexual acts while they watch, or threatens that they are going to sexually abuse you.

Were you abused in ways that did not involve touch? What are your thoughts on this issue?

_____

_____

_____

_____

Myth: If it only happens once, it's not really sexual abuse. You should just ignore it.

Another way of thinking: The effects of sexual abuse are devastating and long lasting whether it happens once or many times. Sexual abuse should never be ignored.

Your thoughts about this issue:

_____

_____

_____

_____

Myth: Certain people, such as husbands or boyfriends, can't really be said to have sexually abused their partners because the existence of a relationship prevents the use of that term.

Another way of thinking: Abuse is abuse regardless of who commits it—even if you used to love that person in the past. _Nobody_ has the right to hurt you.

Your thoughts about this issue:

_____

_____

_____

_____

Myth: People who put themselves in dangerous places or situations or who wear revealing clothing are asking for trouble. It's their fault if they are abused.

Another way of thinking: There's nothing you can do or say that would make abuse your fault—even if you inadvertently showed poor judgment.

Your thoughts about this issue:

_____

_____

_____

_____

Myth: It's not sexual abuse if you became sexually aroused or you had an orgasm during the incident.

Another way of thinking: It is sexual abuse if you were forced or manipulated into doing something you didn't want to do. Our bodies are programmed to respond to certain kinds of stimulation in particular ways, and you could have an orgasm without really wanting to. It is not your fault, and it is still sexual abuse.

Your thoughts about this issue:

_____

_____

_____

_____

Myth: Intrusive, but not explicitly sexual, activities cannot be called sexual abuse. (For example, a relative gives a child an enema every night, a male relative checks to see "how the breasts are developing," someone insists they have the right to watch when you are using the toilet, or someone insists on coming in when you are using the shower or tub.)

Another way of thinking: These things are not normal and are abusive.

Your thoughts about this issue:

_____

_____

_____

_____

Myth: If you have been sexually abused, you can never have a strong, intimate relationship because you can never get over the effects.

Another way of thinking: Many women who have been abused do have intimate, loving, healthy relationships and have relieved the effects of their abuse. There are many ways to heal, including self-help books; self-help skills and strategies learned from a women's class; and individual and group treatment programs that are designed to empower the person who has been abused, validate her experiences, and help her establish connections with people who are loving and affirming.

What have you done to help yourself relieve the effects of sexual abuse? Your thoughts about this issue:

_____

_____

_____

_____

If you can, it helps to talk about these myths and your thoughts about sexual abuse with a trusting friend. If this is not possible, and you think it would be helpful, write about it in your journal.

How Prevalent Is Sexual Abuse?

Until recently, the extent and impact of sexual abuse in our society was not acknowledged. Sexual abuse often was not reported because people feared reprisals from the abuser, or that they would not be believed, or that their report might be too upsetting to others. Sexual abuse is still rampant in our society, but it is now recognized as a very serious problem. As more and more abusers are prosecuted, people have become more willing to come forward and report it.

Current estimates reveal that one fifth to one half of U.S. women were sexually abused as children at least once, most of them by an older male relative. However, truly accurate figures are difficult to gauge because although many women have signs that they may have been abused, they may not remember it at all.

Many school districts have instituted campaigns to raise student awareness about unwanted touch and to coach them on how to respond. Some schools now have counselors available who can work with abused children. Yet our efforts toward prevention remain limited, and money for abused children tends to go toward parent aid, education, and social casework rather than individual or family counseling.

For adult survivors there are many more innovative treatments that address the traumatic stress symptoms of sexual abuse. Some treatments attempt to integrate bodywork with traditional therapy (*hakomi* integrative somatics, for example); others, such as eye movement desensitization and reprocessing (EMDR), focus on helping the individual reprocess traumatic memories; and still others try to protect the survivor against the impact of traumatic stress. While many of these therapies are still in the developmental stages, they hold interesting promise. If you want to pursue a trauma-specific treatment, check with your local mental health agency and make sure any clinician you choose has been fully trained in the technique he or she is using.

Hearing about Sexual Abuse

Many people who have been sexually abused avoid reading articles about it in the newspaper, listening to stories about it on the television or radio, and will walk out of a movie that they find to be upsetting. That's okay—it is a great way to take care of yourself. If people you are with are talking about sexual abuse and it is making you feel uneasy or uncomfortable, you should feel free to ask the person or people to change the subject as it is very upsetting to you, or you could excuse yourself until they are finished talking. Most people will be very understanding. If they aren't, you may be spending time with the wrong people. How do you feel when you read or hear about sexual abuse?

_____

_____

_____

_____

How do you deal with these feelings?

_____

_____

_____

_____

Telling Your Story

As in topic 14, we'd like to invite you to write down your story of sexual abuse. Again, you certainly don't have to write it in the space below—if you're more comfortable doing so, use a separate sheet of paper that you will dispose of when you're done, because the value of this exercise is in getting the experience outside of yourself, not in having something to reread at a later time.

My Story of Sexual Abuse

by _____

_____

_____

_____

_____

_____

_____

_____

_____

_____

Using a separate piece of paper and a pencil, pen, colored markers, or paints, make a picture that illustrates your feelings when you are telling your story of sexual abuse.

Ending Ritual

Describe something you are looking forward to that is happening soon.

_____

_____

Describe something you are looking forward to that will happen in the more distant future.

_____

_____

Optional Activities

1. Tell your story of sexual abuse to a person or people you trust. You can begin by just telling them a sentence or two—just enough to let them know something happened to you. You can tell them more at other times. Doing it slowly will help you feel more comfortable and trusting.

2. Write in your journal about each of the statements in the next section, Things to Remember Every Day.

3. Do an art project using the materials of your choice (fabric, sequins, beads, paper, feathers, leaves, sticks, pictures, and so on) that honors your courage and strength.

Things to Remember Every Day

- I am a strong and powerful person.

- The sexual abuse was not my fault.

- I never owe sex to anyone.

- I can have a good, intimate relationship.

- I can get over the effects of sexual abuse.

Topic 16

Physical Safety

Beginning Ritual

To begin work on this topic, write four good things that happened to you in the last two days:

_____

_____

_____

_____

     People who have been sexually abused may never have learned how to keep themselves safe. As a result, they are often subject to abuse over and over again throughout their lives. It doesn't have to be this way. While no one can ever absolutely protect themselves from future abuse, you can learn to change the way you do things and the way you live your life to minimize the chances that you will be abused. This chapter is an inventory of the current circumstances of your life, how you deal with them, and, if you decide it is necessary, how you might change them to provide yourself with more protection from abuse. There are many possible actions included here. You won't be able to do all of them—use the ones that feel right for you.

Keeping Yourself Safe from Abuse

The way you present yourself can make a big difference in whether an abuser considers you to be a potential target. You can present yourself as a person with low self-esteem and a lack of self-confidence who is weak and vulnerable, or you can present yourself as a strong, powerful, confident woman who can take care of herself. The following factors influence how others see you. Place a check mark next to those you feel you need to work on.

Posture

Walk around for a minute, noticing how you do so. How did you feel about yourself as you were walking?

_____

_____

What message did the way you were walking convey to others who might be looking at you?

_____

_____

Walk around again for a minute, this time repeating over and over to yourself, "I am a strong, powerful, confident woman who can take care of herself."

How did repeating this affirmation affect the way you walked?

_____

_____

What message do you think you were giving to others when you were walking this way?

_____

_____

Practice saying this affirmation over and over to yourself when you feel unsure of yourself or unsafe.

Clothing

The clothes you wear can affect how you feel about yourself and how others see you. Review the outfits you commonly wear. Which ones make you feel strong and in charge of your life?

_____

_____

What colors are they? What style are they?

_____

_____

What message do you think you give to others when you wear these clothes?

_____

_____

Go to a store you like and try on different outfits. Notice how they make you feel about yourself. Think about the message they might be giving to others.

Keeping Healthy and Fit

You'll be better able to defend yourself if you are strong and fit. Every woman should be able to run at least a quarter mile—fast—to get away from a bad situation. If you aren't sure you could do this, give it a try. Make a quarter mile your goal and practice until you reach it. Then run that quarter mile at least a couple of times a week to keep yourself in shape. This won't require much of your time, and the benefits are definitely worth it. (Of course, as with any new exercise regime, you should consult your doctor if you have any physical problems that could affect your ability to run.)

Do you feel that you look physically strong and healthy to others? If not, what could you do about it? Could you gain or lose some weight? Get more exercise? Pay more attention to your personal hygiene?

Other ideas you might have:

_____

_____

_____

Would it be possible for you to take a martial arts or self-defense course? There are many different types of courses available, and many offer women-only sessions, if that would make you feel more comfortable. Contact your local women's crisis center, the Yellow Pages, or the Internet for information.

Physical Safety in Your Living Space

Your home or living space should be a place where you feel comfortable and safe from abuse. However, many people are abused in their own homes. The following section will help you discover how you can decrease the likelihood that that will happen to you.

Would it be hard for intruders to enter the space where you live? If for any reason you think it might be easy, what could you do to correct that?

_____

_____

Would it be hard for intruders to enter the place where you sleep? Do you feel safe in the place where you sleep? If this is a problem for you, is there some way you could arrange to sleep in a safer place? How and when could you do this?

_____

_____

_____

Do you live with people who are nonabusive and who would try to protect you from abuse from others? If not, what could you do to change that situation and when are you going to do it?

_____

_____

_____

_____

Which of the following guidelines for keeping your living space safe do you need to work on?

- Put up curtains or blinds so people can't look in from the outside.

- Use the locks on your doors *and* windows—and install new or more security devices where needed, including dead bolts and chains (if you live in a rental unit, ask your landlord to do this).

- Install good outdoor lighting—perhaps a motion sensor.

- Know your neighbors so you can be watchful and protective of each other.

- Use an initial rather than your first name in the phone book to prevent callers from knowing more than you would like them to.

- If you live in a multiunit building, don't ever buzz delivery people in—go to the main door to meet them. Also, never let in somebody who claims to be visiting someone else.

- Do not give your address to telephone solicitors.

Below, list living-space issues you need to work on along with information on how and when you plan to take action.

_____

_____

_____

_____

_____

_____

If you are without a living space, the following suggestions may help keep you safe from abuse:

- Do not get involved in drinking or doing drugs with anyone.

- If you are staying in shelters, choose those that are well staffed and help you feel comfortable and safe. Look for one with a no-alcohol policy.

- Keep yourself as strong and healthy as possible—eat at soup kitchens and take advantage of other services that will help you maintain your wellness.

- Spend time and share sleeping spaces with people who protect each other.

- Avoid people with whom you feel uncomfortable.

- Avoid spending time where you are totally isolated.

- Take advantage of whatever services will help get you out of this situation.

What other things can you think of to protect yourself from abuse if you are without a living space?

_____

_____

_____

_____

If you are currently without a living space, or living in a space where you are not safe, what are you doing to correct the situation?

_____

_____

_____

What can you do to make your current circumstances as safe as possible?

_____

_____

_____

Physical Safety in Your Community

You should be able to be out and about in your community, whether it be a big city or a small rural village, without fear of abuse. The following inventory will help you assess your safety in the community, and determine action you can take so that you feel safer.

Do you surround yourself with people in your community who care about you, are well intentioned, who would not abuse you, and who, if possible, would protect you against harm or abuse? If not, why not? What could you do to change those circumstances? When could you do it?

_____

_____

_____

Do you spend time in your community in places where you feel safe? If not, are there safe places you can think of where you could be spending time? Could you arrange to spend more time there and less time in places that are unsafe?

_____

_____

_____

_____

Are there places in your community that you should avoid? If so, where are they?

_____

_____

What would you have to do to make it possible for you to avoid these places and when could you make these changes?

_____

_____

When you walk outdoors alone at night, are you able to avoid places that might be unsafe, such as places where drug deals are made or where people tend to gather and drink? If for some reason you occasionally find yourself unable to avoid such areas and you can't find people to accompany you, there are things you can do to protect yourself:

- Walk with vigor and with a clear sense of purpose and direction—avoid meandering or strolling.

- Have a clear destination and know just how you are going to get there.

- Go into a public place immediately if you feel you are being watched or followed.

- Avoid walking through groups of people that are crowding the sidewalk—cross the street instead.

- Carry a whistle, Mace, and/or pepper spray to use if you find yourself in trouble.

- Hold a key between your second and third finger to jab a possible assailant.

- Avoid wearing high-heeled shoes, clogs, restrictive skirts, or any other type of restrictive clothing that might keep you from moving quickly when you need to.

- Walk with a dog.

- As discussed earlier under Keeping Healthy and Fit, be able to run at top speed for at least a quarter of a mile. This may take some practice, but it is a worthwhile goal.

- Avoid making eye contact.

- Stay alert to what is going on around you so you can move out of the area quickly if the need should arise.

- If you carry a pocketbook or bag, keep it strapped to you in a way that makes it inaccessible to others. Better yet, carry money or other valuables in a packet under your clothing so nobody can see it.

Below, list any ideas that you intend to work on to keep yourself safe in your community.

_____

_____

_____

_____

_____

Traveling

When you are traveling, the risk of abuse from strangers increases, partly because you'll have a harder time determining where you are safe and where you are not if you don't know the city well. To keep yourself safe, you will need to have a heightened awareness of your surroundings, be alert to signs of danger, and move out of areas quickly when you feel you are at risk. Using the following strategies where they are applicable will help you keep yourself as safe as possible.

- When you walk from a store or other building to your vehicle, have the keys in your hand, ready to open the car when you get there.

- Park in open and well-lit areas where there are other people around, even if it means a longer walk.

- Always keep car doors locked, even if you're only leaving the car for a minute or two.

- Also keep the car doors locked when you are driving.

- Avoid calling attention to yourself by refraining from interactions and gestures with other drivers and by driving as safely and courteously as possible.

- Avoid late-night driving as much as possible.

- Do not pick up hitchhikers and do not hitchhike.

- Keep your vehicle in good repair to reduce the likelihood of getting stranded—take care of routine maintenance, keep at least a quarter tank of gas at all times, and make sure you have plenty of wiper fluid.

- Carry a safety kit in your car that includes a flashlight and flares.

- Buy a cell phone for use in emergencies.

- If someone stops to help you, open your window only for someone who can prove they are a law-enforcement officer—some criminals impersonate police.

- Avoid public transportation at night.

- When using a public rest room, be aware of who else is in the room with you—you may want to wait until they leave.

- When staying in a hotel, don't let *anyone* in—if a person says they are there to fix something in the room, first call the front desk to verify that someone has been sent. Keep the doors locked and bolted at all times.

- Listen to your intuition! Avoid areas where you feel intuitively unsafe even if you can't think of a good reason for your feeling.

List the strategies that you feel you most need to be aware of when you travel.

_____

_____

_____

_____

_____

Your work on this topic may have shown you that you there are many changes you can make to increase your safety. However, making many changes at the same time can be very difficult. Review this topic and pick out those that you feel are most important to begin work on right away. What are they?

_____

_____

_____

_____

_____

Review this topic regularly to check your progress.

Ending Ritual

Describe something you are looking forward to that is happening soon.

_____

_____

Describe something you are looking forward to that will happen in the more distant future.

_____

_____

Optional Activity

Browse through the section at your local hardware store that offers locks and security systems. Look for an item that you could add to your home to make you feel safer. You may not realize how many innovations there are in home safety and how easily you can add a sense of security to your living situation.

Things to Remember Every Day

- I can do the things I need to do to keep myself safe.
- I have some control over how much danger there is in my life.

Topic 17

What Is Emotional Abuse?

Beginning Ritual

To begin work on this topic, write four good things that happened to you in the last two days:

_____

_____

_____

_____

What Is Emotional Abuse?

You've now looked at the issues of physical and sexual abuse. Perhaps you've found yourself thinking, "I know what I experienced wasn't physical abuse or sexual abuse, but I know something was really wrong in my childhood and/or in that relationship." In this topic you will explore another kind of abuse that can have long-lasting and devastating effects—emotional abuse.

Emotional abuse occurs when the people you depend on to provide you with care, love, and protection, such as parents, other relatives, and teachers, say and do things that make you feel bad about yourself. When you were a child you had no ability to get out of these emotionally abusive relationships—after all, you couldn't leave your parents or drop out of school. If this abuse happened to you as an adult, you may have felt that you couldn't leave the relationship for financial or family reasons. The person who is the abuser always has some kind of power. The power may come from age (such as an older sibling or schoolmate) or position (such as a spouse, parent, or a member of the clergy).

Keep in mind that knowing whether the abuse was emotional, physical, or sexual is not really necessary for the purposes of getting better. All you need to know is that something bad and wrong happened to you and that it has affected how you feel about yourself and the way you live your life.

Jody, a thirty-five-year-old writer and musician, has had problems with severe anxiety and depression for as long as she can remember and says she has no self-esteem. She remembers that, as a child, her mother punished her for childish sloppiness or eating too much by making her scrub the kitchen floor with a toothbrush.

The Emotional-Abuse Inventory

Review each of the terms below and decide whether or not they describe what happened to you at some time in your life. If so, write down what it was and how you think it has affected your life.

Neglect or deprivation—Needs that you had for basic care such as clothing, food, shelter, and positive loving attention were not always met because people were not available to care for you.

_____

_____

_____

_____

_____

_____

Abandonment—You were left alone to care for yourself for long periods of time.

_____

_____

_____

_____

_____

_____

_____

_____

Dysfunctional parents due to alcoholism, depression, or some kind of illness—Your parents were not able to provide you with care because of their own problems, and their behavior may have been disruptive and/or abusive to you and other family members.

_____

_____

_____

_____

_____

Isolation—You had no contact with other people for long periods of time.

_____

_____

_____

_____

_____

_____

Role reversals—You took over responsibilities for your parents or other adults in your life, assuming adult responsibilities when you were still a child.

_____

_____

_____

_____

_____

Severe criticism—You were told repeatedly that what you did or were doing wasn't right, and there seemed to be no way you could satisfy him or her.

_____

_____

_____

_____

_____

Shaming—You were made to feel that you were guilty or should be ashamed of things you didn't do and that were not your fault or that were normal behaviors.

_____

_____

_____

_____

_____

_____

_____

_____

Manipulation—You were made to do things or to do particular things a particular way, even though it wasn't what you wanted to do.

_____

_____

_____

_____

_____

_____

Extreme control—Someone else always told you what to do and how and when to do it; you were not allowed to make any choices for yourself.

_____

_____

_____

_____

_____

_____

_____

Witnessing the abuse of others—You saw other family members, neighbors, or people in the community being physically, sexually, or emotionally abused.

_____

_____

_____

_____

_____

_____

_____

Harsh punishments—You were treated cruelly or made to do very difficult tasks for supposed misdeeds.

_____

_____

_____

_____

_____

_____

_____

Inconsistent discipline—You were sometimes punished severely for certain behaviors, but the same behaviors were ignored or even praised at other times.

_____

_____

_____

_____

_____

_____

List other examples of emotional abuse you have experienced. Describe what happened and how it affected your life.

_____

_____

_____

_____

_____

_____

_____

Emotional abuse often consists of cruel comments, being lectured, or being yelled at. One woman who is now forty-five years old still remembers her father telling her over and over again that she was a no-good, lazy brat who should never have been born.

Make a list of cruel things that were said to you along with a list of things you wish had been said to you instead. For example, "You are a rotten kid." What you wish had been said: "You are such a special and smart kid."

_____

_____

_____

_____

_____

_____

Coping with Emotional Abuse

When people are emotionally abused, they develop strategies to cope with the abuse—strategies that help them get by. You may have developed strategies to cope with emotional abuse that met your needs at that time in that they got you by, but you may have continued to use these strategies as an adult even though you no longer needed to. Some of these strategies may be healthy, such as leaving the area when someone is constantly yelling at you. Other strategies may be harmful. For instance, as an adolescent you may have started using alcohol and illegal drugs to help yourself feel good as a way of coping with your mother's constant criticism and neglect. Now that you are an adult you find that you are addicted to alcohol. Or, because you weren't given enough food and clothing, you may have done some shoplifting. As an adult you have been arrested several times for shoplifting. These arrests are preventing you from taking advantage of some career advancement possibilities.

List healthy coping strategies you developed to deal with emotional abuse.

_____

_____

_____

_____

List unhealthy strategies you used to cope with emotional abuse.

_____

_____

_____

_____

Are any of these strategies still a problem for you? If so, list them below and describe what you could do to help yourself stop.

_____

_____

_____

_____

_____

_____

_____

Ending Ritual

Describe something you are looking forward to that is happening soon.

_____

_____

Describe something you are looking forward to that will happen in the more distant future.

_____

_____

Optional Activities

1. Write about one of the following in your journal: how you deserved to be treated as a child, how you would treat a child of your own, or how you think a child should be treated.

2. Create some art that shows your feelings about the emotional abuse you experienced.

Things to Remember Every Day

- I was a good child.
- I have always been a good person.
- I refuse to let others define who I am.
- I deserve to be treated with dignity, compassion, and respect at all times.
- I have always deserved to be treated fairly and well.
- I had a right to be a child, and to act the way children act. I had a right to have a childhood.
- I have learned how to avoid abusive people.
- I have learned healthy ways to cope with emotional abuse.

Topic 18

Institutional Abuse

Beginning Ritual

To begin work on this topic, write four good things that happened to you in the last two days:

_____

_____

_____

_____

What Is Institutional Abuse?

Many of us, in our search for ways to relieve the disturbing aftermath of trauma, reach out for help to the mental health system and to other kinds of service providers. By reaching out we are often able to access programs and treatments that can be helpful for the short or long term. However, sometimes we are treated in ways that are not at all helpful, that actually worsen the symptoms and add to the experience of abuse. For example, women have reported being searched, physically restrained for short or long periods of time, denied access to their supporters, forced to undergo harsh or punitive treatments, or told things about themselves that undermine their self-esteem. Some people have even reported physical, emotional, or sexual abuse at the hands of the very people assigned by public institutions to help them. This kind of abuse can happen in schools, churches, hospitals, welfare agencies, and other kinds of public institutions. You may have been abused in one of these institutions when you were a child.

By their very nature, these institutions are hierarchical. There is an assumption that the people in these institutions are in some way superior to you—through their position, experience, educational background, and sometimes even sex and age. In truth, these external markers of status do not make any human being superior to another human being. A non-abusive institution views those who reach out for help as equals who need advice, information, and support. If you reach out to an agency with the attitude that you are inferior and need them to fix you, you may be setting yourself up for a continuation of the abuse.

Repeat the following over and over to yourself, or think about it and write about it: I am just as valuable, intelligent, and capable as the person or people to whom I am reaching out for help. I deserve to be treated as an equal, with dignity, compassion, and respect.

Asking Institutions for Help

Don't avoid using these services because you are afraid of abuse. Instead, in this topic, you will learn what your rights are when receiving services, what to do when violations of your rights occur, and how you can help assure that others will act in your best interest in the future.

Before you reach out for help from agencies, learn about them. Ask the agency for a detailed description of the services they provide and for references from others who have used their services. Find out what kind of a reputation this agency has in the community, and find out if any complaints against it have been lodged with the Better Business Bureau—all you have to do is call your local BBB for this free information.

In order to use the agency you're considering, would you have to agree to terms that would restrict your freedom in any way? For example, if you're thinking about an in-patient mental health treatment facility, ask them if they use restraints, seclusion rooms, straitjackets, or other punitive methods of treatment. These harsh methods of treatment can be retraumatizing. If the agency uses these kinds of procedures, or is not acceptable to you in any way, look elsewhere for help.

Some people who have suffered trauma may have been given unhelpful diagnoses that obscured the real problem. A woman may be treated for depression or anxiety or anger and given only medication when she might benefit from a chance to process what she has been through and share her experience with other survivors.

In some systems you will need a diagnosis in order to receive insurance reimbursement for your care. In those cases, work with a health care provider to choose a diagnosis that fits and that you can live with.

Knowing Your Rights

In the course of dealing with the effects of trauma, you may have forgotten you have certain basic human rights—or perhaps you never knew you had them. When you don't know what your rights are, it is easy for violations of your rights to occur. Consider each of the following rights carefully, then write down your thoughts about it, bearing in mind that violation of any of them is abuse.

The only time you lose any of these basic human rights is if you are a danger to yourself or to others—if you have seriously hurt yourself or are threatening someone else.

You have the right to be treated with dignity, compassion, and respect at all times and not to be emotionally, physically, or sexually abused. It is not acceptable to be judged, criticized, blamed, shamed, or made to feel guilty.

_____

_____

_____

_____

You have the right to determine what you will and will not do. You are in charge of your own life. If anyone tries to take away your control over your life, they are violating your rights and perpetuating abuse. For example, sometimes when people receive mental health treatment, they are told things they must do: they must confront their abuser, take a certain medication, undergo a certain treatment, leave a spouse, avoid contact with family members or friends, or go into the hospital. They may even be threatened with a loss of services if they do not comply. This is not acceptable.

_____

_____

_____

_____

You have the right to be treated as a fully competent adult who is making good choices for herself in very difficult circumstances. Being treated in a condescending and patronizing manner is not acceptable, nor is it acceptable for others to accuse you of things such as "manipulative behavior" or "noncompliance" if you are trying to take good care of yourself and make decisions in your own behalf.

_____

_____

_____

_____

You have the right to be part of your own treatment planning and to have the final say on what will and will not be included in this plan. You have the right to determine your own priorities.

_____

_____

_____

_____

You have the right to refuse any medication or treatment you don't want. If a medication or treatment is suggested and you are uncertain how you feel about it, learn all you can about it—from the library, the Internet, the health care provider, your pharmacist, and so on. Then you can make a good decision for yourself. There is a worksheet in the appendix (Questions to Ask the Doctor about Medication) that will guide you through this process.

_____

_____

_____

_____

You have the right to make decisions based on your feelings. Only you know what is right and best for you, and your feelings are often the best indicator of what you need.

_____

_____

_____

_____

You have the right to choose your own friends and whom you will spend time with, including whom you wish to be romantically involved with.

_____

_____

_____

You have the right to say no, to refuse to do things you don't want to do, or to refuse to meet demands you don't want to meet.

_____

_____

_____

_____

You have the right to follow your own values and standards, and to pursue the religious and spiritual path of your choice as well as your own educational, vocational, and/or career goals.

_____

_____

_____

_____

You have the right to express your feelings—to laugh and be joyous, to cry and be sad, to be angry and let others know you are angry.

_____

_____

_____

_____

You have the right to privacy to perform personal hygiene tasks, not to be subjected to invasive search procedures, and to refuse invasive medical procedures.

_____

_____

_____

_____

You have the right to change and grow.

_____

_____

_____

_____

You have the right to obtain a second opinion without fear of reprisal and to change health care providers without fear of reprisal.

_____

_____

_____

_____

You have the right to have the person or people of your choice be with you when you are seeing your doctor or other health care worker.

_____

_____

_____

_____

Make a list of other rights you can think of and any feelings you have about them:

_____

_____

_____

_____

_____

_____

Dealing with Rights Violations

If a service provider or person in a position of authority tells you that in order to fully recover you must engage in some kind of sexual activity with the provider, leave immediately and report the provider, for your own protection and the protection of others who might be at risk. This is never acceptable and is not part of any treatment program.

If you feel your rights have been violated in any way, you can:

1. Ask the person or people who are violating your rights to stop, describing to them clearly how you want to be treated.

2. File a grievance with the agency and request a response. Most agencies have a grievance procedure—ask about it when you are learning about the agency and deciding whether or not you want to work with them.

3. Every state has an Agency of Protection and Advocacy and a Human Rights Commission. If you feel your grievance has not been addressed, contact them through your Yellow Pages.

4. Depending on the severity of the violation, you may want to contact a lawyer and the police.

Advance Planning for Difficult Times

You probably don't like to think about it, but there may be times in your life when you cannot take care of yourself and others will need to take over responsibility for your care and make decisions in your behalf. If this has happened to you in the past, or you think it might happen in the future, it is helpful to develop a crisis plan to prevent further traumatization from poor or abusive treatment and to insure that your needs will be met in the most effective ways. Your crisis plan keeps you in control even when it feels to you as though things are out of control. It gives you the opportunity to clearly state what would be most helpful, what you would like to have done, and who you would want to do it.

There is a nine-part Personal Crisis Plan in the appendix of this book for you to complete at a later time, if you wish. Meanwhile, the information that follows will get you thinking about that plan and what you might like it to say. This is just a beginning. Keep working on your plan until you feel it would really be helpful in a hard time. Sometimes two or three months are required to come up with a good plan. If possible, ask a friend you trust or a health care professional to work on it with you. Develop this plan slowly when you are feeling well, and don't rely on anyone else to do it for you. When you have completed your crisis plan, keep a copy and give other copies to the people you would like to take over responsibility for your care.

Part 1: What I'm like when I'm feeling well

Your crisis plan may be used by someone in an agency who has never met you before, or who doesn't know you well. This listing of words that describe you when you are well will keep them from getting confused about what you are usually like versus what you are like when you are having a hard time. Some words you might use include: talkative, quiet, outgoing, withdrawn, adventurous, cautious, outspoken, reserved, ambitious, laid back, humorous, sensible, practical, and energetic.

Words that describe you:

_____

_____

_____

_____

Part 2: Symptoms

This part is very important, as it is the part that really keeps you in control. Here's where you describe when you want others to take over. Make sure you are very clear. Symptoms or signs that others have used include:

- uncontrollable pacing, unable to stay still;

- severe agitated depression;

- inability to stop compulsive behaviors;

- catatonic—unmoving for long periods of time;

- neglecting personal hygiene (name for how many days);

- not cooking or doing any housework (name for how many days);

- extreme mood swings daily;

- destroying property;

- not understanding what people are saying;

- thinking I am someone I am not;

- self-destructive behavior;

- abusive or violent behavior;

- criminal activities;

- substance abuse;

- threatening suicide or acting suicidal;

- not getting out of bed at all; or

- refusing to eat or drink.

What are your symptoms or signs that others would need to take over for you?

_____

_____

_____

_____

_____

Part 3: Supporters

List at least five people you want to take over for you when the symptoms or signs you list come up. Include family members, friends, and health care professionals. These should be people you trust and who are responsible, honest, sincere, knowledgeable, calm, compassionate, and understanding. If you don't have five people, write down the people you do have and add to the list as you develop new friends and supporters.

People I want to take over for me when I am having a hard time:

_____

_____

_____

_____

You may also want to include a list of people you _don't_ want involved who you are afraid might inadvertently get involved if others don't know your wishes—certain relatives or health care professionals who are not helpful or who have been difficult to deal with in the past. Whether or not you write down _why_ you don't want them involved is entirely up to you.

I do not want the following people involved in any way in my care or treatment:

_____

_____

_____

_____

Part 4: Medication

List the medications you are currently using and why you are taking them. If you are not taking any at this time, list those that you would prefer to take if it became necessary and why you would choose them. Also list those medications that should be avoided along with your reasons.

Medications you are currently using (including daily dosage), and why you are using them:

_____

_____

_____

_____

Medications you would be willing to take if necessary:

_____

_____

_____

_____

Medications that should be avoided, and why:

_____

_____

_____

_____

Part 5: Treatment

List those treatments you would like in a crisis situation and those that you would want to avoid. Include alternative therapies that have helped as well as those that have not.
Treatments that will help:

_____

_____

_____

Treatments to avoid:

_____

_____

_____

_____

Part 6: Home care or respite center

Not too long ago, when you had symptoms or signs that you were unable to take care of yourself, the only option was hospitalization, often psychiatric hospitalization. Today, while psychiatric hospitalization may be necessary, there are a variety of options available that will assure that you get the care you want. If you stayed at home, for example, are there people who could take turns staying with you around the clock, following the instructions in this plan, until you felt better? Is there a safe place in the community—perhaps a crisis center or partial-hospitalization program—where you could spend part of the day, and the rest of the day at home with family members and friends providing for your care? Is there a crisis-respite center or are there respite beds available for your use? Check out all of these options, then write your detailed preferences in the plan.

I know I could make use of the following resources if I need care:

_____

_____

_____

_____

I need to learn more about the following options to see if I could use them in a crisis:

_____

_____

_____

_____

Part 7: Hospital or other treatment facilities

If hospitalization became necessary, which facilities in your area would you prefer, and which would you want to avoid? Consider those facilities you have used in the past and facilities others have told you about. You may want to call the facility and get an information packet to help you in your decision making.

Facilities I would prefer:

_____

_____

_____

_____

Facilities I want to avoid:

_____

_____

_____

_____

Part 8: Help from others

If you are having a crisis, there are certain day-to-day tasks and responsibilities that you may not be able to take care of. List these tasks and who you would want to take care of them. (If it doesn't matter who does it, you don't need to list a specific person.) Examples of such tasks include child care, pet care, watering plants, paying bills, buying groceries, mowing the lawn, and doing the laundry.

What are the specific tasks I need others to do for me in a crisis, and who would I like to do them?

_____

_____

_____

_____

When you are having a hard time, there are things that others can do that would help you feel better. Some ideas include:

- Listen to me without giving me advice, judging me, or criticizing me.

- Hold me.

- Let me pace.

- Encourage me to move around.

- Lead me through a relaxation or stress-reduction exercise.

- Peer counsel with me.

- Take me for a walk.

- Provide me with materials so I can draw or paint.

- Give me the space to express my feelings.

- Don't talk to me (or do talk to me).

- Encourage me; reassure me.

- Feed me good food.

- Make sure I get out in the sun and fresh air for at least one portion of the day.

List those things that others could do that would help you feel better.

_____

_____

_____

_____

_____

_____

Make a list of those things that would not help or might even make you feel worse. Some examples include:

- forcing me to do anything;

- trying to entertain me;

- chattering;

- playing certain kinds of music;

- playing certain videos;

- getting angry with me;

- being impatient;
- invalidating my perceptions; and
- not hearing me.

The following things would *not* help and might make me feel worse:

_____

_____

_____

_____

_____

_____

_____

Part 9: Inactivating the plan

Of course you are going to feel better very soon, and your supporters will no longer need to follow this plan. Develop a list of indicators that your supporters can use to determine that they no longer need to follow this plan. Some examples include:

- when I have slept through the night for three nights;
- when I eat at least two good meals a day;
- when I am reasonable and rational;
- when I am taking care of my personal hygiene needs;
- when I can carry on a good conversation;
- when I keep my living space organized; and
- when I can be in a crowd without being anxious.

My supporters no longer need to use this plan when:

_____

_____

_____

_____

You have now completed the notes that you'll need to fill out the complete crisis plan in the appendix. Update it when you learn new information or change your mind about things, and give your supporters new copies of your crisis plan each time you revise it.

You can help assure that your crisis plan will be followed by signing it in the presence of two witnesses. Appointing and naming an attorney you like and trust will further increase the plan's potential for use. Since the legality of these documents varies from state to state, you cannot be absolutely sure the plan will be followed. However, it can be your best assurance that your wishes will be honored and that you will not be subject to institutional abuse.

Ending Ritual

Describe something you are looking forward to that is happening soon.

_____

_____

Describe something you are looking forward to that will happen in the more distant future.

_____

_____

Optional Activity

Using the guide in the appendix, develop your Wellness Recovery Action Plan. Use this plan regularly.

Things to Remember Every Day

This is a good time to review the list of rights that appears in topic 2. Did you copy the list on a separate piece of paper and carry it with you to read from time to time? Was this helpful for you? If you did not pursue this exercise in topic 2, give it a try this week.

Topic 19

Psychological or Emotional Symptoms

Beginning Ritual

To begin work on this topic, write four good things that happened to you in the last two days:

_____

_____

_____

_____

Experiencing Symptoms Caused by Abuse

If you were abused, you probably developed certain symptoms in response. The symptoms may have happened right away or, in some cases, months or even years after the abuse.

Some symptoms, such as fear, anger, or sadness, are obviously connected to the abuse. Other symptoms, such as paranoia, dissociation, or panic attacks, may have caused a bit more confusion for you. The feelings and behaviors may have been so upsetting and over-whelming at times that you felt as if you were going crazy. In fact, all of these symptoms were signs that abuse had occurred. Some were immediate responses to the abuse, others were attempts to cope with the abuse and prevent it from happening again, and still others were ways to deny that it had ever happened at all so that you could go on living.

As you begin to think about your symptoms differently, it will be up to you to decide what you want to do about particular feelings and behaviors. Some you will want to control yourself, some you will need help from medication or counseling to control. Some symptoms will be easy for you to let go. In other cases, you might decide to hold on to a symptom for a while, in case you need it.

Many signs of abuse have been mistaken for symptoms of mental illness or biochemical brain imbalances, such as chronic depression, bipolar disorder, manic depression, or schizophrenia. If you've sought help from health care providers, perhaps you were told that your symptoms were signs of a disease or a mental illness instead of being the markers of abuse. You may have been given a diagnosis and some medication and never even asked about your abuse. It may be tempting to focus on one view of the problem, but when you see your emotions, biology, and everyday experiences as part of an integrated whole, your recovery will make more sense to you.

Some traumatized women receive treatment at mental health clinics for years for symptoms of anxiety, withdrawal, and dissociation, receiving diagnoses of major depression, bipolar disorder, and borderline personality disorder. Meanwhile, the underlying problem is ignored. Rather than help, diagnoses that obscure the role of trauma just make many women feel bad about themselves. When a woman begins to see her symptoms as connected to years of physical and emotional abuse, she may feel an enormous sense of relief, as if a cloud of confusion had lifted. She may also, however, feel sad and angry because her underlying problem—the trauma—was never really treated.

In this topic, some of the symptoms and feelings associated with abuse will be described. (Addictive and compulsive behaviors will be addressed in topic 20.) For any of the symptoms you have, or have had in the past, write down your answers to the series of questions we've listed. At the end of the exercise there are additional spaces for you to write about other symptoms or feelings that are not listed here.

Dissociation—Feeling as though you are out of your body, watching what is happening to you from a distance. For example, when Ann's counselor mentioned troubling times in Ann's childhood, Ann would protect herself by feeling disconnected from her body. She found she could relieve this symptom by telling the counselor she wanted to change the subject and discuss something pleasant that was happening in her life now, like the course she is taking or an outing with a good friend.

I currently have, or have in the past had, this symptom.

_____ Yes

_____ No

Why is this feeling hard for you?

_____

_____

_____

_____

Where do you think it may have come from?

_____

_____

_____

_____

How have you tried to help yourself feel better when you experience this symptom?

_____

_____

_____

_____

How effective has it been?

_____

_____

_____

_____

Excessive anxiety—Worry accompanied by feelings of nervousness or jitteriness and sometimes shortness of breath, weakness in the arms and legs, and profuse sweating. For example, Nancy experienced anxiety every time she went to visit her parents because she anticipated that an uncle would stop by who had been abusive to her when she was a child. To relieve this anxiety, Ann asked her parents to tell the uncle in advance of her visit that he was not welcome. She learned deep breathing and relaxation and stress-reduction exercises that she practiced regularly. In addition, she cut down on the amount of caffeine she was using.

I currently have, or have had in the past, this symptom.

_____ Yes

_____ No

Why is this feeling hard for you?

_____

_____

_____

_____

Where do you think it may have come from?

_____

_____

_____

_____

How have you tried to help yourself feel better when you experience this symptom?

_____

_____

_____

_____

How effective has it been?

_____

_____

_____

_____

Disturbed sleep—Having a hard time falling asleep, waking often during the night, or waking very early and being unable to get back to sleep. This may be the result of recurring nightmares, even though a woman sometimes can't remember them when she wakes. Mary Ellen has addressed this problem by doing relaxation exercises several times during the day, doing journal writing before going to bed, and taking herbal supplements recommended by a health care professional.

I currently have, or have had in the past, this symptom.

_____ Yes

_____ No

Why is this feeling hard for you?

_____

_____

_____

_____

Where do you think it may have come from?

_____

_____

_____

_____

How have you tried to help yourself feel better when you experience this symptom?

_____

_____

_____

_____

How effective has it been?

_____

_____

_____

_____

Losing track of time—You can't account for where you were and what you were doing at certain times. For example, Marcy kept finding clothes in her closet that she couldn't remember buying. Sometimes people came up to her on the street, acting as if they knew her well, and she had no recollection of who they were. She is dealing with this in three ways: through counseling with a therapist who has experience treating people who have been abused, by practicing being in the moment (discussed in topic 7), and by involving herself in grounding activities such as cooking and cleaning when she is feeling stressed.

I currently have, or have had in the past, this symptom.

_____ Yes

_____ No

Why is this feeling hard for you?

_____

_____

_____

_____

Where do you think it may have come from?

_____

_____

_____

_____

How have you tried to help yourself feel better when you experience this symptom?

_____

_____

_____

_____

How effective has it been?

_____

_____

_____

_____

Fear of leaving the safety and security of your living space—In extreme cases, you might be unable to go outdoors at all. For example, Robin only felt safe in the house because of traumatic events that had happened when she left the security of her home. She worked on relieving this problem by leaving the house for short periods of time and going only to safe places, often accompanied by a supporter. She very gradually increased the length of time she could be away and the number of places she could go, and eventually began spending more time away from home on her own.

I currently have, or have had in the past, this symptom.

_____ Yes

_____ No

Why is this feeling hard for you?

_____

_____

_____

_____

Where do you think it may have come from?

_____

_____

_____

How have you tried to help yourself feel better when you experience this symptom?

_____

_____

_____

How effective has it been?

_____

_____

_____

_____

Hypervigilance—Feeling as though you are always on edge, expecting something bad to happen, always expecting the worst, and feeling tense all over in anticipation. For example, Patsy grimaced every time someone touched her because she expected the touch to be abusive. Patsy explained the problem to several friends and worked with them, practicing being touched without grimacing until she was able to enjoy friendly touch. Whenever this issue comes up she reminds herself that she is no longer in the abusive situation that she believes was responsible for this symptom.

I currently have, or have had in the past, this symptom.

_____ Yes

_____ No

Why is this feeling hard for you?

_____

_____

_____

_____

Where do you think it may have come from?

_____

_____

_____

_____

How have you tried to help yourself feel better when you experience this symptom?

_____

_____

_____

_____

How effective has it been?

_____

_____

_____

_____

_____

Uncontrollable rage—Yelling, screaming, or hollering at someone, something, or nothing. For example, Jan would have screaming fits toward her husband. Sometimes these fits were unprovoked, and other times they began as the result of a minor incident or misunderstanding. She felt this rage was left over from the physical and emotional abuse she experienced as a child. She learned to deal with this symptom by noticing early warning signs that she was getting stressed; sometimes she was able to recognize a certain circumstance that was likely to lead to an outburst. She would then stop what she was doing, go to a quiet place she had designated in the house, listen to quiet music, and do a relaxation exercise.

I currently have, or have had in the past, this symptom.

_____ Yes

_____ No

Why is this feeling hard for you?

_____

_____

_____

_____

Where do you think it may have come from?

_____

_____

_____

_____

How have you tried to help yourself feel better when you experience this symptom?

_____

_____

_____

_____

How effective has it been?

_____

_____

_____

Flashbacks—When you experience a vision of a past traumatic ~~event along with~~ strong feelings relating to the trauma. For example, while she was involved in some enjoyable activity, Diane would suddenly see in her mind a frightening incident of abuse with her ex-husband. This seemed to drain away all her energy and fill her with fear. Diane learned to deal with this symptom by immediately reminding herself that flashbacks are "old news" that have nothing to do with her present circumstance. She would then take a few deep breaths before resuming her other activities.

I currently have, or have had in the past, this symptom.

_____ Yes

_____ No

Why is this feeling hard for you?

_____

_____

_____

_____

Where do you think it may have come from?

_____

_____

_____

_____

How have you tried to help yourself feel better when you experience this symptom?

_____

_____

_____

_____

How effective has it been?

_____

_____

_____

_____

Hallucinations—Seeing, hearing, feeling, and thinking things that are not based in reality. For example, Marlene had times when her whole life felt out of control. Nothing seemed real. All of her senses seemed to be distorted. She would tell others about things she had seen and heard that made her upset and they knew these things had not really happened. Marlene learned to watch for possible triggering events and early signs of hallucinations. When they occurred, she took time off from work and spent one or several very quiet days at home, doing relaxation exercises, journaling, and engaging in activities she enjoys.

I currently have, or have had in the past, this symptom.

_____ Yes

_____ No

Why is this feeling hard for you?

_____

_____

_____

Where do you think it may have come from?

_____

_____

_____

_____

How have you tried to help yourself feel better when you experience this symptom?

_____

_____

_____

_____

How effective has it been?

_____

_____

_____

_____

Low self-esteem—Feeling as though you have little or no value as a person. For example, Jodie kept trying and trying to do things that would make her feel good about herself. She got a doctorate as well as a master's degree, had a successful career, and she still couldn't feel like she had any value. She felt this was because she was told over and over as a child that she was "no good for anything." Jodie worked on raising her self-esteem by repeating over and over the affirmation, "I am a wonderful person with lots of talents to share with others." In addition, she started avoiding people who gave her negative feedback about herself, spending more time with people who were positive and affirming.

I currently have, or have had in the past, this symptom.

_____ Yes

_____ No

Why is this feeling hard for you?

_____

_____

_____

_____

Where do you think it may have come from?

_____

_____

_____

_____

How have you tried to help yourself feel better when you experience this symptom?

_____

_____

_____

_____

How effective has it been?

_____

_____

_____

_____

Inability to trust—Being unable to connect closely and bond with others because of fears of rejection or abuse. For example, Jane often felt lonely and separated from others. However, whenever people attempted to establish a connection with her she would become fearful, avoiding the person and not responding to their invitations. She felt she was unable to trust others because when she was a child her parents had physically and emotionally abused her and neglected her basic needs. To address this issue in her life, she interviewed several counselors until she found one with whom she felt comfortable. They worked together to develop a trusting relationship. The counselor then introduced Jane to a support group of other women who had been abused. In this group she learned to share personal information with others who had similar experiences and who respected her confidentiality. She developed close friendships with several of the women in the group, getting together with them for walks and movies. With these successful trusting relationships, she began to take more risks, becoming friendly with people at work and at her church.

I currently have, or have had in the past, this symptom.

____ Yes

____ No

Why is this feeling hard for you?

_____

_____

_____

_____

Where do you think it may have come from?

_____

_____

_____

How have you tried to help yourself feel better when you experience this symptom?

_____

_____

_____

_____

How effective has it been?

_____

_____

_____

_____

Use the following spaces to address other symptoms and feelings you experience as a result of abuse.

Feeling or symptom:

_____

Why is this feeling hard for you?

_____

_____

_____

_____

Where do you think it may have come from?

_____

_____

_____

How have you tried to help yourself feel better when you experience this symptom?

_____

_____

_____

How effective has it been?

_____

_____

_____

Feeling or symptom:

_____

Why is this feeling hard for you?

_____

_____

_____

_____

Where do you think it may have come from?

_____

_____

_____

How have you tried to help yourself feel better when you experience this symptom?

_____

_____

_____

How effective has it been?

_____

_____

_____

Feeling or symptom:

_____

Why is this feeling hard for you?

_____

_____

_____

_____

Where do you think it may have come from?

_____

_____

_____

How have you tried to help yourself feel better when you experience this symptom?

_____

_____

_____

How effective has it been?

_____

_____

_____

_____

Your List of Tools

As you review the responses to your symptoms above, you will discover that you developed some successful tools for relieving symptoms and feelings associated with abuse. What are they?

_____

_____

_____

_____

_____

_____

_____

You will find other ways to relieve symptoms in topics 6, 7, and 13. Review the work you did in those topics and make a list of the tools you have started to use or plan to try.

_____

_____

_____

_____

_____

_____

You may want to make a copy of this list of tools to hang on your bulletin board or refrigerator for easy reference. Use them whenever you have emotional or psychological symptoms or feelings that are uncomfortable or distressing. The more you practice these skills, the easier they will be to use. After a while you will notice that you are using them almost automatically. Your symptoms will become less of an issue in your life and you will feel better and enjoy your life more. This change happens gradually over time.

Ending Ritual

Describe something you are looking forward to that is happening soon.

_____

_____

Describe something you are looking forward to that will happen in the more distant future.

Optional Activities

1. Spend at least one hour each day doing something you really enjoy. Note how you feel before and after this activity.

2. The next time a symptom or a bad feeling occurs, stop, write the name of the symptom or feeling on a piece of paper, and put the paper in a safe place. As you are doing this, tell yourself, "I can control this feeling. I don't need to experience this right now if I don't want to."

Things to Remember Every Day

- I'm not crazy. The symptoms and feelings I experience are normal responses to trauma and abuse.

- I recognize symptoms of trauma and abuse. I relieve them by using the tools I have discovered on my own and through this work.

Topic 20

Addictive or Compulsive Behaviors

Beginning Ritual

To begin work on this topic, write four good things that happened to you in the last two days:

_____

_____

_____

_____

   Addictive and compulsive behaviors are very difficult to control—they may even seem impossible to control. Do you ever feel driven to do certain things, even if the behavior is hurting you and you desperately want to stop? These behaviors may be a response to trauma or abuse. They become a problem when they cause you to do things that are physically harmful and dangerous (such as cutting yourself, drinking excessive amounts of alcohol, or using potentially lethal drugs) and/or keep you from doing the things you want to do and being the kind of person you want to be.

   You may have begun using these behaviors to:

- feel better (at least temporarily) and get some relief from the pain or symptoms and feelings related to abuse,

- give you the courage to do difficult things,

- give you some feeling of control over your life, and/or

- keep yourself from thinking about difficult things.

Why do you think you may have begun using these behaviors?

_____

_____

_____

_____

By the time you realize these behaviors are not helpful and are destructive, they may have already become habits or addictions that are very hard to break.

Admitting the Behaviors Are a Problem

Sometimes it's hard to admit that behaviors are addictive or compulsive and that some parts of our lives are out of control. Has this been a problem for you? If so, which of the following statements have you used to try to convince yourself or others that you don't have a problem? Place a check mark next to those that apply.

- I can stop whenever I want.

- It's just something I really enjoy—I have a right to do things I enjoy.

- I can handle it.

- Who's it hurting?

- It's my business.

- It makes me feel better.

- I don't want to think about all that stuff.

- Everyone else is doing it.

- Who cares?

- There's nothing else to do.

- It makes it easier to talk to people; I'm not as shy; I can dance.

- I'm old enough to do what I want to; I'm an adult and I can do what I want.

- I deserve it.

List other statements you have used to justify addictive or compulsive behaviors:

_____

_____

_____

_____

What's wrong with statements like this? Why aren't they helpful?

_____

_____

_____

_____

Next, let's look at specific addictive or compulsive behaviors that might be issues for you. Again, place a check mark next to those that apply.

- working all the time (workaholic);
- the need for excessive or promiscuous sex;
- harming yourself (cutting or burning);
- repeatedly washing your hands or some other part of your body;
- shoplifting;
- excessive exercising, even when it is causing you physical pain;
- eating large amounts of foods—sometimes particular kinds of foods, such as sweets;
- drinking or eating lots of caffeine-containing foods (coffee, tea, soda, diet soda, chocolate);
- eating very little food;
- being very weight conscious;
- overeating;
- pulling your hair out;
- needing to be perfect;
- gambling;
- watching TV all the time;
- excessive cleaning;
- excessive shopping;

- excessive smoking;

- excessive alcohol use;

- excessive use of illegal drugs; and

- excessive use of prescription medicines such as tranquilizers and sedatives.

Are there any other compulsive or addictive behaviors that are issues in your life?

_____

_____

_____

_____

Sharon admits she is addicted to exercise. She walks or runs at least fifteen miles every day, taking longer runs whenever possible. She does over 500 sit-ups every morning. In addition she rides her bike, swims, and skis whenever possible. She finds it very hard to stop exercising, even when she wants or needs to do other things or is physically hurting. This addiction has affected her family life—her partner and children want more time and attention. At work she is constantly plagued with thoughts that she needs to be exercising. In addition, she needs hip and knee surgery as a result of not paying attention to her body's need for rest.

Marcy is a writer who loves her work. She feels good when she's writing, and it keeps her from thinking about other things. She has gotten into the habit of writing from sixty to eighty hours a week. She writes instead of taking care of her other responsibilities and uses it as an excuse for avoiding contact with other people. Sometimes she feels as though her life is really empty. Recently she has noticed she has begun having panic attacks.

Mindy is a successful businesswoman. Several years ago her doctor prescribed pain medication for a chronic pain condition. She noticed that she felt more comfortable interacting with people when she took this medication—she didn't get the sweaty palms and butterflies in her stomach she normally experienced when meeting with people she doesn't know well. She kept getting the prescription refilled until her doctor would no longer fill it for her. She then changed doctors and got a new prescription. In the last two years she has changed doctors three times and goes from pharmacy to pharmacy to keep getting the medication. If she doesn't take it, she becomes very anxious and disoriented.

If reading these stories reminds you of problems you have had with addictive or compulsive behaviors, write your own story here. You can use separate sheets of paper if necessary, or you could make a tape recording or tell the story to someone you trust.

_____

_____

_____

_____

_____

_____

_____

_____

_____

_____

Strategies for Letting Go of These Behaviors

People have devised many successful ways of getting rid of addictive and compulsive behaviors. They all take hard work, consistency, time, and patience. You can begin doing this work now, or you can just begin thinking about it now and come back to it at a later time. You can live with the behavior the rest of your life if that is what you want to do and if it is not illegal or life threatening.

If you are going to work on getting rid of this behavior, there are many options you can choose depending on your preference and what you know works well for you. As you make these choices, be wary of anyone who tells you what you "must" do. This is your life and the choices are up to you. If you choose to become involved in any kind of organized treatment program or self-help group, continue to listen to yourself in making decisions about what you will and will not do. Don't do anything that doesn't feel right to you and don't let anyone else try to control your life.

The following list includes some options for getting rid of addictive or compulsive behaviors. If there are some that you might want to explore further, you can get more information about such techniques from self-help resources such as books or the Internet.

Rewards: Devise a system for yourself so that when you avoid the behavior for a length of time you specify, you give yourself a reward (going to a movie, going out for lunch, taking an hour off in the middle of the day to read a good book, or spending some time in a museum).

Support: Tell someone you trust that you've decided to break your compulsion and arranging to contact them whenever you feel tempted to do what it is you are trying to avoid doing.

Replacing the unwanted behavior with self-soothing activities: Review the self-soothing activities in topic 7. Whenever you are tempted by your addictive or compulsive behavior, do a self-soothing activity instead.

Diversionary activities: Diversionary activities are things you really enjoy doing—things that will divert your attention away from your addictive or compulsive behavior. Whenever you feel pulled toward the behavior you want to avoid, do a diversionary activity instead. Hang a list of things you like to do on your refrigerator so you can refer to it quickly whenever you need to.

Incremental steps: Develop a series of small incremental steps or goals that will take you toward your bigger goal of letting go of the behavior. For instance, if you are working on letting go of addictive eating patterns, your first step might be that you would avoid foods that are high in fat or sugar for two days in one week. The next week you avoid them for three days, and so on. A notebook or journal can help you keep track of your progress.

Wellness Recovery Action Plan: This plan was introduced as an optional activity in topic 18. It is fully described in the appendix. Develop one of these plans to deal with your specific addictive or compulsive behavior.

Medical help/consultation: Ask your doctor or another health care professional for information and advice on how they recommend relieving addictive or compulsive behaviors.

Treatment programs: There are a variety of treatment programs for dealing with addictive and compulsive behaviors, and many are covered by health insurance. The best known are those that deal with alcohol and drug addictions. Ask for complete information about any treatment program before enrolling.

Counseling: Often, the assistance and support of a specially trained counselor will help assure success in treating your behavior.

Support groups: There are support groups to deal with many kinds of addictive and compulsive behaviors. They help by giving you the opportunity to talk openly about what you are doing and how you are feeling, and to get ideas from others who are trying to do the same things. Learn what is available in your area through the newspaper, the Internet, a local information line, a hospital, a mental health agency, or a crisis center.

Twelve-step groups: Twelve-step groups are a specific type of highly structured support group. You will be led through a series of well-defined steps designed to help you give up your addictive or compulsive behavior. Such groups have been very helpful to many people, but you'll want to attend several meetings before you decide this is the right strategy or group for you.

Which strategies that you know of would you like to use in getting rid of addictive or compulsive behaviors that are troublesome to you? When and how will you go about getting involved in these strategies?

Is This the Right Time for You?

If your compulsive or addictive behaviors are not dangerous or illegal and are not seriously affecting your health, you may want to deal with other more pressing issues in your life before addressing the behaviors. Certain life changes might make addressing your behaviors right away very difficult—for example, if you are under a lot of stress, moving, changing jobs, getting a divorce or leaving a relationship, being abused, expecting a child (unless the behavior is dangerous to the unborn child), physically sick, or close to someone who is ill or needs caretaking.

What issues, if any, do you need to deal with before addressing your addictive and compulsive behaviors?

_____

_____

_____

_____

_____

_____

The best time to address your troubling behaviors is when you are feeling physically well and are taking good care of yourself, you have people in your life who are supportive, you have learned self-soothing techniques to use when you are having a hard time, and you feel you are strong and self-confident.

It's normal to want to get rid of all your addictive and compulsive behaviors as quickly as possible, but that's not a good idea. It's too hard to let go of all your crutches at the same time. You may want to begin with the one that is most troublesome right now. Or, you may want to deal with the one that you think would be easiest, so that you experience some success right away.

Of course, certain addictions or compulsions should be dealt with right away, regardless of the circumstances of your life. As we've mentioned previously, behaviors that place you and others in imminent danger cannot be ignored. Such behaviors include: excessive alcohol or drug use, promiscuous sex, severe anorexia or bulimia, wanting to hurt yourself, excessive smoking, and stealing.

If you can think of any addictions or compulsions that are so serious that you need to work on them right away, even if the circumstances of your life will make this difficult, list them here:

_____

_____

_____

_____

Setting Goals

Review the list of your addictive and compulsive behaviors and the possible strategies for letting go of them. Use the following format to develop plans for letting go of one or more of these behaviors.

Behavior:

_____

Why do I want to get rid of this behavior?

_____

_____

_____

Long-term goal: By _____ , I plan to:

_____

_____

_____

Short-term goal: By _____ , I plan to:

_____

_____

_____

I will begin to work toward meeting these goals [when]

_____

Strategies I will use to meet my goals:

_____

_____

Behavior:

Why do I want to get rid of this behavior?

Long-term goal: By _____ , I plan to:

Short-term goal: By _____ , I plan to:

I will begin to work toward meeting these goals [when]

Strategies I will use to meet my goals:

Behavior:

_____

Why do I want to get rid of this behavior?

_____

_____

_____

Long-term goal: By _____ , I plan to:

_____

_____

_____

Short-term goal: By _____ , I plan to:

_____

_____

_____

I will begin to work toward meeting these goals [when]

_____

Strategies I will use to meet my goals:

_____

_____

_____

_____

You may have made a strong commitment to working on getting rid of compulsive or addictive behaviors. You may have already begun to do the work. But there are things that can get in the way of achieving your goals, and you may find that despite your best efforts, things are not going well. The following list will help you explore some things that may be getting in your way.

1. Negative self-talk—you may be giving yourself negative messages (such as those that follow) that make the work more difficult. If so, develop positive responses to these negative messages to repeat over and over every time you find yourself thinking negatively.

   Negative thought: I've messed up once so I'm never going to be able to do this. Positive response: It's okay to mess up. I'll just try again. If I don't succeed right away, I'm sure I will eventually.

   Negative thought: I'll never get through the first week. Positive response: I can do it. It may be hard but I'm strong enough to succeed.

2. Negative support—family members, friends, and/or health care professionals might tell you that you can't do it or might even be subtly or actively encouraging you to continue the addiction. If this is an issue for you, let them know that they are not being helpful. If they won't stop, avoid them as much as possible, spending time with people who are supportive and affirming. You can find people who are supportive and affirming in support groups and at crisis centers.

3. Low self-esteem and lack of self-confidence—perhaps you don't feel good enough about yourself or your abilities. If this is an issue for you, keep reminding yourself that you are a great person and you deserve to have your life the way you want it to be. Refer to topic 6 for ideas on helping yourself feel good about yourself.

4. Not using the right strategies—perhaps the strategies you have chosen to do this work are not the best ones for you. Assess what you are doing. Does it feel right to you? If not, review the list of ways to get rid of these behaviors and revise your plan.

5. Current abuse—it is very difficult to give up addictive and compulsive behaviors if you are being abused. As we've emphasized throughout this book, you deserve to be treated well and if you are currently being abused in *any* way, and you are not working with a counselor to correct this situation, contact your local mental health agency or crisis center right away.

Remember, you had to be creative to come this far in your life. Use your strength, power, and creativity to design and use a strategy for making your life just the way you want it to be.

Ending Ritual

Describe something you are looking forward to that is happening soon.

_____

_____

Describe something you are looking forward to that will happen in the more distant future.

_____

_____

Optional Activities

1. Make a list of all the skills and strategies you have discovered that might help relieve your addictive or compulsive behaviors. If you've developed a Wellness Recovery Action Plan, add these skills and strategies to the plan.

2. Do at least one thing to really celebrate yourself—paint a picture, sing an inspirational song, spend extra time pampering yourself, or look in the mirror and repeat over and over "I am great"—whatever makes you feel really good.

Things to Remember Every Day

- I deserve to have my life the way I want it to be.

- I can do the work I need to do to get control of addictive or compulsive behaviors.

- I am in charge of when and how I will work on getting rid of my own addictive and compulsive behaviors.

Topic 21

Abuse and Relationships

Beginning Ritual

To begin work on this topic, write four good things that happened to you in the last two days:

_____

_____

_____

_____

From the time you were old enough to appreciate being a woman, you probably dreamed of being in a healthy relationship. The fantasy of the beautiful bride in her long white gown and veil leaving the church with her handsome groom and going on to live "happily ever after" in a vine-covered cottage is a dream experienced by countless young girls. However, as you grow and learn, you realize that this vision is only a fantasy—that life has its ups and downs and there is no "happily ever after." You may have had or now have a long-term relationship or some shorter relationships that are rich and fulfilling, or you may live a good life by yourself. On the flip side, your life story may be even further removed from that fantasy. You may find yourself in an abusive and unfulfilling relationship that has gone on for many years, or perhaps you've had a series of shorter, unhealthy relationships. As each relationship ends, your hopes may remain high that the next relationship will be better.

List words and phrases that you would use to describe a healthy relationship. Words you might use could include "equal," "fair," "honest," and "trusting."

_____

_____

_____

_____

Recognizing Abuse in Relationships

Because of your history, you may have a hard time recognizing abuse in a relationship. You may feel or know that something is really wrong in the relationship, yet try to justify it. You may say things to yourself such as, "He didn't really mean it that way." "She was exhausted." "If I don't do this again, I'm sure it won't happen again." Or maybe it's absolutely clear to you that this is an abusive relationship but you feel stuck in it—you can't see your way out.

The following words will help you understand what an abusive relationship is.

Manipulation—someone using deception or other devious means to get you to do things you don't want to do or that are destructive.

What does the word "manipulation" mean to you? Describe circumstances in current or past relationships where you have been manipulated, and explain how it made you feel.

_____

_____

_____

_____

Intimidation—someone frightening, scaring, coercing, or terrorizing you to get you to do what they want you to do or be the way they want you to be.

What does the word "intimidation" mean to you? Describe circumstances in current or past relationships where you have been intimidated, and explain how it made you feel.

_____

_____

_____

_____

Aggression—someone attacking you or using force against you.

What does the word "aggression" mean to you? Describe circumstances in current or past relationships where aggressive behavior has been used against you, and explain how it made you feel.

Domination—someone else using what they perceive as their power to control you and your life. In such situations, the other person's needs are always more important than yours.

What does the word "domination" mean to you? Describe circumstances in current or past relationships where you have been dominated, and explain how it made you feel.

Linda has been married to Joe for twenty-five years. Every morning Joe has uncontrollable rage in which he rants and yells, telling Linda and their two adolescent sons everything they have ever done wrong. He threatens them with taking away their "privileges" and forcing them to do things they don't want to do. Sometimes he hits them. At work and in the evening, however, he is warm and friendly.

Kate has been living in a committed long-term relationship with June for ten years. June lost her job several years ago, and Kate continues to work full-time to support both of them. June spends all day at home watching television. She refuses to do any housework or help with meal preparation. In addition, she will not turn off the television when Kate asks her to and frequently changes the channel when Kate is watching a program she enjoys.

Theresa has lived with Frank for seven years. They have three small children. Theresa likes the house to be neat but is not terribly fussy about it. Frank doesn't care what the house looks like and piles books, magazines, and electronic equipment everywhere. Occasionally Theresa likes to have several friends come in for lunch. Before they come she spends several days cleaning the living room and dining room. Frank resents this and thwarts her efforts by piling his things in the places she has just cleaned. Theresa feels so discouraged by this she has decided it isn't worth it to have her friends come in because she is too embarrassed.

Are there aspects in any of these stories that seem familiar to you? If so, what are they? What other stories of abuse have you seen or experienced?

———————————————————————

———————————————————————

———————————————————————

———————————————————————

———————————————————————

Margaret is sixty years old. As a child she had been abused and neglected by several family members. In her early twenties, Margaret married a man with whom she spent the next twenty years of her life. He was generally regarded by others as an outstanding member of the community. While he was not outwardly abusive, he found subtle ways to constantly remind Margaret that she was "incompetent and not as good" as other women with whom he was in regular contact. She left this marriage for a man who bought her nice things and took her out to dinner. Compared to her former marriage, this new situation seemed like heaven. By the time Margaret realized that this man was alcoholic and very abusive, she had married him and they had purchased a home together. It took five years for her to get up the courage to literally hide from this man and begin a new life. When Margaret was in these relationships, she felt there was some truth in what these men were telling her about herself—that if she could figure out how to be the way they wanted her to be, the abuse would stop. Even though she had a good job, she felt convinced she couldn't make it on her own. Now, after many years of counseling, she is in a relationship based on equality, where she feels valued and supported.

Why do some women seem to turn from one abusive partner to the next? In looking back, women who have been in one or more abusive relationships give the following reasons for being in those relationships:

- I didn't see what was happening to me as abuse. It was the way I had always been treated.

- I never knew what a healthy relationship should look like.

- I was "sucked in" by good treatment early in the relationship, and by the time I realized it was abusive we were married and I was pregnant.

- I never felt I deserved anything better.

- I had really low self-esteem and didn't think anyone else would want me.

- I didn't think there were any other options.

If you have been in one or several abusive relationships, why do you think that is?

———————————————————————

———————————————————————

———————————————————————

_____

_____

Perhaps you have had the frustration of seeing a friend or relative get repeatedly involved in abusive relationships. Why do you think your friend did this?

_____

_____

_____

_____

Staying or Leaving

If you are in an unhealthy relationship, do you need to leave? The answer to this question is very personal and only you can provide the answer. Of course, if your life or the lives of others are in danger, you may need to leave at once. (Possible preparations for such a move are described in the next section.) If you choose to stay, there are some things you can do to improve the situation—for example, you could talk to your partner openly about changes you'd like to see in the relationship, or you could ask your partner to see a counselor with you.

If you decide to talk to your partner about changing his or her behavior, write down the reasons that this seems like a good idea to you, as well as the reasons that this might *not* be a good idea:

_____

_____

_____

_____

_____

If you decide to ask your partner to see a counselor with you, write down the reasons that this seems like a good idea to you, as well as the reasons that this might *not* be a good idea:

_____

_____

_____

_____

_____

_____

Would you like to change the way you respond to the abuse?

_____ Yes

_____ No

To change the way I respond, I would:

_____

_____

_____

This seems like a good idea because:

_____

_____

This is not a good idea because:

_____

_____

Describe other good ways you can use to improve your relationship.

_____

_____

_____

Leaving an Abusive Relationship

While you may understand that you deserve to be treated well, and know that you are being abused, leaving an abusive relationship is not easy.

Check off the reasons you have stayed in abusive relationships:

_____ threats to yourself, other family members, or pets;

_____ a sense of commitment to the relationship;

_____ a belief that things will get better;

_____ religious beliefs;

_____ children;

_____ pets;

_____ financial security;

_____ personal insecurity, such as feeling you can't take care of yourself;

_____ feeling no one else would ever want you;

_____ liking your home and being unable to get the abuser to leave.

What are the factors keeping you (or that have kept you) in an abusive relationship?

_____

_____

_____

_____

_____

Only you will know when it is the right time, and when you are ready, to leave a relationship. Others in your life may want you to do it right away and may not understand your hesitation. Remind them that you are in charge of your life and you need to make these decisions based on what feels right, comfortable, and safe to you.

The biggest consideration when leaving an abusive relationship is your safety and the safety of others. Some abusive people may threaten to hurt you or others you care about when you announce your intention to leave. If this is even a remote possibility, you will need to plan your leaving very carefully to ensure the safety of everyone involved. For help in planning, consider talking with a crisis counselor who has experience in helping people leave abusive situations.

Marli knew she needed to leave her abusive husband. His alcoholic rages were becoming more frequent and his abuse was becoming more violent. She was constantly afraid for her own safety and that of her two daughters, ages six and eight. Her husband threatened that if she left, he would keep her daughters and never let her see them again. Marli contacted her local crisis center and made arrangements to go there with her daughters when she was ready. She opened a checking account with a mailing address at the crisis center, making regular deposits of the money that was left after buying groceries. She took some clothing, personal items, and pictures, along with some of her daughters' clothes, to the crisis center before she actually left. She and her daughters left right after her husband went away on a business trip when she knew he would be gone for several days, giving them several days to adjust. She immediately got a restraining order against her husband. She and her daughters hid out in the crisis center until she made arrangements to move out of the area.

Things to arrange ahead of time if you need to leave an abusive relationship:

- Where will you stay for the short and long term? Options include renting a home, staying with friends or relatives, or staying at a safe house or crisis center.

- Arrange to have some money available. Depending on your circumstances, you may need to hide some money—give it to a family member or friend for safekeeping, or open a checking account and arrange for mail to be sent to a post office box or other safe place.

- Get a credit card in your name and, again, arrange for mail to be sent to a post office box or other safe place.

- What about your children—can they leave when you do, or do you need seek help from the courts to terminate or limit your ex-partner's access to the children?

- What about your pets? If you can't keep them and you're sure they're unsafe with your partner, can you find another home for them or arrange temporary housing for them?

- Personal belongings—if removing all of them will be difficult, can you remove just the items that are important to you ahead of time?

- Personal support—do you have friends, family members, health care professionals, or crisis workers who will help and support you through this time?

- Do you need to let the authorities know that you or others are at risk? Do you need to get a restraining order against your partner?

- Getting your abuser to leave your home may be a very daunting task that may put you and others at risk. You may have to sacrifice your home or use legal means to keep control of your property.

If you are thinking of leaving an abusive relationship, describe the preparations you need to make before leaving.

_____

_____

_____

_____

_____

Avoiding Abusive Relationships

When you first become involved in a relationship, you see the world and your new lover through rose-colored glasses. At first you think the two of you are perfect for each other. Sometimes, abuse doesn't become apparent until you have been together for quite a while. By that time you may have made a major commitment to each other that is hard to break, such as getting married or having a child together. Your lives may have become intertwined—you live together and share activities, responsibilities, family, and friends. How can you avoid getting into relationships that turn sour down the road and become difficult to end?

Consider the following possible answers to that question. Would taking these actions have kept you from getting into an abusive relationship in the past?

- Taking time to get to know each other well before becoming sexual or making any kind of permanent commitment, such as living together or having a child.

- Observing how this person treats their children, other family members, and friends.

- Watching for early signs that the potential partner might be manipulative, domineering, aggressive, or intimidating.

- Learning about the person's relationship history. Has he or she ever been served with a restraining order or been accused of stalking?

- Having your own interests and resources so you are not dependent on a relationship for your survival.

- Building your own self-esteem and self-confidence so you don't need another person's approval to feel good about yourself.

What actions could you take to avoid getting into abusive relationships?

_____

_____

_____

_____

_____

Being Abusive Yourself

Having a history of being abused is an explanation for being abusive to others, but it is not an excuse. If you know that you manipulate, intimidate, dominate, are aggressive, or have behavior patterns that are damaging to others, you need to take corrective action right away. You can begin by seeing a counselor and asking for help. If you don't have one, call your local mental health agency for a referral. If cost is an issue, ask about low-cost or free options.

Either before you see the counselor or with the counselor, make a very accurate assessment of your abusive behaviors. Being honest with yourself in this regard is essential. Becoming aware of your abusive behaviors and writing them down is an important first step in resolving this issue, so list your abusive behaviors below.

_____

_____

_____

_____

You will now need to work intensively on avoiding these behaviors. It helps if you have people in your life you can talk to about your problem and what you are doing about it, and whom you can talk to when you need support and courage to go on.

Let the person or people you have been abusing know that you are trying to stop. Tell them why you are doing it, and ask for their help and support as you work to change.

When you feel as though you are going to be abusive, try one of the following:

• Take a few deep breaths.

• Call and talk to a friend.

• Do something you enjoy.

• Get away from the person or people you were going to abuse.

• Sit alone quietly until the feeling passes.

Other ideas you have for avoiding abusive behavior:

_____

_____

You may want to set up a system of rewards for yourself, giving yourself a bonus after you have avoided certain behaviors for a predetermined length of time.

Keep a daily journal of your progress in avoiding abusive behavior. Have a personal celebration when you need to affirm yourself and the important work you are doing.

Ending Ritual

Describe something you are looking forward to that is happening soon.

_____

_____

Describe something you are looking forward to that will happen in the more distant future.

_____

_____

Optional Activities

1. (For people who live with others) Think about what your life would be like if you lived alone and didn't have to consider another person's needs. Can you make some changes so your life is the way you want it to be without infringing on the rights of the person who live with?

2. (For people who live alone) Think about what your life would be like if you lived with others. Are there any changes you could make to more closely match your ideal? For example, are there people or relationships you want to add to your life? How might you accomplish this?

3. Make an art object that expresses your frustrations about relationships.

Things to Remember Every Day

- I deserve to be treated well at all times.

- I treat others well.

- I can do what I need to do to keep myself and others safe.

Part 3

Creating Life Changes

Topic 22

Family Myths and Distortions

What Are Family Myths and Distortions?

Family myths and distortions are stories that develop within the family to keep others from knowing the reality of what is *really* going on in the family. These myths and distortions are used, for example, to hide abuse, cover up specific information about relationships within the family, and make the family look good to others. Sometimes these myths and distortions have been going on for so long and have so much power that people within the family forget that they are not real. These family stories often keep women from seeing themselves and their relationships as they really are. You sometimes may find yourself perpetuating the myths and distortions you grew up with. In this topic you will take a close look at the family that raised you. Seeing that family as it really was will help you see yourself and your current relationships more honestly.

Taking a Closer Look

To begin the process of seeing your family as it really is or was, it helps to take a look at the family from the vantage point of what you think an outsider probably thought.

Someone outside of Marcy's family might have said the following: When Marcy was a child she lived in a suburban community on the outskirts of a large city. Her family consisted of her father, mother, her mother's sister, an older sister, and a younger sister. It was a tight-knit family that enjoyed being together and working together. Her father was highly regarded because he was a deacon in the church and volunteered at the local hospital, and because he had "taken in" his wife's sister, who had "a hard time learning." Her mother was easygoing and hard-working—she worked nights in a nursing home. The aunt took care of the children. The children were quiet, well-behaved, and happy.

Describe your family as if you were seeing it as someone else who lived in your community.

_____

_____

_____

_____

_____

_____

However, the way Marcy's family was seen by others in the community was vastly different from the reality of the family.

Marcy's father had a previous family with two sons and two daughters that few people knew anything about. He was not allowed any contact with the daughters because he had been convicted of molesting both of them. He had escaped a prison sentence through a mistake in the court system. He was having a sexual relationship with the aunt while Marcy's mother worked at the nursing home. Marcy's mother and the children knew of this relationship but were instructed not to mention it to anyone. Her mother felt she couldn't get along without her husband. The father was also having sex with two of his daughters. The aunt controlled all the activities of the daughters and resented their relationships with their father, often verbally and physically abusing them. One daughter became very obese, another developed severe anorexia, and the third has gone through years of counseling that have given her the strength she needed to leave her family and build a life for herself that is built on reality.

If you had written the true story of your family when you were a child and anyone in your family saw it, you might have gotten into serious trouble. You might have risked serious abuse. But now you are an adult and you are safe. Of course, when you write the true story of your family you may still feel very uncomfortable and frightened. If this exercise feels too uncomfortable or frightening, either write just a line or two or skip it. You can write more at some other time if you want to.

Here is the _true_ story of my family.

_____

_____

_____

_____

_____

_____

_____

_____

_____

How did it feel to write the true story of your family?

_____

_____

_____

_____

_____

Why do you think you felt this way?

_____

_____

_____

_____

_____

Uncovering and Debunking Your Family's Myths and Distortions

In this section you will work to uncover your families myths and distortions and develop some ideas on ways you could reduce the effects of the myths on your life. There are five steps in this process.

1. Identifying the myth and/or distortion.

2. Naming the person or people who taught you this myth, and assessing that person's believability.

3. Thinking about the purpose of the myth or distortion and who or what it was meant to protect.

4. Considering how this myth or distortion has affected your life. What have you done or what can you do to reduce the effects of this myth or distortion on your life?

5. Developing a positive response to the myth.

1. Identifying the myth or distortion.

Think about the things you learned from your family that were not true or were distortions of the truth. List the myths and distortions you uncover. For instance, the myths or distortions Marcy discovered included:

- I have a normal family.

- I am only good for sex and for working around the house.

- Women are second-class citizens.

- Men are more important than women.

- Dad is a great guy and knows best.

List your family's myths and distortions.

_____

_____

_____

_____

_____

_____

Later, you will look at these myths by using the five-step method. First, here's how Marcy completed steps 2 through 5 for her first myth: I have a normal family.

2. Who taught you this myth?

My father, mother, and aunt. How believable are these people based on what you now know about them? *They are not believable. My father is an abusive man, and very dishonest, manipulative, and aggressive. My mother is passive and doesn't even feel she can take care of herself. My aunt is vicious and cruel.*

3. What was the purpose of this myth? What was it meant to do? Who or what was it meant to protect?

This myth was meant to keep the dysfunction and abuse from public view and to protect my father from being prosecuted for ongoing abuse.

4. How has this myth or distortion affected your life?

It has distorted my view of family life. I grew up thinking that all families were like mine. I also was unclear about what abuse is. I got into several very abusive relationships. What have you done or what can you do to reduce the effects of this myth or distortion on your life? *I have been in counseling for many years. I have also been part of positive family activities and celebrations through a new relationship. This has given me new insight into the realities of family life.*

5. Develop a positive response to this myth.

My family was very abusive and dysfunctional. Now, through counseling and participation in positive family activities with my partner, I have developed clarity regarding normal family life.

Use the following spaces to fill in your responses to the questions. You can look at as many or as few myths or distortions as you feel comfortable doing at this time. If you want to, you can return to this section at another time.

Myth number 1:

1. _____

2. Who taught you this myth?

_____

How believable is this person based on what you now know about them?

_____

_____

_____

3. What was the purpose of this myth? What was it meant to do? Who or what was it meant to protect?

_____

_____

_____

_____

4. How has this myth or distortion affected your life?

_____

_____

_____

What have you done or what can you do to reduce the effects of this myth or distortion on your life?

_____

_____

_____

_____

5. Develop a positive response to this myth.

_____

_____

Myth number 2:

1. _____

2. Who taught you this myth?

_____

How believable is this person based on what you now know about them?

_____

_____

_____

3. What was the purpose of this myth? What was it meant to do? Who or what was it meant to protect?

_____

_____

_____

_____

4. How has this myth or distortion affected your life?

_____

_____

_____

What have you done or what can you do to reduce the effects of this myth or distortion on your life?

_____

_____

_____

_____

_____

5. Develop a positive response to this myth.

_____

_____

_____

Myth number 3:

1. _____

2. Who taught you this myth?

_____

How believable is this person based on what you now know about them?

_____

_____

_____

3. What was the purpose of this myth? What was it meant to do? Who or what was it meant to protect?

_____

_____

_____

_____

4. How has this myth or distortion affected your life?

_____

_____

What have you done or what can you do to reduce the effects of this myth or distortion on your life?

_____

_____

_____

_____

_____

5. Develop a positive response to this myth.

_____

_____

_____

Myth number 4:

1. _____

2. Who taught you this myth?

_____

How believable is this person based on what you now know about them?

_____

_____

_____

3. What was the purpose of this myth? What was it meant to do? Who or what was it meant to protect?

_____

_____

_____

_____

_____

4. How has this myth or distortion affected your life?

_____

_____

_____

What have you done or what can you do to reduce the effects of this myth or distortion on your life?

_____

_____

_____

_____

5. Develop a positive response to this myth.

_____

_____

_____

Myth number 5:

1. _____

2. Who taught you this myth?

_____

How believable is this person based on what you now know about them?

_____

_____

3. What was the purpose of this myth? What was it meant to do? Who or what was it meant to protect?

_____

_____

_____

_____

_____

4. How has this myth or distortion affected your life?

_____

_____

_____

What have you done or what can you do to reduce the effects of this myth or distortion on your life?

_____

_____

_____

_____

5. Develop a positive response to this myth.

_____

_____

_____

Reinforcing Your Positive Responses

Myths and distortions you learned as a child are hard to unlearn because you learned them from people whom you trusted at the time and because they were reinforced every day. Time, creativity, and persistence are needed to permanently change these myths and distortions to the positive responses you developed in step 5 of the preceding exercise. You will discover many ways to reinforce these positive responses and gradually you will notice that the myths and distortions become less real for you. Here are some of the ways that others have successfully used:

- Write the positive responses on a piece of paper you carry with you and then read them over and over every time you have a few extra minutes.

- Repeat the positive responses over and over every time you notice that you are thinking about the myths or distortions.

- Repeat the positive responses five times when you first get up in the morning and five times before you go to sleep at night.

- Write the positive responses over and over using different styles of handwriting, using your right hand for some and your left for others.

- Write in your journal about the positive responses.

- Make signs with the positive responses and hang them in places where you will see them often. Read them every time you see them.

List other ways you have thought of that would help reinforce your positive responses.

_____

_____

_____

_____

_____

Optional Activities

1. Make a list of the myths and distortions you learned in your family, then destroy it to symbolize letting go of the misinformation.

2. Using an artistic medium that feels right to you, express how you feel about your family's myths and distortions.

3. Talk to a trusted friend about your family's myths and distortions.

4. Ask a trusted sibling to share any family myths or distortions they recall. Are they the same or different from yours? Why do you think that is?

Things to Remember Every Day

- I see myself and my relationships as they really are.

- I can successfully get rid of the effects of the myths and distortions I learned as a child.

Topic 23

Current Family Life

Effects of Abuse on the Family

Abuse affects the family and influences how family members relate to each other long after the abuse is over—and this is true even if the abuse happened outside of the family. If you have been abused, it may be very hard for you to make decisions about your relationships with members of your family. It may be especially hard for you to make decisions about your relationship to the person who abused you. The exercises in this topic will help you determine what kind of relationships you can have with family members that will help avoid disappointments and further abuse. The exercises will also help you discover what kinds of precautions you need to take if and when you decide to have contact with your family.

Thought Patterns to Consider

Some of the following thoughts may affect the way you relate to your family. However, these thoughts may have been learned when you were a child and were not able to accurately assess what you were taught by others. Consider them again now to see if you might respond to them in a way that would feel better to you.

Old thought: It's my obligation.
New way of thinking: It's up to me to decide what is an obligation and what is not. I don't have any obligation to see people I don't want to see or who have hurt me, or to do things I don't want to do.
How do you feel about this?

_____

_____

_____

What changes are you going to make in the way you do things because of this new way of thinking and how you feel about it?

_____

_____

_____

_____

Old thought: I can't stay away from this person—he or she is my [father, mother, brother, sister, aunt, uncle, cousin, grandparent] after all!

New way of thinking: I can stay away from anyone I want to. I don't have to spend time with people or be where they are just because I am related to them.

How do you feel about this?

_____

_____

_____

What changes are you going to make in the way you do things because of this new way of thinking and how you feel about it?

_____

_____

_____

_____

Old thought: It's best to forgive and forget.

New way of thinking: I need to heal from the bad things that have happened to me. I don't need to forgive anyone I don't wish to, and forgetting is impossible.

How do you feel about this?

_____

_____

_____

What changes are you going to make in the way you do things because of this new way of thinking and how you feel about it?

_____

_____

_____

_____

Old thought: I can't survive without them. They are the only family I have.

New way of thinking: I can do anything I need to do to take care of myself and support myself. I can even create a new family for myself.

How do you feel about this?

_____

_____

_____

What changes are you going to make in the way you do things because of this new way of thinking and how you feel about it?

_____

_____

_____

_____

Old thought: I just want the whole family to be together.

New way of thinking: Getting the whole family together may be a very bad idea. I can arrange to spend time with only those people who treat me well.

How do you feel about this?

_____

_____

_____

What changes are you going to make in the way you do things because of this new way of thinking and how you feel about it?

_____

_____

_____

_____

Old thought: I must not hurt this family member's feelings.
New way of thinking: I need to take good care of myself. If that means I have to hurt someone else's feelings, I may need to do that.
How do you feel about this?

_____

_____

_____

What changes are you going to make in the way you do things because of this new way of thinking and how you feel about it?

_____

_____

_____

_____

Old thought: I can't stand up to this family member or set limits for family members.

New way of thinking: I can do anything I need to do to take care of and protect myself and others I care about, and this includes setting limits for family members.

How do you feel about this?

_____

_____

_____

What changes are you going to make in the way you do things because of this new way of thinking and how you feel about it?

_____

_____

_____

_____

Old thought: If a family member threatens me or people I love, I have to do what they want. I can't say no to members of my family.

New way of thinking: I have the right to contact the police and get protection for myself in such situations. I can also reach out to the local crisis services and public services for protection, assistance, and support.

How do you feel about this?

_____

_____

_____

What changes are you going to make in the way you do things because of this new way of thinking and how you feel about it?

_____

_____

_____

_____

_____

Old thought: If a family member abuses me, I just have to put up with it because if I told someone, it might hurt the feelings of other people in the family and/or those other people might get angry with me.

New way of thinking: I can tell anyone I want, including the police, and family members have no right to get angry with me about this. If they are not supportive of me, I need to stay away from them and spend time with people who are supportive.

How do you feel about this?

_____

_____

_____

What changes are you going to make in the way you do things because of this new way of thinking and how you feel about it?

_____

_____

_____

_____

You can use this method to analyze any thoughts or thought patterns you have that you feel need to be changed. Use the following spaces if you can think of any now.

Old thought:

_____

_____

_____

New way of thinking:

_____

_____

_____

How do you feel about this?

_____

_____

What changes are you going to make in the way you do things because of this new way of thinking and how you feel about it?

_____

_____

_____

_____

Old thought:

_____

_____

_____

New way of thinking:

_____

_____

_____

How do you feel about this?

_____

_____

_____

What changes are you going to make in the way you do things because of this new way of thinking and how you feel about it?

_____

_____

_____

_____

Old thought:

_____

_____

New way of thinking:

_____

_____

_____

How do you feel about this?

_____

_____

_____

What changes are you going to make in the way you do things because of this new way of thinking and how you feel about it?

_____

_____

_____

_____

_____

Improving Your Relationships with Family Members

People generally want to have loving relationships with most of the members of their family. In your case, this may seem impossible. However, there are some things you can do to improve relationships with individual members of your family or with your whole family. Of course, you are the only person who will know what would help improve relationships with people in your family. Which of the following do you think you could use to help ease your relationships with people in your family?

- Talk to one or more of my family members about family issues that are disturbing to me. Make specific requests regarding changes I would like.

  Would this work in your family? Why or why not?

  _____

  _____

  _____

- Go to a counselor with one, several, or all family members to discuss strategies for addressing problems in the family and to get information and advice on how to deal with family problems.

  Would this work in your family? Why or why not?

  _____

  _____

  _____

- Hold a family meeting. Get family members together to discuss family relationships and possible strategies for improving relationships.

  Would this work in your family? Why or why not?

_____

_____

_____

- Plan a special family gathering where the focus is on doing a fun activity such as taking a hike, eating together, playing ball, or planting a garden.

  Would this work in your family? Why or why not?

  _____

  _____

  _____

- Give extra attention to family members who are having a hard time.

  Would this work in your family? Why or why not?

  _____

  _____

  _____

- Take responsibility for planning a holiday gathering and set it up in a way that would feel comfortable to me.

  Would this work in your family? Why or why not?

  _____

  _____

  _____

- Make regular phone calls or set up regular contact with certain family members.

  Would this work in your family? Why or why not?

  _____

  _____

  _____

- If I feel I am always receiving help from certain family members, turn the tables and do some things to help them out.

  Would this work in your family? Why or why not?

  _____

  _____

  _____

- If I feel that I am always giving to others and not getting anything back, ask family members to give me a hand with certain tasks and projects.

  Would this work in your family? Why or why not?

  _____

  _____

  _____

- Are most of my interactions with family members concerned with trying to "fix" things? If so, I will stop doing that for a while and notice what happens. If things get better I may want to stop "fixing things" permanently.

  Would this work in your family? Why or why not?

  _____

  _____

  _____

- Do certain family members nag me a lot? If so, ask them to stop for three days. See if that improves my relationship with that family member. If it does, I will try asking them to stop nagging me for good.

  Would this work in your family? Why or why not?

  _____

  _____

  _____

- Do I nag certain family members a lot? If so, I will stop for three days and see if that improves my relationship with that family member. If it does, I will try to stop nagging them for good.

Would this work in your family? Why or why not?

_____

_____

_____

• List any other ways you think you could improve relationships with members of your family.

_____

_____

_____

_____

_____

_____

_____

Setting Up a New Family for Yourself

Many people grow discouraged with trying to improve their relationships with their families and give up. This is often a very good thing to do and is part of making a commitment to spend time with people who treat you well. However, if you have done this or are thinking of doing this, you may notice that it makes you feel very lonely and sad. You can set up a new family—a family of choice—by asking people you know, like, and trust if they would fill family roles for you. For instance, if there is an older woman who treats you as you wish your mother had treated you, you could ask her to fill that role in your life. Perhaps you can think of other people to be your father, siblings, aunts, uncles, or even children.

Some women try for many years to heal relationships with their families, but in spite of their efforts the families continue to be emotionally abusive. Finally they may decide they have had enough and stop having any contact with the families—no longer going to their homes for family gatherings and refusing to talk with them on the phone. By asking neighbors, friends, or church members to act as substitute parents, many women find that they can talk, share fun activities, and spend holidays together without the tension and abuse they experience with their families.

You may not feel ready to do this now. If not, just keep the idea in the back of your mind and do it whenever it feels right to you. If you would like to create a new family for yourself, who would you want in your family—mother, father, sister? Do you have people in mind for these roles? Below, write down the roles you'd like filled and the people you have in mind to fill them.

_____

_____

_____

_____

_____

_____

Spending a Holiday with Your Family

Imagine that tomorrow is a holiday and you will be spending the day with the family who raised you. Spend several minutes thinking about the day.

How do you feel about spending this holiday with your family?

_____

_____

Is this something you would normally do? Why or why not?

_____

_____

What would be hard for you about this day?

_____

_____

What would you like about the day?

_____

_____

_____

Who would you most look forward to seeing and why?

_____

_____

_____

Is there anyone you would want to avoid? Who would it be and why do you feel that way about them?

_____

_____

_____

If there is anyone whom you think would not want to see you, who would it be and why do you think they wouldn't they want to see you?

_____

_____

_____

Is there anything you could do to make this day more pleasant for yourself?

_____

_____

_____

Is there anything that others could do to make this day more pleasant for you if you asked them to?

_____

_____

_____

Is there anyone who you would be afraid of? If so, is there anything you could do to protect yourself?

_____

_____

_____

Did you gain any insights about your family from this exercise? If so, describe them below.

_____

_____

_____

_____

_____

_____

_____

Optional Activities

1. Design an ideal holiday celebration with your family. What would it be like? What would you do together? Who would you invite and why? Who would you not invite and why?

2. Look through old photos. Make a display of pictures of those family members who have always treated you well.

3. Look through old magazines and cut out pictures of people who represent family members you never want to see again. Then destroy these pictures to symbolically represent getting them out of your life.

Things to Remember Every Day

- I can take care of myself and meet my needs.

- I choose to spend time with people who treat me well.

- I do only what feels right to me.

- I set my own limits and boundaries.

- I can do what I need to do to protect myself and others.

Topic 24

Decision Making: Trusting Your Judgment

Why Decision Making Can Be Hard

In previous topics you've explored various myths, distortions, secrets, and other family interactions that can occur when any kind of abuse is part of your life. Because these influences are based on distorted reality, you may have learned to ignore or not to trust your own feelings and perceptions about things. Perhaps you often let others make decisions for you because it feels easier, because you think you don't have a choice, or because you don't trust your ability to make good decisions for yourself. As part of the healing process, you may feel that you now want to learn to trust your own judgment, take back your right to make decisions for yourself, and learn how to make decisions that serve your best interests.

Steps for Good Decision Making

While it is not possible to be sure that every decision you make will turn out well, the following five steps will help you make decisions for yourself that will increase the likelihood of a positive result. The more positive experiences you have in decision making, the more you will learn to trust your judgment.

1. List the options.

2. Ask yourself the following questions:
   - What do I really want to do?
   - Which option has the best chance of working out well?
   - Does the option keep me safe?
   - If I choose this option, is there a chance that I will be hurt or disappointed in the future? If so, is this a risk I am willing to take?

- If I choose this option, would I be doing a really good thing for myself?
- Will this option affect anything else I have planned or want?
- What are the long-term benefits of this option?
- What are the short-term benefits of this option?
- Is money a factor in making this choice? If so, can I think of a way to make any money problems manageable?
- Does this option fit with long-term goals I have for myself?
- Does this option affect any short-term goals I have for myself?
- Who else do I need to consider in making this decision?
- If I feel there are people who need to be considered, am I sure that I'm not considering them out of old habits from the past (such as checking in with your mother before you make a decision)?
- Is this situation like one I have been in before? What happened then? Is there anything I have learned from that experience that will help me make this decision?
- If I feel pressured to make this decision quickly, before I have had time to think it through, is there any way I could arrange more time to think about it?

List any other questions you feel you should ask yourself before you make decisions.

_____

_____

_____

_____

_____

3. Is there anyone you trust whom you could ask for guidance, such as a counselor or close friend?

4. Choose the option that feels best to you.

5. Think about the option you have chosen. Sit in a quiet, comfortable place. Take a few deep breaths. Does the option still seem right to you? If not, what has changed?

Looking at Old Decisions in New Ways

When you look back on your life, you probably wish you had done certain things differently or made different choices.

Sarah met Brian at work. After working with him for several weeks on a project, he asked Sarah to go out to dinner and he told her that he wanted to spend more time with her because he found her to be really attractive. He said he was married and had several children but that he no longer got along with his wife and was going to ask her for a divorce.

Sarah became sexually involved with Brian. He kept telling her he was going to get divorced but never seemed to get around to it. Eventually, Brian's wife found out about the relationship and made threatening phone calls to Sarah. Brian continued to pursue his relationship with Sarah even though she tried to end the relationship. She finally felt she had to leave her job, which she had enjoyed, and move to a new place away from her network of friends.

Describe an experience in your life (a relationship, a job, a living situation, or a health issue, for example) that didn't turn out the way you wanted it to.

_____

_____

_____

_____

_____

What decision or decisions did you make that affected the outcome of this experience?

_____

_____

_____

_____

What do you think the outcome would have been if you had made different decisions?

_____

_____

_____

_____

Using the five steps outlined above, analyze one of the decisions you made to see if, through using this process, you might have made a different decision.

1. List the options.

_____

_____

_____

_____

_____

2. Ask yourself the following questions:
   - What do I really want to do?

   _____

   _____

   - Which option has the best chance of working out well?

   _____

   _____

   - Does the option keep me safe?

   ____ Yes

   ____ No

   - If I choose this option, is there a chance that I will be hurt or disappointed in the future? If so, is this a risk I am willing to take?

   ____ Yes

   ____ No

   - If I choose this option, would I be doing a really good thing for myself? If not, why not?

   _____

   _____

   - Will this option affect anything else I have planned or want? If so, what, and how will it be affected?

   _____

   _____

- What are the long-term benefits of this option?

- What are the short-term benefits of this option?

- Is money a factor in making this choice? If so, can I think of a way to make any money problems manageable?

- Does this option fit with long-term goals I have for myself?

- Does this option affect any short-term goals I have for myself?

- Who else do I need to consider in making this decision?

- If I feel there are people who need to be considered, am I sure that I'm not considering them out of old habits from the past (such as checking in with your mother before you make a decision)?

_____

_____

_____

- Is this situation like one I have been in before? What happened then? Is there anything I have learned from that experience that will help me make this decision?

_____

_____

_____

- If I feel pressured to make this decision quickly, before I have had time to think it through, is there any way I could arrange more time to think about it?

_____

_____

_____

List any other questions you feel you should ask yourself (along with the answers), before you make this decision.

Questions:

_____

_____

_____

_____

Answers:

_____

_____

_____

_____

_____

3. Is there anyone you trust whom you could ask for guidance? If so, whom?

_____

_____

4. Choose the option that feels best to you.

5. Think about the option you have chosen. Sit in a quiet, comfortable place. Take a few deep breaths. Does the option still seem right to you? If not, what has changed?

_____

_____

_____

Use these steps whenever you make decisions over the next few weeks or months. Soon you will notice that you feel better about making good decisions for yourself.

Making a New Decision

Now you will use the five steps to analyze a decision you need to make right now. The decision could be anything, large or small—perhaps you are thinking about starting a new job or hobby, asking your husband for a divorce, or going to spend two weeks with your parents.

What is the decision you'd like to make now?

_____

_____

_____

1. List the options.

_____

_____

_____

_____

_____

2. Ask yourself the following questions:

   • What do I really want to do?

   _____

   _____

   • Which option has the best chance of working out well?

   _____

   _____

   • Does the option keep me safe?

   ____ Yes

   ____ No

   • If I choose this option, is there a chance that I will be hurt or disappointed in the future? If so, is this a risk I am willing to take?

   ____ Yes

   ____ No

   • If I choose this option, would I be doing a really good thing for myself? If not, why not?

   _____

   _____

   • Will this option affect anything else I have planned or want? If so, what, and how will it be affected?

   _____

   _____

   _____

   • What are the long-term benefits of this option?

   _____

   _____

- What are the short-term benefits of this option?

- Is money a factor in making this choice? If so, can I think of a way to make any money problems manageable?

- Does this option fit with long-term goals I have for myself?

- Does this option affect any short-term goals I have for myself?

- Who else do I need to consider in making this decision?

- If I feel there are people who need to be considered, am I sure that I'm not considering them out of old habits from the past (such as checking in with your mother before you make a decision)?

- Is this situation like one I have been in before? What happened then? Is there anything I have learned from that experience that will help me make this decision?

_____

_____

_____

- If I feel pressured to make this decision quickly, before I have had time to think it through, is there any way I could arrange more time to think about it?

_____

_____

_____

List any other questions you feel you should ask yourself (along with the answers), before you make this decision.

Questions:

_____

_____

_____

_____

Answers:

_____

_____

_____

_____

3. Is there anyone you trust whom you could ask for guidance? If so, whom?

_____

_____

4. Choose the option that feels best to you.

5. Think about the option you have chosen. Sit in a quiet, comfortable place. Take a few deep breaths. Does the option still seem right to you? If not, what has changed?

_____

_____

_____

Optional Activities

1. Create some art that celebrates your progress in your healing journey.

2. Many people notice that they feel more calm when they draw something with their nondominant hand. Using your left hand if you are right handed, or your right hand if you are left handed, draw a picture of an object you can see right now—like a leaf, a flower, a chair, or a shoe. How did you feel afterward? If you felt more calm after this exercise, you may want to repeat it from time to time. If this works for you, you might be interested in exploring the book *Drawing on the Right Side of the Brain,* by Betty Edwards (New York: Tarcher/Putnam, 1989).

Things to Remember Every Day

- I am in charge of my life.

- I make many good decisions that keep me safe.

- I make decisions that are in my best interest.

- I trust my judgment.

Communication: Making Yourself Understood

A history of abuse affects the way you communicate with others. You may have learned negative or indirect ways of communicating, or you may have avoided communicating to protect yourself and others. Now you may find that you have a hard time sharing information about yourself with others; talking about your observations, thoughts, and feelings; and letting others know what you want and need. This can cause difficulties in all areas of your life, including family, relationships, work, and school. Fortunately, positive changes can occur very quickly when you learn ways of communicating that make it easy for others to understand what you are saying.

Communication Styles to Avoid

First, consider the following kinds of communication that don't help and will often make the situation worse.

Sarcasm—cutting or bitter comments that make the other person feel bad. For example, "Yeah! Right! Sure you're going to get an A on that paper!"

Reminding of past experiences—reminding the other person of bad things he or she has done in the past rather than addressing what is happening right now. For example, "I remember that time when you yelled at her just because she was five minutes late."

Hurtful labels—using hurtful words such as "stupid," "lazy," "good-for-nothing," "brat," "fool," and so on to label someone. For example, "You are really crazy!"

Negative comparisons—comparing a person to another person in a bad way. For example, "If only you were smart like your brother."

Judgmental "you" messages—speaking to the other person in an accusatory way. For example, "You always mess everything up! You never treat me right!"

Describe any other communication styles you can think of that don't work well for you.

_____

_____

_____

_____

_____

Kinds of Communications

Our communications include a mix of observations, thoughts, feelings, and needs. Clear communication styles can be learned and used consistently by understanding the parts of communication and effective communication guidelines.

Observations—telling someone else exactly what you saw, heard, read, or experienced. It is a statement of fact. In clear communication you will give accurate feedback about your observations; you share something exactly the way it is or was. For example,

- The sun shone brightly all day today.

- I had tomato soup and cheese for lunch.

- My wallet is made of brown leather.

Thoughts—conclusions you have drawn from things you have observed or experienced. They may include value judgments, wishes, and desires. For example,

- I would get along better with my husband if I stopped smoking.

- Janie is a good girl because she always obeys her parents.

- It would be nice to have a vacation next fall.

- I wish I lived in a bigger house.

Feelings—expressions of emotions. They can be very difficult to share, and others may not want to hear them. People may act bored or upset when you share your feelings, or they may just hear what they want to hear and ignore the rest. Because of this, you may have decided to keep your feelings to yourself. Yet when you share your feelings with others, that helps them understand you, and it may help them better meet your needs. You might want to practice sharing feelings that have to do with the information you are trying to communicate. For example,

- I'm really upset about losing my job.

- I feel nervous every time I talk to my father.

- I really miss having my children at home.

- I'm afraid of the dark.

Needs—communicating what you need lets others know what is important for you. This may be very hard for you. Women who have been abused are not used to asking for or getting what they need. You may feel you are bad to ask for anything you need. When you need something, practice making straightforward requests. For example,

- I need to have some time by myself.

- I need to get some extra work done.

- I need to avoid people who treat me badly.

- I need to spend some time with my friends.

What do you need?

_____

_____

_____

Wants—sometimes you just want something. It may be something small or frivolous, like a hot fudge sundae or a new pair of earrings. Or it may be something larger, such as more free time or a better job. These are wants, not necessities. Many people are confused about the difference between needs and wants. Because of your history, you may feel you have no right to wants that are not also needs. Have you thought about the fact that you are entitled to wanting things that will make your life more fun, easy, or interesting? For example,

- I want to go to the beach for a week.

- I want a new rug for my house.

- I want to have time to draw.

- I want to take a photography class.

What do you want?

_____

_____

_____

Guidelines for Clear Communication

1. Give whole messages that include all important pieces of information. Don't leave important information out.

2. Use "I" statements such as, "I feel angry," "I am upset," and "I like being with you."

3. Ask yourself the following questions about the communication:

- What am I observing, thinking, or wanting in this communication?
- What is the purpose of this communication?
- Is the stated purpose the same as my real purpose?
- What am I afraid of saying?
- What do I need to communicate?

4. Watch the response you get from the person or people you are talking to. Check their body language so you can know if this is the right time to be sharing this, or if the subject matter is right for this person. You may need to change what you are saying according to the response you observe.

5. Depending on the communication, you may want to talk to this person in a private, congenial, and comfortable place with few distractions where you won't be interrupted.

The following examples will help you understand the difference between clear and unclear communications.

Unclear: You talk too much.

Clear: I need some quiet time.

Unclear: You always say the wrong thing.

Clear: I don't agree with what you said.

Unclear: I'm sick of you.

Clear: I need some time alone.

Unclear: You are just a jerk.

Clear: When you said I wasn't trying hard, it made me feel upset.

Unclear: You don't know how to dress.

Clear: I don't like the color of your dress.

Unclear: I'm really pissed off.

Clear: When you tell me I am not doing my job, I feel angry.

One woman's husband came home late for supper for the third night in a row. By the time he got home, she had already fed the children, dinner was cold, and she was busy getting the children ready for bed. She said in a very irritated voice, "You are a real jerk. How could you do this to me?"

How can this communication be changed so that it is clear and direct?

Observation: Her husband was late for the third night in a row.

Thought: When my husband comes home late, it upsets my routine and is an inconvenience.

Feelings: I feel angry and irritated.

Needs: I need him to either come home on time or let me know he will be late so I can adjust my schedule accordingly.

Wants: I want to have more time with him in the evening.

A clear statement to her husband might be, "You have come home late three nights in a row. By the time you get home the children have been fed, dinner is cold, and I am busy getting the children ready for bed. It upsets my routine and is an inconvenience to me. I feel angry and irritated. I need you to either come home on time or to let me know you will be late so I can adjust my schedule accordingly. I would also like more time alone with you in the evening."

Analyze three verbal interactions you have had recently. Choose interactions that felt difficult for you. If you can't think of a recent interaction, you can come back to this exercise another time.

1. Describe an experience you had recently that involved talking to someone about something that was difficult.

_____

_____

_____

_____

_____

What happened or what did you observe?

_____

_____

_____

Describe what you thought and concluded from this interaction.

_____

_____

_____

How did it make you feel?

_____

_____

_____

What were your needs regarding this situation?

_____

_____

_____

Develop a clear statement you could have used in communicating with the other person.

_____

_____

_____

2. Describe an experience you had recently that involved talking to someone about something that was difficult.

_____

_____

_____

_____

What happened or what did you observe?

_____

_____

_____

Describe what you thought and concluded from this interaction.

_____

_____

_____

How did it make you feel?

_____

_____

_____

What were your needs regarding this situation?

_____

_____

_____

Develop a clear statement you could have used in communicating with the other person.

_____

_____

_____

3. Describe an experience you had recently that involved talking to someone about something that was difficult.

_____

_____

_____

_____

What happened or what did you observe?

_____

_____

_____

Describe what you thought and concluded from this interaction.

_____

_____

How did it make you feel?

What were your needs regarding this situation?

Develop a clear statement you could have used in communicating with the other person.

Effective Communication: A Test

Refer back to the clear statements you developed for each of the three examples you developed in the last section. Were you able to answer yes to the following questions?

Example 1.

1. Have I expressed what I actually know to be fact? ____ Yes ____ No

2. Have I expressed and clearly labeled my inferences and conclusions? ____ Yes ____ No

3. Have I shared my feelings without blame or judgment? ____ Yes ____ No

4. Have I shared my needs without blame or judgment? ____ Yes ____ No

5. Have I been able to say what I want? ____ Yes ____ No

Example 2.

1. Have I expressed what I actually know to be fact? ____ Yes ____ No

2. Have I expressed and clearly labeled my inferences and conclusions?
   ____ Yes ____ No

3. Have I shared my feelings without blame or judgment? ____ Yes ____ No

4. Have I shared my needs without blame or judgment? ____ Yes ____ No

5. Have I been able to say what I want? ____ Yes ____ No

Example 3.

1. Have I expressed what I actually know to be fact? ____ Yes ____ No

2. Have I expressed and clearly labeled my inferences and conclusions?
   ____ Yes ____ No

3. Have I shared my feelings without blame or judgment? ____ Yes ____ No

4. Have I shared my needs without blame or judgment? ____ Yes ____ No

5. Have I been able to say what I want? ____ Yes ____ No

   Is this way of communicating new to you? ____ Yes ____ No

   Does this way of communicating feel comfortable to you? Why or why not?

   _____

   _____

   _____

   What have you learned about communication from this exercise?

   _____

   _____

   _____

Saying No

There are times in your life when you need to say no, or be firm or insistent about what is and is not okay with you. When you were abused, you may not have been able to say no, or if you did it was not heard. You may find that you still have a hard time saying no or being firm when necessary. However, there are times when you must say no and mean it. You may need to practice this over and over again in front of the mirror, or whenever you have some free time.

Sometimes, another person will try to talk you into whatever it is they want even after you say no. Don't argue or try to convince them your way is right. If you are clear that the answer must be no, just keep saying no over and over again. If this is hard for you, it may help to repeat this affirmation to yourself: "No one can talk me into doing things I don't want to do, or that are not okay with me."

List some times when no is all you need to say.

_____

_____

_____

_____

List times in the past when you wish you had said no or when someone convinced you to change your mind and you wish you hadn't.

_____

_____

_____

_____

Self-Disclosure

Talking about yourself and your experiences to a person who is trustworthy and supportive helps the recovery process. However, women who have been abused are often reluctant to share personal details of their lives with others. You may be afraid that others will not want to hear the truth about your life, don't care enough to listen, or will invalidate or trivialize significant life experiences. You may be afraid that the listener will disapprove of what you are saying or will reject you if they know about your life. There are many benefits of sharing information about yourself with others, however:

- Increased understanding of yourself—often our thoughts, feelings, and needs are confused until we put them into words. In order for someone else to understand what you are saying, you have to organize your thoughts in ways that can also help you better understand yourself.

- Closer relationships—relationships deepen when you share intimate details of your life with someone you care about.

- Improved communication—as you share more openly with others, you will notice that they share more openly with you.

- Alleviation of guilt—women who have been abused often feel so guilty that their self-esteem and life enjoyment are affected. When you share feelings of guilt you no longer have to keep your guilt hidden and you can look more closely at the reality of the guilt. Self-disclosure begins the process of letting go of feelings of guilt.

- Increased energy—keeping important information about you and your life hidden inside you takes energy. As you share with others you will notice feelings of relief, which leads to higher energy levels.

You might begin the process of sharing the details of your life with a counselor or one or more close friends. Or, you might join a support group where you can share with others who have had similar life experiences. Many people use peer counseling to effectively share information about themselves in a safe and supportive way. Following is information about this; you may wish to give it a try.

Peer Counseling

Peer counseling is a structured way of sharing the intimate details of your life. It can help you express your feelings, understand your problems, discover some helpful action you can take, and eventually feel better. It provides an opportunity to express yourself any way you choose, while supported by a trusted friend. When used consistently, it is a free, safe, and effective self-help tool. Peer counseling also provides you with an opportunity to give support to someone else and hear the details of his or her life. Both of these aspects of peer counseling will help you.

Peer counseling is not the same as working with a professional counselor, therapist, or mental health worker. A counselor or therapist has special skills and experience that they use to provide you with assistance in dealing with issues in your life. A peer counselor only listens and does not give advice.

Peer counseling is not the same as conversation in that no attempt is made to insure equal time; there is no give and take. Instead, in a peer counseling session, two people who like and trust each other agree to spend a previously agreed upon amount of time together, dividing the time equally, addressing and paying attention to each other's issues. For instance, if you have decided you will spend an hour together, the first half hour is focused on one person and the second half hour on the other person. Sessions can be as short or as long as the two participants would like them to be. Often the length of time is predetermined by the demands of busy lives and hectic schedules. Various formats can be powerful and effective in their own way. Most people choose to do it for one hour, with each person sharing for half an hour.

Mary Ellen spends at least one afternoon a week peer counseling for an hour with her friend Laura. "We have been doing this for about four years. I always look forward to it. It's a special time for both of us and relieves stress in our busy lives. Recently when I found myself feeling overwhelmed with worry about one of my children, I called her and arranged some extra peer counseling time."

The content of these sessions is strictly confidential, of course. Information that a person shares in a session is never shared with *anyone*. Judging, criticizing, and giving of advice by the listener are not allowed. When someone is speaking, the listener should only make an occasional neutral comment such as, "I understand," "I'm sorry you are having such a hard time," or "I am here for you."

Sessions are held in a comfortable, quiet place where there will be no interruption or distraction and where the session cannot be heard by others. Disconnect the phone, turn off the radio and television, find someone to watch the children, and do whatever else is necessary to eliminate distractions. While most of us prefer face-to-face sessions, phone sessions can also be held when necessary.

The content of the session is determined by the speaker, who can use his or her time any way he or she chooses. This may include crying, trembling, ranting, indignant storming, laughter, yawning, shaking, singing, or punching a pillow. You may want to spend some time planning your life and goals.

You may find it useful to focus on one issue and keep coming back to it despite feelings of wanting to avoid it. At other times you may find yourself switching from subject to subject. At the beginning of a session you may want to focus on one particular issue, but as you proceed, you may find other issues coming up that take precedence. All of this is up to you. The person who is listening and paying attention needs to do only that.

At the beginning of a session the listener can ask the speaker to share several good things that have happened in the last week (or day, or month). This provides a positive starting point for the session. At the end of the session, to provide a positive ending point, the listener should ask the speaker to share something she is looking forward to.

In peer counseling, the expression of emotion is *never* seen as a symptom of a psychiatric illness or an indication that something is wrong. Instead, emotion is viewed as a vital part of the wellness process. You may have been treated inappropriately for expressing emotion and may have learned not to express emotion because it is not safe, which interferes with your wellness process. Peer counseling can help change that.

Optional Activity

Learn more about good communications from *Messages: The Communication Skills Book,* by M. McKay, M. Davis, and P. Fanning (Oakland, Calif.: New Harbinger Publications, 1983).

Things to Remember Every Day

- I can share my observations, thoughts, feelings, needs, and wants with others in a clear and direct way.

- By sharing information about my life I will increase my understanding of myself, develop closer relationships with others, improve my communication skills, relieve feelings of guilt, and feel more energetic.

- I can say no and mean it.

- No one can talk me into doing things I don't want to do or that are not okay with me.

Topic 26

Self-Destructive Behaviors

Self-destructive behaviors are things you intentionally do to yourself that may physically hurt or even kill you, have the potential to hurt or destroy things that are important to you, or that may make your life circumstances very difficult. Women who have been traumatized or abused often develop such behaviors as ways of dealing with uncomfortable or painful feelings such as confusion, shame, guilt, fear, anger, disappointment, low self-esteem, and self-hatred. They become habits that may be very hard to break, can harm every aspect of your life, and keep you from living the kind of life you want to live. They include:

- excessive use of drugs or alcohol;
- starving yourself;
- binge eating;
- doing things that worsen a physical problem, such as eating lots of sweets if you are diabetic;
- cutting or burning yourself;
- trying to kill yourself;
- doing things that are very risky, such as driving very fast or dodging in and out of traffic;
- doing things that will make good opportunities turn bad;
- smoking cigarettes;
- raging;
- promiscuous sex; and
- spending time in unsafe areas.

List the self-destructive behaviors you engage in:

_____

_____

_____

_____

_____

As with any kind of addictive or compulsive behaviors, self-destructive behaviors are difficult to get rid of. It takes patience, persistence, and courage.

Have you ever gotten rid of a self-destructive behavior? If so, what was it? How did you get rid of it?

_____

_____

_____

_____

_____

Even if you accomplished this remarkable feat many years ago, and even if you still have other persistent self-destructive behaviors, take time now to celebrate your success. Congratulate yourself. If someone you love is nearby, have them give you a hug. You have accomplished something quite wonderful.

Understanding Your Self-Destructive Behavior

All of our behaviors make sense—even the self-destructive ones. Think about your self-destructive behaviors. Do they help you cope with anxiety, despair, or feelings of numbness? Do they provide comfort, company, distraction? When you understand these behaviors you may be better equipped to get rid of them and substitute other, healthier, behaviors.

Example: Self-destructive behavior: smoking cigarettes

Purpose of the behavior: _calms me down_

Another way to achieve the same end: _go for a walk_

1. Self-destructive behavior:

_____

Purpose of the behavior:

_____

Another way to achieve the same end:

_____

2. Self-destructive behavior:

_____

Purpose of the behavior:

_____

Another way to achieve the same end:

_____

3. Self-destructive behavior:

_____

Purpose of the behavior:

_____

Another way to achieve the same end:

_____

4. Self-destructive behavior:

_____

Purpose of the behavior:

_____

Another way to achieve the same end:

_____

Techniques

There are many techniques for getting rid of destructive behaviors, and you will have to figure out which techniques will work best for you. Most people use several different ways to get rid of these behaviors. Following are methods that other people have used to get rid of self-destructive behaviors. However, you have probably developed or know of other ways that have been or would be really useful to you in ridding yourself of these behaviors. After you have reviewed this list, write down other ideas that you have.

- Attend Twelve-Step Groups
  Twelve-step groups are structured support groups that meet regularly to help people let go of self-destructive behaviors. The best known of these groups is Alcoholics Anonymous. However, there are twelve-step groups for dealing with many other issues. Check your newspaper or call your local mental health agency to get more information about these groups.

- Attend Survivors Groups
  Survivors groups are for people who have been abused or experienced some other kind of traumatic life event or events. You are supported by others who have similar issues while you work to get rid of self-destructive behaviors.

- Work with a Counselor
  Arrange to see a counselor in your area who works with women who have been traumatized and who has helped others let go of self-destructive behaviors. Other women who have been traumatized can let you know who the best counselors are.

- Talk to a Friend
  Talking to a person you like and trust about self-destructive behaviors helps. Ask them if they have some time to listen—from five minutes to an hour, perhaps. Then talk about your self-destructive behavior and why you want to get rid of it. Talk about your successes and your hard times. Ask the friend not to interrupt with advise, corrections, or criticism. (The best way to do this is to use the peer counseling format.)

- Do Something You Enjoy
  When you feel as though you must use a self-destructive behavior, do something that diverts your attention and feels good instead. This might be something as simple as brushing your hair. Bonnie, for example, decided to try this when her symptoms became serious. While at a crisis respite center, she went in the shower with all her clothes on. When asked why, she said she had had an overwhelming urge to hurt herself and the only thing that could stop it was to jump in the shower very quickly—even with her clothes on. The staff applauded her resourcefulness in finding a strategy that helped her avoid self-destructive behavior.

  Make a list of things you could do instead of your self-destructive behavior. Hang it on your refrigerator or put it in some other place where you will see it frequently.

Things I could do instead of _____

_____

_____

_____

_____

_____

_____

- Change Negative Self-Talk to Positive

  In topics 3 and 6 you learned how to change negative thoughts into positive ones. You can use the same techniques now—think of the desire to do something self-destructive as a negative thought, and change that thought into something positive. With practice and persistence, you will find that you will think these positive thoughts instead of thinking about hurting yourself.

  Begin by listing the negative, self-destructive thoughts you have. Then, next to each negative thought, write a positive response that contradicts the self-destructive thought. Use "I," "me," or your own name in the positive response. For example,

  I want to cut myself. I keep myself safe.
  I want to have a drink. Alcohol makes me feel terrible.
  I am not going to eat supper. I am going to eat healthy food.

_____

_____

_____

_____

_____

_____

  Use the two-step technique you learned in topics 3 and 6.

- Read Self-Help Books

  There are many self-help books that focus on getting rid of self-destructive behaviors. Some of them are listed in the Resources section at the end of this book, and others can be found by doing searches online.

- Use Self-Soothing Activities

  Review topic 7 and make a list of self-soothing activities that you think you could use whenever you are thinking about doing something self-destructive. For example, get some exercise, do something routine such as washing your hair or doing the dishes, do a relaxation exercise, or play with a pet.

_____

_____

_____

_____

_____

Examining Self-Destructive Behaviors

In the following exercise you will examine self-destructive behaviors that are troublesome for you and decide what you are going to do about them. Begin by reading through the following example.

Self-destructive behavior—*eating way more than I need to, eating lots of foods that are unhealthy.*

How does this behavior interfere with your life? *It makes me fat so no one is interested in having a relationship with me or even getting to know me. I can't exercise and do other things I like to do. I can't even dance anymore. I can't wear pretty clothes. Nothing looks good on me. People make fun of me. I feel lousy about myself.*

If you don't stop doing this, what bad things could happen? *I could develop heart disease or diabetes. I could end up never having a close relationship. I could become more and more of a couch potato, never doing the things I want with my life.*

Are you ready to work on getting rid of this behavior? If so, when are you going to start? *Right now.*

How are you going to do that? *I am going to join a support group for people who have weight problems and follow their weight-loss plan. I am going to reduce my fat intake by avoiding fast-food restaurants and not buying any high-fat or high-sugar foods for myself.*

If you are not ready to get rid of this self-destructive behavior, what is getting in your way? *Nothing is getting in the way, I think I can tackle this behavior now.*

What do you think would help you get over this hurdle? *Not applicable.*

Why might somebody not be ready to get rid of a self-destructive behavior? There can be many reasons: they might be working on other things, or they might have too many other uncomfortable symptoms. They might say they need more support or resolution of another particular problem to get over this hurdle. Remember, when you decide why a behavior exists, you have the right to understand the reason without holding on to the destructive behavior. For example, suppose you are gaining a lot of weight because you don't want a relationship. You have a right to avoid a close relationship without having to hurt yourself in the process. It may be a relief just to say, "I don't want a relationship just now."

Analyze your self-destructive behaviors in the spaces below.

1. Self-destructive behavior:

   _____

   How does this behavior interfere with your life?

   _____

   _____

If you don't stop doing this, what bad things could happen?

_____

_____

_____

Are you ready to work on getting rid of this behavior? If so, when are you going to start?

_____

How are you going to get rid of this self-destructive behavior?

_____

_____

_____

If you are not ready to get rid of this self-destructive behavior, what is getting in your way?

_____

_____

_____

What do you think would help you get over this hurdle?

_____

_____

_____

2. Self-destructive behavior:

_____

How does this behavior interfere with your life?

_____

_____

If you don't stop doing this, what bad things could happen?

_____

_____

_____

Are you ready to work on getting rid of this behavior? If so, when are you going to start?

_____

How are you going to get rid of this self-destructive behavior?

_____

_____

_____

If you are not ready to get rid of this self-destructive behavior, what is getting in your way?

_____

_____

_____

What do you think would help you get over this hurdle?

_____

_____

_____

3. Self-destructive behavior:

_____

How does this behavior interfere with your life?

_____

_____

If you don't stop doing this, what bad things could happen?

_____

_____

_____

Are you ready to work on getting rid of this behavior? If so, when are you going to start?

_____

How are you going to get rid of this self-destructive behavior?

_____

_____

_____

If you are not ready to get rid of this self-destructive behavior, what is getting in your way?

_____

_____

_____

What do you think would help you get over this hurdle?

_____

_____

_____

Things to Remember Every Day

- I am in charge of my life.

- I can do what I need to do to get rid of self-destructive behaviors.

- I deserve the very best that life has to offer.

Topic 27

Blame, Acceptance, and Forgiveness

In this topic you will explore your feelings about three issues that are important to the process of healing from the effects of abuse—blame, acceptance, and forgiveness. You may have received confusing messages about these issues from your abuser or abusers, family members, friends, mental health workers, schools, or religious organizations. The following exercises are designed to help you decide what you think and to consider any action you may want to take. Addressing these issues should help you reach a deeper level of understanding about what happened to you, and to think about ways to move past these issues so the abuse is just a small part of your life story, not your whole story.

Blame—Whose Fault Was It?

Women who have been abused often blame themselves for the bad things that have happened to them—things that are *never* their fault. In addition, others may have blamed you for being abused. In our society, women are often blamed and made to feel guilty for the bad things that have happened to them. This lowers your self-esteem and can get in the way of your healing and recovery.

Following are some of the situations in which women or children erroneously feel they are to blame for the abuse.

It was my fault because I was wearing that dress or those shoes, and because I put on makeup.

It was my fault because I was walking alone on the street at night.

It was my fault because I didn't keep quiet enough.

It was my fault because I cried too much.

It was my fault because I didn't help out enough.

It was my fault because I smiled at someone.

It was my fault because I talked with someone.

It was my fault because I wanted to get a job.

It was my fault because I was asking for it.

List circumstances in which you were told (or you told yourself) it was your fault but you now know that it was someone else's fault.

_____

_____

_____

_____

Remember: It is not your fault if you had to hurt someone to keep them from hurting you, from hurting you more than they already have, or from hurting someone else. It is normal to feel bad if you accidentally hurt someone. Apologizing and doing something to help the person you hurt may help make you feel better.

Who is really to blame for what happened to you?

_____

_____

How does it feel to put the blame where it belongs?

_____

_____

_____

Many women report that after they put the blame where it really belongs—on their uncle, cousin, or stranger—they feel worse than they did before. If this is the case for you, there may be some other steps related to acceptance and forgiveness that will help you feel better.

Use the following imagery exercise, or develop your own similar activity, to help you feel better about putting the blame where it really belongs.

Take a few deep breaths. Imagine that it is a warm, sunny spring day. You are standing in a meadow surrounded by beautiful wildflowers. Birds are flying overhead. You feel safe and comfortable as a cloud comes over and it starts to rain. It is a very warm and soothing rain. The rain flows over you. It feels wonderful. It makes you feel wonderful. As the rain washes over you it takes with it all those feelings of blame and shame that don't belong to you. When the sun comes out again, your clothes dry quickly and you feel great.

Design an imagery exercise or an activity that would help you let go of blame.

_____

_____

_____

_____

_____

Acceptance

Sometimes you may feel as though you are stuck—you can't do the things that you want to with your life because of memories, symptoms, thoughts, feelings, and life circumstances that are either a direct or indirect result of the abuse. You may feel as though you are losing your whole life to the abuse.

Write one or several of the following statements (whichever ones feel right to you) on a piece of paper or write similar statements in your own words. Carry the paper with you and repeat the statements over and over to yourself whenever you get a chance.

I accept the abuse as part of my life story. My journey in working to get over the effects of this abuse has made me strong. Now I am in charge of my life. I am going to do whatever I need to do to make my life the way I want it to be.

The things that happened to me were terrible and should never have happened to me. But they did. Now it's time to get my life back—to be the kind of person I want to be and to do the things I want to do.

The abuse happened a long time ago. I am no longer being abused. I am in charge of my life and I am doing the things I want to do.

The abuse was then. This is now. I am doing good work in getting over the effects of the abuse. I am ready to move on with my life.

My life story acceptance statement:

_____

_____

_____

_____

_____

Answering the following questions should assist you in the process of acceptance and moving past the abuse.

How would you like your life to be?

_____

_____

_____

Now that you know you are strong and that the abuse is just part of your life story, what are you going to do to make your life the way you want it to be?

_____

_____

_____

_____

Make a list of all the things you are looking forward to:

_____

_____

_____

_____

Make a list of all the things you enjoy in your life the way it is right now.

_____

_____

_____

_____

_____

Forgiveness

Of these three issues—blame, acceptance, and forgiveness—forgiveness is probably the most confusing. When you reported the abuse, you may have been told to forgive and forget. In church you may have been taught to forgive those who have hurt you or to turn the other cheek. Your counselor may have told you that you need to forgive your abuser in order to heal or recover. Other people you respect may have told you there is "no way" you can forgive someone who abused you. You may want to believe all of these people. The only way to resolve this dilemma is for you to decide for yourself how you feel.

If you've been told you need to forgive your abuser before you can really heal from the trauma, think about the following statement: _I never have to forgive someone who hurt me. I can heal and still know that another person abused me._

How do you feel about this?

_____

_____

_____

The following list contains some options for dealing with the issue of forgiveness.

- I will never forgive my abuser, but I am going to get on with my life and do the things I want to do.

- I forgive my abuser because I realize bad things must have happened to him to have made him act that way.

- I forgive my abuser but I will never have anything to do with him.

- My abuser has died and that makes me feel really good.

List any other options for dealing with forgiveness that you can think of.

_____

_____

_____

To help clarify your thinking about forgiveness, spend five to ten minutes writing about it. Write whatever comes into your mind. Try not to censor or edit it in any way. If you think it or feel it, write it.

_____

_____

_____

_____

_____

_____

_____

Describe any changes that you notice in your feelings about forgiveness from doing these exercises.

_____

_____

_____

_____

You might decide to forgive the abuser. This may mean just doing that in your mind, having a phone call or face-to-face conversation, or sending a letter. Or, you may not want to forgive the abuser at all. However, you may be just as determined to move ahead with your life and do the things you want to do. If you have decided to forgive your abuser, how and when would you do it? Remember, if you decide to forgive your abuser, you will need to determine if having contact with him or her is a good and safe idea.

_____

_____

_____

_____

There may be other people in your life who did not abuse you, but whom you may feel had some responsibility for what happened to you. Your feelings about this may have come from the perspective of a child who felt unprotected, rather than from the perspective of an adult.

One woman's mother went into a state psychiatric facility when the child was eight years old, and did not come home for eight years. This woman blamed her mother for the abuse she endured while her mother was away. She felt if her mother had been there to protect her, the abuse would not have happened.

Another woman we spoke with was abused by several older boys in her neighborhood. She blamed her parents for the abuse because they had hired these boys as baby-sitters. Other women blame an older sibling for the abuse because that sibling was too busy with his or her own life to offer any protection or support.

Think about people in your life whom you have blamed for your abuse. Perhaps now you realize that these people should not have been blamed. Some action on your part could help improve these relationships and enrich your life. For instance, the woman whose mother was away for eight years never told her mother she blamed her for the abuse. She doesn't want to bring it up with her now. Instead, she decided to write extensively in her journal about this issue until she felt she had stopped blaming her mother. The woman who was abused by the baby-sitters handled her feelings differently. Because her parents learned about the abuse when she was an adult, she decided to talk with them about it and let them know she understood they didn't know what those boys were doing and that she forgave them.

1. Name a person in your life, other than the abuser, whom you blame (or blamed) for the abuse.

   _____

   Why do you (or did you) blame this person for the abuse?

   _____

   _____

   As you see it now, from an adult perspective, were they really at fault? Why or why not?

   _____

   _____

   _____

   Would forgiving them now be a positive step in your recovery or healing? If so, how would you do that?

   _____

   _____

   _____

2. Name a person in your life, other than the abuser, whom you blame (or blamed) for the abuse.

_____

Why do you (or did you) blame this person for the abuse?

_____

_____

As you see it now, from an adult perspective, were they really at fault? Why or why not?

_____

_____

_____

Would forgiving them now be a positive step in your recovery or healing? If so, how would you do that?

_____

_____

_____

3. Name a person in your life, other than the abuser, whom you blame (or blamed) for the abuse.

_____

Why do you (or did you) blame this person for the abuse?

_____

_____

As you see it now, from an adult perspective, were they really at fault? Why or why not?

_____

_____

_____

Would forgiving them now be a positive step in your recovery or healing? If so, how would you do that?

_____

_____

_____

Optional Activities

1. Develop a ceremony to let go of the blame you are holding for the abuse.

2. Draw a picture of the new you—that person who believes in herself, who accepts her life story, and who honors herself for the strength and courage she has used to work on making her life the way she wants it to be.

Things to Remember Every Day

- The abuse was not my fault.

- I accept the abuse as part of my life story. My abuser is no longer in control of my life—I am.

- I don't have to forgive my abuser.

- I don't have to confront my abuser and make him or her apologize.

- I can take whatever action I feel is best to forgive people I blamed who did not deserve it.

Topic 28

Feeling Out of Control

When you were being abused you probably felt as though your life was out of your control. At that time it was true—your life *was* out of your control. Now you are in charge of your life, but there may still be times when you feel that way—when you can't control the way you feel and the way you behave, when you feel overwhelmed with anger and emotions, or when you feel that you are going crazy. Everyone has times like this. But because you have been abused and are dealing with its aftereffects on a day-to-day basis, you may feel out of control more often than you think you can deal with. You may feel that being out of control is ruining your relationships or making it hard for you to do your work and take care of your children. You may feel embarrassed and ashamed.

In this book you have learned many ways of doing things that will help keep you in control. However, there are times when things happen and you just can't remember what to do to stay in control or regain control. In topic 19 you made a list of tools for maintaining wellness, relieving uncomfortable symptoms, and dealing with difficult situations. It included tools you learned in topics 6, 7, and 13, along with tools you may have discovered yourself. In this topic you will learn a simple system for organizing and using these tools and other strategies to:

- Keep yourself in control when you want.

- Recognize and respond to triggers that might cause you to begin to feel out of control.

- Identify early signs that things are starting to get out of control.

- Know when things are getting much worse.

A plan such as this is commonly referred to as a wellness recovery action plan.

This topic will help you develop your plan. However, you may find it easier to use the plan if you transfer the information you write here into a three-ring binder with tabs for each section of the plan.

Before you begin work, understand that fully expressing your emotions is healthy and that there are times when it is perfectly acceptable to be out of control. Again, everyone feels that way sometimes. Common scenarios include laughing hysterically over a funny incident;

being overcome with grief after hearing about a horrible tragedy; getting really angry at someone who deserves your anger, such as a person who is abusing you or someone else; or sharing something difficult with a good friend.

List some times when you have felt out of control but it has been okay:

_____

_____

_____

_____

_____

_____

Daily Maintenance Plan

When you were a child, your family life may have been hectic, chaotic, and disorganized, making your life very difficult in that you may not have had an opportunity to learn many of the skills you need as an adult to accomplish your goals and make your life the way you want it to be. A daily maintenance plan can provide the structure, organization, and discipline you need to make your life more organized and keep you in control.

As you've worked your way through this book, you've hopefully learned a variety of skills and strategies that will help you feel well. These things are different for each of us. For instance, Mary Ellen thinks she would feel quite well if she does the following things every day.

- Eat three healthy meals and two healthy snacks.

- Drink six eight-ounce glasses of water.

- Exercise for at least half an hour.

- Get at least half an hour of outdoor light.

- Do something I enjoy for at least half an hour—play the piano, read a good book, or paint a picture.

- Spend a few minutes talking to a close friend or supporter.

- Avoid secondhand smoke, caffeine, and sweets.

What do you think you would need to do every day to feel well?

_____

_____

_____

_____

_____

_____

_____

Try doing the things on your list every day, and notice how you feel. After a while these things will become good habits. Copy this list and hang it on your refrigerator as a daily reminder, if you think that will help.

There may be some unpleasant things you need to do sometimes that cause you stress when you forget to do them, such as paying the bills, buying groceries, doing housework, or calling a family member. Include in your plan time to do these less pleasant things, so that they aren't forgotten and don't cause you more stress in the long run.

Make a list of things you need to consider doing each day.

_____

_____

_____

_____

_____

_____

Triggers

Triggers are external events or circumstances that may make you feel as though you are losing control. These need to be responded to and dealt with in some way, or you may begin feeling as though you have less and less control over your life.

Make a list of your triggers. Here are some common ones:

- anniversary dates of losses or trauma;

- seeing something or someone that reminds you of the trauma;

- flashbacks (seeing in your mind a vivid picture of a traumatic event);

- traumatic news events;

- sexual harassment or references by others to sexual acts;

- disagreements or fights with family members, friends, or co-workers;

- a relationship ending;

- spending too much time alone or feeling left out;

- things that remind you of abandonment or deprivation;

- being judged, criticized, or teased;

- physical illness;

- aggressive-sounding noises;

- intimacy;

- excessive stress;

- someone trying to tell you how to run your life;

- self-blame;

- extreme guilt; and

- substance abuse.

My triggers list:

_____

_____

_____

_____

_____

_____

Now, develop a plan that you can use when you have "been triggered" that you feel will help you stay in control. A plan might include:

- Make sure I do everything on my daily maintenance list.

- Call a support person and ask them to listen while I talk about the trigger.

- Do a half hour of relaxation exercise.

- Go for a twenty-minute walk.

- Play my guitar for a half hour.

My triggers action plan:

_____

_____

_____

_____

_____

_____

_____

Early Warning Signs

Early warning signs are uncomfortable or distressing feelings inside you that indicate you may be starting to lose control but that seem unrelated to external events in your life. You may begin to notice these signs even though you are doing everything on your daily mainte-nance list and taking action whenever triggers come up. You can help yourself stay in con-trol by identifying these early warning signs when they first appear and responding to them before they worsen.

Make a list of your early warning signs. Here are some common ones:

- an increase in anxiety;
- being more forgetful than usual;
- not being able to enjoy things;
- not feeling like doing anything;
- feeling slowed down or speeded up;
- avoiding doing things you need to do to take care of yourself;
- not caring about people you usually care about;
- avoiding others or choosing to be alone more than usual;
- being obsessed with things that don't really matter;
- thinking thoughts that are not based in reality;
- feeling unconnected from your body;
- being more irritable or negative than usual;
- increasing your smoking, drinking, or eating;
- doing things without thinking;
- experiencing more aches and pains;

- feeling discouraged, hopeless, or worthless;

- failing to buckle your seat belt; and

- losing things you normally keep track of.

My early warning signs:

_____

_____

_____

_____

_____

_____

Develop a plan that will help you relieve your early warning signs and feel more in control. A plan might include:

- Do the things on my daily maintenance plan whether I feel like it or not,

- Tell a supporter/counselor how I am feeling and ask for their advice.

- Peer counsel at least once a day until early warning signs diminish.

- Do at least one focusing exercise a day.

- Do at least three ten-minute relaxation exercises each day.

- Write in my journal for at least fifteen minutes each day.

- Spend at least one hour involved in an activity I enjoy.

- Ask others to take over my household responsibilities for a day.

- Go to a support-group meeting.

My early warning signs action plan:

_____

_____

_____

Things Are Breaking Down or Getting Worse

Perhaps one day, in spite of your best efforts, you'll begin feeling more and more out of control. You'll still be able to take some action to help yourself stay in control, but you'll need to do so right away.

Make a list of feelings or symptoms that indicate things are getting much worse despite all of your efforts. Here are some common feelings or symptoms:

- feeling very oversensitive, fragile, and needy;

- having irrational responses to situations and/or the actions of others;

- feeling very angry all the time;

- being unable to sleep for several days, or sleeping all the time;

- ceasing to eat, or eating everything you can get your hands on;

- wanting to be totally alone;

- taking risks such as driving too fast or having unprotected sex;

- thinking of hurting yourself;

- excessive use of alcohol or other drugs;

- being obsessed with very negative thoughts;

- behaving in unusual or bizarre ways;

- dissociating (blacking out, spacing out, losing time);

- seeing things that aren't there;

- taking out your anger on others; and

- being unable to feel anything.

Signs that I'm breaking down:

Now, develop a plan that you can use when you feel you are breaking down. A plan might include:

- Call my doctor or other health care professional and follow their instructions.

- Follow my early warning signs action plan every day.

- Check in with at least two of my supporters.

- Do at least five ten-minute relaxation exercises each day.

My "things are breaking down" action plan:

Using Your Wellness Recovery Action Plan

In order to use your plan successfully so that you will feel in control most of the time, at first you will need to review it every day. Many people like to do so at the start of each day, such as before or after breakfast. As you become familiar with your plans, you will find that the review takes less and less time, until eventually you'll know how to respond to certain symptoms without even referring to the plan.

In the beginning, you may notice things that you had not noticed before that you need to add to your plan. You may also find that some of your plan works well while other parts need to be revised. Change whenever you feel you need to.

Optional Activity

Do a week-long "dry run" of one of the plans you have developed for dealing with daily maintenance, triggers, early warning signs, or signs that things are breaking down.

Things to Remember Every Day

- Sometimes it's okay to feel out of control.
- I can do the things I need to do to stay in control of myself and my life because I am in charge of my life.

Topic 29

Relationships

Our relationships and connections with others make our lives rich. However, developing and keeping relationships strong can be difficult for women who have been abused. You may find that developing healthy connections with others and keeping these connections healthy is work that will continue all your life. In this topic you will consider issues related to your connections with others as you work toward surrounding yourself with people who treat you well and who are positive, loving, and supportive—whether they are casual acquaintances, friends, co-workers, colleagues, children, brothers and sisters, parents, other family members, boyfriends, or girlfriends.

Healthy Relationships and Connections

You need and deserve at least a few people in your life with whom you have healthy relationships, people whom:

- you like, respect, and trust, and who like, respect, and trust you;

- make you feel good about yourself;

- listen to you without sharing personal information about you with others;

- you can tell anything;

- allow you to talk freely and express your feelings and emotions without judging you, criticizing you, teasing you, or putting you down;

- give you good advice when you want and ask for it, and who work with you to figure out what to do next in difficult situations;

- allow you the space to change, grow, make decisions, and make mistakes;

- accept you as you; and

- share fun activities with you.

List other things that are important to you in relationships with others:

_____

_____

_____

_____

_____

_____

_____

Describe your healthy relationships.

Person:

_____

Relationship:

_____

Why do you feel this is a healthy relationship?

_____

_____

_____

Person:

_____

Relationship:

_____

Why do you feel this is a healthy relationship?

_____

_____

_____

_____

Person: _____

Relationship: _____

Why do you feel this is a healthy relationship?

_____

_____

_____

Person: _____

Relationship: _____

Why do you feel this is a healthy relationship?

_____

_____

_____

Unhealthy Relationships

Following is list of indicators of an unhealthy relationship. Are there any indicators that you are willing to tolerate? Think about them carefully, because while your first impulse may be to reject all of them, you, like many women who have been abused, may almost subconsciously tolerate some of them at least some of the time:

- sexual abuse of yourself or others;

- emotional abuse of yourself or others;

- physical abuse of yourself or others;

- drug or alcohol abuse;

- criminal activity;

- violation of your boundaries;

- threats;

- dishonesty;

- being controlled;

- criticism, judging, teasing, put-downs, or ridicule;

- a lack of caring from your partner;

- being treated unfairly;

- lack of commitment;

- betrayal; and

- abandonment.

List other things you will not tolerate in a relationship.

_____

_____

_____

_____

_____

If you are in relationship with someone who does any of the above things, realize that you can make choices about how you'll deal with it. Your choices will depend on your connection with that person and the seriousness of their actions. For instance, if your partner is sexually abusing you or your children and is threatening your life, you'll need to make very specific plans to get away from that person and to keep him from finding you. On the other hand, if an acquaintance is very critical of you, you may choose to talk with that person about it rather than avoiding him or her—though that is of course an option, too.

Following are some choices you can make in addressing unhealthy relationships.

- Get safely away from the person and make a plan that includes how you'll keep him from finding you and others who are with you.

- Refuse to have further contact with that person.

- Ask the person not to come to your home again.

- Change jobs.

- Talk about the problems and work together to make changes.

- Go to counseling together.

- Limit your involvement.

- Stop going to places where that person might be and ask that person not to go to places where you will be.

- Tell the other person what is not okay in the relationship and ask them to make changes—avoiding contact in the future if changes are not made.

- Wait until a better time to plan and take action.

List the ways that you would like to address the unhealthy relationships in your life:

_____

_____

_____

_____

To help you think about your unhealthy relationships and what you are going to do about them, answer the following questions.

Person with whom I have an unhealthy relationship:

_____

Why is this an unhealthy relationship?

_____

_____

_____

What action do you need to take concerning this relationship?

_____

_____

_____

When are you going to take this action?

_____

_____

If you are not going to take this action right away, why are you waiting? (There may be very good reasons why you are not going to take action right away.)

_____

_____

_____

Person with whom I have an unhealthy relationship:

_____

Why is this an unhealthy relationship?

_____

_____

_____

What action do you need to take concerning this relationship?

_____

_____

_____

When are you going to take this action?

_____

_____

If you are not going to take this action right away, why are you waiting? (There may be very good reasons why you are not going to take action right away.)

_____

_____

_____

Person with whom I have an unhealthy relationship:

_____

Why is this an unhealthy relationship?

_____

_____

_____

What action do you need to take concerning this relationship?

_____

_____

_____

When are you going to take this action?

_____

_____

If you are not going to take this action right away, why are you waiting? (There may be very good reasons why you are not going to take action right away.)

_____

_____

_____

Developing Positive Connections with Others

Many people who have been abused have few, if any, healthy relationships. You may feel lonely much of the time. Many women report that they can't feel strongly connected to anyone. In this section you will explore steps you can take to build new and healthy connections in your life. You can use these steps if you just want more casual friends or acquaintances, want to develop some closer friendships, or if you want to get into a committed relationship. Developing positive connections with others takes a long time. You will want to proceed very slowly. If you make one close friend in the next year, that is a remarkable accomplishment. Depending on your situation, or the relationships with people you already have in your life, you may not need to take all of these steps.

Step 1: Meeting people

- Attend a support group. This could be a group for people who have similar health issues or challenges, or a generic group for people of a particular sex or age.

- Go to community events. Let yourself be seen and known in the community.

- Join a special-interest club. This might be a group that is focused on hiking, bird watching, stamp collecting, cooking, music, literature, church, or sports.

- Take a course. Adult-education programs, community colleges, and universities offer courses that will help you meet new people. Another benefit is that you will learn something interesting that might even open the doors to a new career, or a career change.

- Volunteer. Offer to assist at a school, hospital, or organization in your community.

Step 2: Beginning to get closer

You may begin to develop a special interest in one or several of the people with whom you come in contact. Observe them. Notice how they interact with others. Ask yourself, "What is it about this person that appeals to me?" Don't forget to also ask yourself about danger signs—are there things that indicate this person might not be someone you want to feel close to?

Step 3: Beginning to do things together

When you feel you have developed a special rapport with another person that feels like real friendship, and when the person seems equally interested and eager to spend time with you, make a plan to get together. The first time you meet could be for a low-key activity such as eating lunch together or taking a walk.

Don't overwhelm the person with phone calls. Use your intuition and common sense to determine when to call and how often. Don't ever call late at night or early in the morning until you both have agreed to be available to each other in case of emergency. As you feel more and more comfortable with the other person, you will find that you talk more and share more personal information, but make sure you have a mutual understanding that anything personal the two of you discuss remain absolutely confidential.

Remember, you can always get out of a relationship if it begins to feel uncomfortable or unsafe to you. Bearing in mind the skills you've developed in other topics in the book, how would you end the relationship with this hypothetical person?

_____

_____

_____

_____

Step 4: Developing a meaningful and lasting friendship

When your relationship progresses to this point, you feel a strong connection. You may notice that you feel disappointed when you and the other person can't get together. You accept the other person as they are. You stay close to each other through the ups and downs that all relationships experience. If this has the potential for being an intimate or committed relationship, you may be making plans for the future together.

If you have had or have relationships that have progressed to this point, how do they make you feel?

_____

_____

_____

What, if anything, makes you uncomfortable about being this close to another person and how can you deal with the discomfort?

_____

_____

_____

Don't forget that no one person can meet all your needs. Do not grow dependent on only one or two people because if that person (or people) are sick, away, or busy with something or someone else when you need them, the situation may cause you undue stress.

One woman said she didn't need to work on developing relationships with others because she was close to her mother and her sister and that was all she needed. She began to feel differently about this when her mother became ill and needed lots of care and support and when her sister became involved with a man whom she later married.

Who are the people to whom you feel closest in your life?

_____

_____

_____

What Can Get in the Way of Relationships?

Problem: You have been hurt so much that you now feel you could never trust anyone enough to feel close.

Possible solution: Remind yourself that you have learned how to make good choices when developing close relationships with people who will treat you well and will use this information when it is needed.

Other solutions that you feel might work for you:

_____

_____

_____

Problem: Feeling that because you don't like yourself, no one else will.

Possible solutions: Remember that even though you don't feel good about yourself right now, others still like you. Also, work on raising your self-esteem. (See topic 6.)

Other solutions that you feel might work for you:

_____

_____

_____

Problem: You are shy and don't know how to reach out to others.

Possible solution: Practice being comfortable with others by joining a school club, church group, or community group. It's always hard to go the first time. You may feel that you'll stand out like a sore thumb. Ignore those feelings and force yourself to go to activities that interest you. When you have talked to the same person at several activities, ask that person to join you in an activity of mutual interest. That's how friendships develop.

Other solutions that you feel might work for you:

_____

_____

_____

Problem: You are oversensitive to any sign of rejection and react to it by giving up on the other person.

Possible solution: Once you're aware of this tendency, make an effort to avoid giving up on people until you are absolutely sure they can't be supportive. Talk to the other person about what you are feeling, and encourage them to share how they are feeling. Work together so you can both feel good in the relationship.

Other solutions that you feel might work for you:

_____

_____

_____

Problem: You have not had the opportunity to develop the social skills necessary to make and keep friends and supporters. Poor social skills that might be a problem are the same kinds of things that you might find offensive in others. They include:

- being overly dependent or needy,

- expecting too much,

- lack of attention to the needs of others,

- blaming and bad-mouthing others,

- gossiping and spreading rumors,

- negativity,

- constant chatter,

- expecting the other person to carry all the conversation,

- inattentiveness when others are talking,

- invalidation of the feelings of others,

- lack of attention to personal hygiene,

- foul language, and

- lying.

What behaviors do you feel might be hampering your relationships?

_____

_____

_____

_____

Possible solution: Again, self-knowledge is the first step—you can begin to fix these behaviors once you're aware of them. Making the above list is a start. Next, work to avoid the behaviors and make a mental note to yourself when you catch yourself slipping.

Other solutions that you feel might work for you:

_____

_____

_____

Keeping Your Relationship Healthy

- Don't expect the other person to know what you want and need. Tell them. Ask them to tell you what they want and need.

- Spend as much time listening and paying attention to the other person as they spend paying attention and listening to you.

- Take turns suggesting and initiating activities.

- Keep regular contact with the people you care about, whether things are going well or not.

What would you like to do to keep your relationships strong?

_____

_____

_____

Optional Activities

1. Have one or more peer counseling sessions with somebody who you've recently built a new relationship with (see topic 25).

2. Volunteer to spend an afternoon with a civic or charitable group whose work you respect.

Things to Remember Every Day

- I surround myself with people who love me and treat me well.

- I recognize unhealthy relationships and can do what I need to do to change them or end them.

- I have several or many healthy relationships.

- I know how to work on developing new relationships.

- I work to solve problems in my relationships.

Topic 30

Goal Assessment

Looking Back and Moving Ahead

Before you begin working on the closing rituals of this part of your healing journey, take a look at what you have accomplished as you worked through the twenty-nine topics of this book. In topic 1 you wrote your goals for this work. In topic 11 you reviewed these goals. Since then you may have eliminated some of them and perhaps added some new ones. In this topic you will take one more look at your goals, assess your progress, and see which of your goals you have achieved, which you need to work on further, and which no longer seem important to you. You may decide to develop some new goals as you end this structured work on your healing and as you integrate the new ways of thinking and new skills you have learned into your life. In addition, you will take a realistic look at yourself, determine the personal strengths that have allowed you to get to this place in your healing journey, look at the challenges you have overcome, and make some decisions about how you want to go forward.

Reviewing Your Goals

Review each of the goals you listed in topic 11, including any new goals. Ignore any goals you decided to eliminate. Using the following format, assess each of these goals.

Goal:

_____

_____

_____

Describe your progress in meeting this goal:

_____

_____

_____

_____

_____

Does it seem important to keep working on this goal? (If not, skip over the next questions and move on to your next goal.)

If you have further work to do in meeting this goal, how will you do it?

_____

_____

_____

_____

_____

If there are new ways of doing things or new skills that you will use to work toward meeting this goal, list them here.

_____

_____

_____

_____

Goal:

_____

_____

_____

Describe your progress in meeting this goal:

_____

_____

_____

_____

_____

Does it seem important to keep working on this goal? (If not, skip over the next questions and move on to your next goal.)

If you have further work to do in meeting this goal, how will you do it?

_____

_____

_____

_____

If there are new ways of doing things or new skills that you will use to work toward meeting this goal, list them here.

_____

_____

_____

_____

Goal:

_____

_____

_____

Describe your progress in meeting this goal:

_____

_____

_____

_____

_____

Does it seem important to keep working on this goal? (If not, skip over the next questions and move on to your next goal.)

If you have further work to do in meeting this goal, how will you do it?

_____

_____

_____

_____

_____

If there are new ways of doing things or new skills that you will use to work toward meeting this goal, list them here.

_____

_____

_____

_____

Goal:

_____

_____

_____

Describe your progress in meeting this goal:

_____

_____

_____

_____

Does it seem important to keep working on this goal? (If not, skip over the next questions and move on to your next goal.)

If you have further work to do in meeting this goal, how will you do it?

_____

_____

_____

_____

If there are new ways of doing things or new skills that you will use to work toward meeting this goal, list them here.

_____

_____

_____

_____

Goal:

_____

_____

_____

Describe your progress in meeting this goal:

_____

_____

_____

_____

_____

Does it seem important to keep working on this goal? (If not, skip over the next questions and move on to your next goal.)

If you have further work to do in meeting this goal, how will you do it?

_____

_____

_____

_____

If there are new ways of doing things or new skills that you will use to work toward meeting this goal, list them here.

_____

_____

_____

_____

If you have more goals, you can assess them on a separate sheet of paper.

New Goals

Because of the healing work you have completed, you may now have some new goals for yourself. For instance, you may have decided to get more education, develop some new interests, meet some new people, move to a different area, or change jobs or careers. Below, list your new goals.

Goal:

_____

_____

_____

How I plan to achieve this goal:

_____

_____

_____

_____

What skills and new ways of doing things will you use in working to achieve this goal?

_____

_____

_____

_____

Goal:

_____

_____

_____

How I plan to achieve this goal:

_____

_____

_____

_____

_____

What skills and new ways of doing things will you use in working to achieve this goal?

_____

_____

_____

_____

Goal:

_____

_____

How I plan to achieve this goal:

_____

_____

_____

_____

What skills and new ways of doing things will you use in working to achieve this goal?

_____

_____

_____

_____

_____

Goal:

_____

_____

_____

How I plan to achieve this goal:

_____

_____

_____

_____

What skills and new ways of doing things will you use in working to achieve this goal?

_____

_____

_____

_____

Challenges

Your work in this book has probably not been easy. As you addressed each topic, you faced new challenges. You may have thought about things you had not thought about in a long time. You may have remembered some things that you had not recalled in the past. You may have done some things you never did before. What were your biggest challenges in doing this work and how did you meet these challenges?

Challenge:

_____

_____

_____

How I met this challenge:

_____

_____

_____

_____

Challenge:

_____

_____

_____

How I met this challenge:

_____

_____

_____

_____

Challenge:

_____

_____

_____

How I met this challenge:

_____

_____

_____

_____

_____

Challenge:

_____

_____

How I met this challenge:

_____

_____

_____

_____

_____

Strengths

What personal strengths have helped you in doing this work, and how will each of those strengths help you as you continue your healing journey?

Strength:

_____

_____

_____

How this strength will help me as I continue my healing journey:

_____

_____

_____

Strength:

_____

_____

How this strength will help me as I continue my healing journey:

_____

_____

_____

Strength:

_____

_____

How this strength will help me as I continue my healing journey:

_____

_____

_____

Strength:

_____

_____

_____

How this strength will help me as I continue my healing journey:

_____

_____

_____

Strength:

_____

_____

_____

How this strength will help me as I continue my healing journey:

_____

_____

_____

Strength:

_____

_____

_____

How this strength will help me as I continue my healing journey:

_____

_____

_____

List additional strengths on a separate sheet of paper.

Optional Activities

1. This week, remind yourself *every day* of the good work you have done.

2. Create something (art, music, writing, or drama) that celebrates where you are in your healing journey right now.

Things to Remember Every Day

- The progress I have made in doing this work is just right for me. I deserve to be proud of myself.

- I have many strengths.

- I continue to meet and overcome challenges in my life.

Part 4

Closing Rituals

Topic 31

Truths and Myths
about Abuse

Everyone is bombarded with information every day—from the media, books, magazines, colleagues, friends, family members, and other people with whom we have contact. Some of this information is true and some is not true. Often it's hard to know the difference. Some of the things you are told are blatantly false, although they may make you pause for a moment. For instance, if a stranger is unkind to you, you may wonder for a second what you did to cause it, but then you can immediately say to yourself, "That person doesn't even know me" and forget the incident. Other messages are much more subtle—such as an advertisement for blue jeans depicting a very slim woman that seems to be saying, "To be okay you have to look like this." Thinking about what you hear or learn, and determining whether or not it is true, is a process that will continue throughout your life. You have the right to determine what you believe and what you don't believe.

As you worked through this book, you had the opportunity to think about things you may have been told by others about yourself. You thought about things others wanted you to believe were true but that you now know were false. You may have had a hard time deciding whether some statements were truths or myths. Even once you made your decisions, you may have found it hard to let go of the myths and replace them with the truths you now understand. In this topic you will get further practice in thinking about what others tell you and determining whether those things are true. You will also learn strategies for letting go of false information so that you can easily do it on an ongoing basis.

Subtle Messages

This exercise will help you learn to think about the subtle messages that you are being given about yourself and the way you should do things. To do this exercise you will need one or several women's magazines or tabloid newspapers.

Using the following format, list five advertisements that are trying to tell you you need to be different than you are, the message the advertisement is trying to give you, and a statement of your reality about that message. For example,

Product: *A bra that hides differences in the size of your breasts.*

Message: *My body is not okay.*

Statement of my reality: *My body is fine the way it is. Who said my breasts are supposed to be the same size?*

Product:

_____

Message:

_____

_____

_____

Statement of my reality:

_____

_____

_____

Product:

_____

Message:

_____

_____

_____

Statement of my reality:

_____

_____

_____

Product:

_____

Message:

_____

_____

_____

Statement of my reality:

_____

_____

_____

Product:

_____

Message:

_____

_____

_____

Statement of my reality:

_____

_____

_____

Product:

_____

Message:

_____

_____

_____

Statement of my reality:

_____

_____

_____

The following exercise will give you more practice in thinking about subtle messages.
Statement: Women are responsible for birth control.
Do you think this statement is true or false? Why do you feel that way?

_____

_____

_____

_____

If it is false, how could you change it to make it true?

_____

_____

_____

Statement: I deserve to be treated with dignity, compassion, and respect at all times.
Do you think this statement is true or false? Why do you feel that way?

_____

_____

_____

_____

If it is false, how could you change it to make it true?

_____

_____

_____

Statement: When a woman is abused, it's because she is asking for it. She could prevent the abuse if she really wanted to.

Do you think this statement is true or false? Why do you feel that way?

_____

_____

_____

_____

If it is false, how could you change it to make it true?

_____

_____

_____

Statement: I have to have a baby to be a valuable woman.

Do you think this statement is true or false? Why do you feel that way?

_____

_____

_____

_____

If it is false, how could you change it to make it true?

_____

_____

_____

Statement: I am in charge of my life.
Do you think this statement is true or false? Why do you feel that way?

_____

_____

_____

_____

If it is false, how could you change it to make it true?

_____

_____

Statement: If you have children, you need to stay with your husband, even if you are being abused.
Do you think this statement is true or false? Why do you feel that way?

_____

_____

_____

If it is false, how could you change it to make it true?

_____

Statement: If a person is drunk and they abuse you, it is not their fault.

Do you think this statement is true or false? Why do you feel that way?

_____

_____

_____

_____

If it is false, how could you change it to make it true?

_____

_____

_____

Myths from Your Life

When Jackie was a small child, she was told by her older brother and a cousin that she was fat and ugly. They told her this over and over, teasing and taunting her. She said it made her feel like she looked "really bad and overweight." Throughout her childhood she was very shy and felt ashamed of the way she looked. She avoided social activities and went on many crash diets. As an adult she has come to understand that she looks fine and her weight is within the normal range. In order to really believe that she looks okay, she has worked on changing the negative thoughts she has about the way she looks to positive ones by repeating affirmations such as, "I look great" and "I am an attractive woman." She has also had treatment for eating disorders.

List things you learned from others that you thought were true that you now know are myths.

Myth:

_____

_____

Where did you learn this?

_____

_____

Why wasn't this a good source of this information?

_____

_____

In what way is it clear to you that this is a myth?

_____

_____

How did believing this myth affect you and your life?

_____

_____

_____

Rewrite this myth to make it a truth.

_____

_____

How have you (or how has your life) changed since you found out this statement is not true or accurate?

_____

_____

_____

_____

_____

Describe any action you have taken so that you believe the truth almost all the time.

_____

_____

_____

Myth:

_____

_____

Where did you learn this?

_____

_____

Why wasn't this a good source of this information?

_____

_____

_____

In what way is it clear to you that this is a myth?

_____

_____

_____

How did believing this myth affect you and your life?

_____

_____

_____

_____

_____

Rewrite this myth to make it a truth.

_____

_____

How have you (or how has your life) changed since you found out this statement is not true or accurate?

_____

_____

_____

_____

Describe any action you have taken so that you believe the truth almost all the time.

_____

_____

_____

Myth:

_____

_____

Where did you learn this?

_____

_____

Why wasn't this a good source of this information?

_____

_____

_____

In what way is it clear to you that this is a myth?

_____

_____

_____

How did believing this myth affect you and your life?

_____

_____

_____

_____

Rewrite this myth to make it a truth.

_____

_____

How have you (or how has your life) changed since you found out this statement is not true or accurate?

_____

_____

_____

_____

Describe any action you have taken so that you believe the truth almost all the time.

_____

_____

_____

You can use this format any time you discover myths that are affecting your life.

Ideas for Letting Go of Myths and Accepting Truths

Even though you may know that a myth is not true, and even though you may fully understand the truth, you may still find it very hard to let go of the myths that have been part of your thought patterns since you were young. Here are some ideas that might help.

1. Make a list of the myths that have been most troublesome to you in your life along with a statement of the truth. (You may have written them in previous exercises in this topic or in other topics in this book.) For example,

   Myth: Girls are supposed to do whatever boys want them to do.
   Truth: Girls decide for themselves what they want to do.

   _____

   _____

   _____

   _____

   _____

   _____

2. On a separate sheet of paper, make a list of those myths you no longer want to believe. Then let the myths go out of your life by destroying the paper—throw it in the rubbish, burn it, throw it in a river, or tear it to shreds.

3. Review the exercise for changing negative thoughts to positive ones (topic 3, under Feeling Better about Your Body).

4. Wear a rubber band on your wrist. Every time you catch yourself believing the myth, snap the rubber band and repeat the truth three times.

5. Write your truths on a piece of paper to carry with you. Read them over and over whenever you have free time. Read them before you go to bed and when you first get up.

6. Make signs that state your truth. Hang them in key places around your home—on the refrigerator door, the bathroom mirror, a bulletin board, or the coat closet door. Read the sign five times every time you see it.

7. Write the truth over and over until you get tired of writing it. Change writing styles as you go along. Use printing and cursive. Use decorative papers and pens.

8. If writing with your nondominant hand has proved helpful for you (see optional activity number 2 at the end of topic 24), write your truth six times with your nondominant hand.

Optional Activities

1. Spend an evening watching television and write down all the myths about women you see in programs or in advertising. Then rewrite these myths to make them truths.

2. Write in your journal for twenty minutes to one hour about how myths have affected your life and what the changes are that you expect in your life now that you believe the truths.

Things to Remember Every Day

- I have the right to determine what I believe and what I don't believe—I decide what is a truth and what is a myth.

- I make decisions in my life based on *my* truths.

- I am fine the way I am.

Topic 32

What It Means to Be a Woman—Revisited

In topic 2 you addressed issues related to being a woman. Since then, your feelings about being a woman may have changed. Before you finish working in this book, you may find it useful to look at this topic again, answering some of the questions and repeating some of the exercises as a way of assessing your progress.

Women You Admire

Think of one or several women whom you admire. Who are they?

_____

_____

_____

Return to topic 2. Are these the same women you said you admired when you were working on that topic? If they are different, why do you think that is?

_____

_____

_____

Through doing this work, do you now see women in a different way? If so, describe how.

_____

_____

_____

Do the following exercise without looking at your responses in topic 2.

Make yourself comfortable. Sit back and relax, take a few deep breaths, then answer each of the following questions with the first word or phrase that comes into your mind. Try not to think about your answer, and don't censor it. If your answer does not make sense to you, that's okay. Just let it be what it is.

What do you think about being a woman?

_____

What do you feel about being a woman?

_____

What is the first sensation you feel when you think about being a woman?

_____

Now, look back at your answers in topic 2 and see how your responses have changed. Describe any changes you notice.

_____

_____

_____

_____

Gender Issues

Answer the following questions from topic 2, again without looking back at your previous answers.

Do you feel there are some advantages to being a male? If so, what are they?

_____

_____

_____

_____

_____

Are you glad you are female? Why or why not?

_____

_____

_____

_____

Now, look back at your responses in topic 2. Describe any changes in your responses.

_____

_____

_____

_____

If your responses have changed significantly, why do you think this is so?

_____

_____

_____

Family Issues

In topic 2 you wrote about how your family has affected the way you feel about being a woman. Describe the way your family influences the way you feel about being a woman now.

_____

_____

_____

_____

Now, look back at your responses in topic 2. Describe any changes in your responses.

_____

_____

_____

_____

Societal Issues

In topic 2 you explored ways in which the media affects how you feel about yourself as a woman. How does society and the way women are depicted in the media affect the way you feel about yourself as a woman now?

_____

_____

_____

When you see an ad or a story in a magazine or newspaper that makes women seem like sex objects or that sends a message that women need to do something to improve themselves, how does it make you feel?

_____

_____

_____

Now, look back at your responses in topic 2. Describe any changes in your responses.

_____

_____

_____

_____

_____

Who Am I?

Have some changes occurred in your life as you worked through these topics? Do you still have the same roles you checked off in topic 2?

Circle all that apply, and add any that are not in the list.

mother / grandmother / aunt / friend / partner / wife / lover / head of household / housekeeper / cook / wage earner / employee / employer / business owner / chauffeur / caretaker / buyer / manager / social director / confidant / supporter

_____

_____

_____

If your roles have changed, how or why did these changes occur?

_____

_____

_____

Make a list of words that describe you.

_____

_____

_____

How would you describe yourself physically?

_____

_____

_____

_____

Now go back to topic 2 and see whether you used most of the same words you used to describe yourself then or whether most of your words now are different. If they are different, why do you think that is?

_____

_____

_____

_____

Feeling Good about Yourself

Write down three things you have achieved in your life that you feel proud of. (List more if you feel like it.)

_____

_____

_____

Now go back to topic 2. Is this list different now, or the same? If it's different, why do you think that is?

_____

_____

_____

Repeat the following exercise from topic 2.

Get a pen and a sheet of colored paper. Spend ten minutes writing down everything good you can think of about yourself. Everything goes, as long as it's positive. If you have a hard time writing good things about yourself for ten minutes, you can repeat the same things over and over, or ask a supportive person to tell you some good things about yourself. When you are done, read what you have written. Then fold it up and put it under your pillow, on your bedside table, or in your pocket. Read it before you go to bed at night, when you first get up in the morning, and whenever you a have a free moment. Read it aloud whenever you can. Read it to a supportive friend.

How does your response differ from the one you wrote in topic 2?

_____

_____

_____

If it is quite different, why do you think that is?

_____

_____

_____

Optional Activities

1. Read one, several, or all of the books about remarkable women in the Women's Lives category of the Resources section at the back of this book.

2. Take another look at all the Optional Activities sections in this book, and pick one or more activities to do now that you didn't do before.

Things to Remember Every Day

- Being a woman is a challenge, but it's a challenge I am ready to take on.

Topic 33

Closing Ritual

You have now completed work on thirty-two topics related to healing from the effects of trauma in your life. This ending is also a beginning—the beginning of living your life with new thoughts, new feelings, new ways of responding to thoughts and feelings, and new ways of doing things. You deserve to celebrate the work you have done and the new life you are anticipating with a ritual you have designed for yourself.

The process of developing a ritual to celebrate yourself is one you can use over and over again—whenever you reach an important milestone in your life, make a change, or begin a new phase of your life. Developing your rituals is a very personal task. This topic will provide you with ideas.

Plan to spend at least the first half hour of your time working on this topic developing your ritual. Use the second half hour (or some other time, if you want) to spend more time actually doing the ritual. This ritual, and other rituals you use in your life, can be as short or as long as you want it to be. For example, after you complete an important project at work, you might want to stop at a florist and buy yourself a flower. After you give up smoking, you might celebrate for a week by taking a vacation from work and/or personal responsibilities and pampering yourself by spending each day listening to music you enjoy, dancing, spending time with good friends, and doing activities you enjoy. When you leave an abusive relationship, you may want to take some time (maybe an hour) out of each day for an entire year to celebrate this momentous achievement.

One woman developed a ritual to celebrate the ending of her structured work on healing from the effects of childhood abuse. Specifically, she wanted to celebrate herself and the changes she had made in her life. She planned a ritual that would take one hour on a weekend afternoon, and she decided to do it alone. She planned to do her ritual in the corner of a room in her home where she had done many of the activities that were part of her healing work. She gathered together the needed supplies and decorated the space in the week prior to her ritual time with some of her favorite plants, pictures of herself at different ages, and a high school sports trophy she had won. Before the ritual she dressed in her favorite colorful skirt and peasant blouse. Her ritual included reading aloud a short story that had been inspirational to her, playing music and dancing, eating a special meal and drinking a favorite herbal tea, making a colorful collage of her life, reading an affirming guided imagery exercise, and ending with a prayer.

This topic contains many ideas for rituals, and you will undoubtedly find that you have many good ideas of your own. Combine them in any way you choose to develop a ritual or celebration that feels just right to you. You may want to read through the entire topic before you make decisions about your ritual.

First, what message do you want to give yourself through this ritual? Perhaps it is one or several of the following (place a check mark next to those that apply):

_____ to celebrate myself

_____ to acknowledge an ending

_____ to acknowledge a beginning

_____ to say good-bye

_____ to say hello

_____ to congratulate myself for an achievement

_____ to acknowledge progress I have made

_____ to say I love myself

_____ to recognize I am loved

_____ to affirm I am a strong, powerful woman

_____ to say I am in charge of my life

_____ to know I can make myself feel better

_____ to say life is great

_____ to honor my courage

_____ to reward my effort and persistence

The message I want to give myself in this ritual or celebration is:

_____

_____

_____

Time

When will you do your ritual or celebration? After working on this topic, you may be inspired to do it right away. Or, you may choose to wait for your favorite time of year, favorite holiday, a special anniversary, the time just before or after your menstrual period, during the full or new moon, or some other such time that feels special. You'll also want to consider whether your ritual will be done just once or numerous times.

I will do my ritual on this day (or days) at this time (or times):

My ritual will be roughly this long in duration:

Other issues related to time that are important to me:

Place

Where do you want to do your ritual? In the same space where you have been doing this work, or in some other special place such as a park, a church, the woods, or near a body of water? You might also consider moving from one place to another as part of your ritual.

Your location should be a place where you feel comfortable making noise and doing whatever you want to do without fear of intrusion by others who are not involved in your ritual, who might not understand, who might inhibit your actions, or who might not respect your right to privacy.

I will do my ritual in the following place or places:

What Will You Do During Your Ritual?

Here are a few ideas; place a check mark next to those activities you might want to include:

_____ reading favorite things you or others have written;

_____ singing songs that have special meaning to you;

_____ playing a musical instrument, perhaps with music you composed yourself;

_____ playing your favorite CD;

_____ moving—dancing, walking, running, skipping, jumping;

_____ drawing, painting;

_____ meditating;

_____ praying;

_____ relaxation exercises;

_____ visualization exercises;

_____ wrapping yourself in something that feels good;

_____ talking to someone who will hear you and listen without interruption;

_____ listening to someone speak to you;

_____ cooking;

_____ yoga;

_____ a game or activity you enjoyed as a child;

_____ massage—either giving or receiving;

_____ sculpting;

_____ making an offering;

_____ gathering flowers, shells, or some other kind of object;

_____ bathing or showering;

_____ making sounds—humming, shouting, or even banging objects against each other;

_____ writing;

_____ sewing, quilting, embroidering, making a doll, or other type of craft.

Other kinds of activities you want to include in your ritual:

_____

_____

_____

_____

_____

Use the following to more clearly define the activities you plan to include in your ritual.
Activity:

_____

Why I want to do it:

_____

How I will do it:

When I will do it (at the beginning, middle, end, after the song, and so on)

Supplies I will need for this activity:

Activity:

Why I want to do it:

How I will do it:

When I will do it (at the beginning, middle, end, after the song, and so on)

Supplies I will need for this activity:

_____

_____

Activity:

_____

Why I want to do it:

_____

_____

How I will do it:

_____

_____

_____

When I will do it (at the beginning, middle, end, after the song, and so on)

_____

Supplies I will need for this activity:

_____

_____

_____

Activity:

_____

Why I want to do it:

_____

_____

How I will do it:

_____

When I will do it (at the beginning, middle, end, after the song, and so on)

Supplies I will need for this activity:

Activity:

Why I want to do it:

How I will do it:

When I will do it (at the beginning, middle, end, after the song, and so on)

Supplies I will need for this activity:

Scheduling Your Activities

You will want to plan the order in which you do the activities that will be part of your ritual. Of course, as you do your ritual, a different order of activities may feel better to you, but it helps to begin with a plan. Review your list of activities and decide which you want to do first, second, third, and so on. If you have a definite ending time for your ritual, make sure that the time required for each activity won't cause you rush through too fast for fear of running out of time. Refer to the following schedule as you plan your ritual.

Activity #1:

_____

Length (optional, depending on whether or not you have a set ending time):

_____

Activity #2:

_____

Length:

_____

Activity #3:

_____

Length:

_____

Activity #4:

_____

Length:

_____

Activity #5:

_____

Length:

_____

Activity #6:

_____

Length:

_____

Activity #7:

_____

Length:

_____

Activity #8:

_____

Length:

_____

Gathering Supplies

You will want to gather supplies for your ritual to decorate the space, to decorate yourself, and to complete the activities you have planned. These supplies and the way you use them help you feel the way you want to feel—so that you clearly hear the message you are trying to give yourself. You may need some time to get these supplies together.

Here are some ideas of things you might use to decorate your ritual space and make yourself feel comfortable:

- candles;

- plants;

- mirrors;

- feathers;

- rocks, stones, or crystals;

- dishes;

- fabric;

- furniture;

- flowers;

- pillows;

- mementos such as stuffed animals, trophies, or pictures; and

- carpets or rugs.

List and describe the things you will use to decorate the space:

_____

_____

_____

_____

_____

_____

What about items that might be used in some way during your ritual? For example,

- art supplies;

- pieces of wood or other items from nature;

- musical instruments;

- a journal;

- various kinds of paper—big, small, colored, plain, heavy weight, light weight;

- books;

- camera and film;

- fragrances or scents;

- foods;

- movies or videos; or

- pictures.

What supplies will you need to do your activities?

_____

_____

_____

_____

_____

Clothing

What will you wear when you do your ritual? What you wear can really affect the way you feel. Also, a particular type of clothing might be needed for one of the activities you have planned, such as a flowing skirt that would be part of a dance. How do you want to feel when you are doing your ritual?

_____

_____

What kind of clothing would help you feel this way?

_____

_____

Perhaps you don't like to think about clothes and you don't plan to wear anything special—that's okay, too. Or, perhaps you'd like to be nude.

If you do plan to wear particular clothing for your ritual, place a check mark next to the kinds of clothing that seem right to you:

_____ sexy

_____ soft

_____ silky

_____ shimmering

_____ brightly colored

_____ subdued

_____ comfortable

_____ feminine

_____ masculine

_____ childish

_____ fancy

_____ lacy

Also, give some thought to accessories that might help you feel the way you want to feel when you are doing this ritual. For example: hats, jewelry, headdresses, hair pieces, and shoes.

List your ideas about the kind of clothing or accessories you want to wear for your ritual.

_____

_____

_____

_____

_____

If you don't have clothing that meets your needs, you might use this occasion to buy some new ones, find some at a thrift store, or borrow from a family member or friend.

I will get the clothing I want to wear during my ritual from:

_____

When I do my ritual I will wear:

_____

_____

During my ritual I will change my clothes [how many] times:

_____

People

Is there anyone you want to join you in your ritual? Sharing your ritual with another person can be very affirming, validating, and powerful if it feels right to you.

I want the following people to join me in my ritual:

Person and reason for inclusion:

_____

_____

_____

What I will ask them to do (if anything)

_____

_____

Person and reason for inclusion:

_____

_____

_____

What I will ask them to do (if anything)

_____

_____

Person and reason for inclusion:

_____

_____

What I will ask them to do (if anything)

_____

_____

Person and reason for inclusion:

_____

_____

What I will ask them to do (if anything)

_____

_____

Things to Avoid During Your Ritual

When planning your ritual, you will want to avoid the following:

- work—either household tasks or work responsibilities outside of your home;
- using the phone;
- the media—television, radio, newspapers.

List other things you will want to avoid during your ritual:

_____

_____

_____

_____

_____

Other Rituals

After you've completed your ritual, ask yourself if there are any things you learned that would help you in planning future rituals—things you would change, or things you would or wouldn't do. If so, what were they, how would you change them, and why would you change them?

What I would change:

_____

_____

_____

How I would change it:

_____

_____

_____

Why I would change it:

_____

_____

_____

What I would change:

_____

_____

_____

How I would change it:

_____

_____

_____

Why I would change it:

_____

_____

_____

What I would change:

_____

_____

_____

How I would change it:

_____

_____

_____

Why I would change it:

_____

_____

_____

Congratulations on all the good work you have done!

Optional Activities

1. Make a list of ways to celebrate yourself that can be done every day.

2. Do something you enjoy every day this week.

3. Spend time every day this week with someone who is loving, affirming, and supportive.

Things to Remember Every Day

- I like myself.

- I am a magnificent woman.

- I am in charge of my life.

- I celebrate myself and my life.

- I do things I enjoy, things that make me feel good.

- I can do whatever I want to do.

- I can set goals for myself and work to meet my goals.

Appendix

Information for the Physician

1. List all medications, vitamins, and health care preparations you are using for any reason.

   Medication:

   Dosage:

   When and how used:

2. Provide a medical history of yourself and your family.

   Your history:

   _____

   _____

   _____

   _____

   _____

   Your mother's side of the family:

   _____

   _____

   _____

_____

_____

Your father's side of the family:

_____

_____

_____

_____

3. Describe recent changes in each of the following.
   Appetite or diet:

   _____

   _____

   _____

   Weight:

   _____

   _____

   Sleep patterns:

   _____

   _____

   Sexual interest:

   _____

   _____

Ability to concentrate:

_____

_____

_____

Memory:

_____

_____

_____

4. Have you recently had any of the following? If so, describe in detail.
   Headaches:

_____

_____

_____

Numbness or tingling anywhere:

_____

_____

_____

Loss of balance:

_____

_____

_____

Double vision or vision problems:

_____

_____

_____

Periods of amnesia:

_____

_____

_____

Coordination changes:

_____

_____

_____

Weakness in arms or legs:

_____

_____

_____

Fever:

_____

_____

_____

Nausea or diarrhea:

_____

_____

_____

Other gastrointestinal problems:

_____

_____

_____

Fainting or dizziness:

_____

_____

_____

Seizures:

_____

_____

_____

Stressful life events:

_____

_____

_____

Additional pertinent information:

_____

_____

_____

Questions to Ask the Doctor about Medication

- Generic name
- Product name
- Product category
- Suggested dosage level
- How does this medication work? What do you expect it to do?

- How long will it take to achieve that result?

- What are the risks associated with taking this medication?

- What kind of an effectiveness track record does this medication have?

- What short-term side effects does this medication have?

- What long-term side effects does this medication have?

- Is there any way to minimize the chances of experiencing these side effects? If so, what are they?

- Are there any dietary or lifestyle suggestions or restrictions I should keep in mind while using this medication?

- Why do you recommend this particular medication?

- Have your other patients used this? If so, how have they done?

- How is this medication monitored?

- What tests will I need prior to taking this medication?

- How often will I need these tests while taking the medication?

- What symptoms indicate that the dosage should be changed or the medication stopped?

- Where can I get more information about this medication?

- Is there any printed information on this medication that I can take home to study?

Wellness Recovery Action Plan
Getting Started

Here's all you need to develop your own recovery monitoring system:

- a three-ring binder with paper and a set of five dividers or tabs,

- a writing instrument of some kind, and

- (optional) a friend or other supporter to give you assistance and feedback.

Completing Your Plan
Daily Maintenance List

Label the first tab Daily Maintenance List. On the first page, describe yourself when you are feeling okay. Do it in list form. Some descriptive words that others have used are: bright, cheerful, talkative, outgoing, boisterous, energetic, humorous, happy, dramatic, athletic, optimistic, reasonable, responsible, competent, industrious, curious, supportive, argumentative, difficult, compulsive, a fast learner, contemplative, calm, introverted, and so on.

On the next page, make a list of things you need to do for yourself every day to keep yourself feeling okay. Here are some ideas (change amounts and times to meet your needs):

- Eat three healthy meals and three healthy snacks (specify what the snack should consist of, if you wish).

- Drink at least six eight-ounce glasses of water.

- Exercise for at least a half hour.

- Get a half hour's exposure to outdoor light.

- Take medications and vitamins.

- Take twenty minutes of relaxation or meditation time.

- Write in my journal for at least fifteen minutes.

- Spend a half hour enjoying a fun, affirming, or creative activity.

On the next page, make a reminder list for things you might need to do. Reading through this list daily will help keep you on track. Here are some ideas:

- Set up an appointment with one of my health care professionals.

- Spend time with a good friend.

- Spend extra time with my partner.

- Be in touch with my family.

- Spend time with children or pets.

- Do peer counseling.

- Get more sleep.

- Do some housework.

- Buy groceries.

- Have some personal time.

- Plan something fun for the weekend.

- Plan a vacation.

- Take a hot bubble bath.

- Go for a long walk.

- Call my sponsor.

- Go to a support group or twelve-step meeting.

Triggers

You may experience external events or circumstances that produce serious symptoms, such as making you feel as though you are getting ill. These are normal reactions to events in your life, but if you don't respond to them and deal with them in some way, they might actually cause a worsening in your symptoms.

Label the next tab Triggers, and on the first page write down those things that might cause an increase in your symptoms. Examples are listed below. Try to think of things that have triggered or increased your symptoms in the past.

If any of the following events or circumstances come up, I will do some of the activities listed on the next page to help keep my symptoms from increasing.

- anniversary dates of losses or trauma,

- traumatic news events,

- being overtired,

- work stress,

- family friction,

- a relationship ending,

- spending too much time alone,

- being judged or criticized,

- being teased or put down,

- financial problems,

- physical illness,

- sexual harassment,

- aggressive-sounding noises (sustained),

- feeling left out,

- things that remind me of abandonment or deprivation,

- intimacy,

- excessive stress,

- self-blame,

- extreme guilt, and/or

- substance abuse.

On the next page, write a Triggers Action Plan to use if any triggers come up. This plan should keep your symptoms from worsening if the triggering event occurs. Here's a sample plan:

If any of my triggers come up, I will do the following:

Must do:

- *Make sure I do everything on my daily maintenance list.*

- *Call a support person and ask them to listen while I talk through the situation.*

- *Do some deep breathing exercises.*

- *Get validation from someone I feel close to.*

- *Do a half hour of relaxation exercise.*

Choices:

- *Journaling.*

- *Do vigorous exercise.*

- *Do my focusing exercises.*

- *Do some peer counseling.*

- *See or talk to my counselor, case manager, or sponsor.*

- *Play my guitar for an hour.*

Early Warning Signs

Early warning signs are internal and may be unrelated to reactions to stressful situations. In spite of your best efforts at reducing symptoms, you may begin to experience early warning signs—subtle signs of change that indicate you may need to take some further action.

Label the next tab Early Warning Signs. On the first page, make a list of early warning signs you have noticed. Here are some examples:

- anxiety,

- nervousness,

- forgetfulness,

- inability to experience pleasure,

- lack of motivation,

- feeling slowed down or speeded up,

- avoiding doing things on daily maintenance list,

- being uncaring,

- avoiding others or isolating myself,

- being obsessed with something that doesn't really matter,

- beginning irrational thought patterns,

- feeling unconnected to my body,

- increased irritability,

- increased negativity,

- increase in smoking,

- not keeping appointments,

- spending money on unneeded items,

- impulsivity,

- aches and pains,

- feelings of discouragement and hopelessness,
- substance abuse,
- failing to buckle my seat belt,
- not answering the phone,
- overeating or undereating,
- weepiness,
- compulsive behaviors,
- feeling worthless or inadequate, and/or
- secretiveness.

On the next page, write an Early Warning Signs Action Plan to use if early warning signs come up. This plan should keep your symptoms from worsening if you experience early warning signs. Here is a sample plan:

Things I Must Do

- *Do the things on my daily maintenance plan whether I feel like it or not.*
- *Tell a supporter/counselor how I am feeling and ask for their advice.*
- *Peer counsel at least once a day until early warning signs diminish.*
- *Do at least one focusing exercise a day.*
- *Do at least three ten-minute relaxation exercises each day.*
- *Write in my journal for at least fifteen minutes each day.*
- *Spend at least one hour involved in an activity I enjoy.*
- *Ask others to take over my household responsibilities for a day.*
- *Go to [number] twelve-step meetings.*

Things I could choose to do if it feels right to me:

- *Check in with my physician or other health care professional.*
- *Surround myself with loving, affirming people.*
- *Spend some time with my pet(s).*
- *Read a good book.*
- *Dance, sing, listen to good music, or play a musical instrument.*
- *Exercise.*

Things Are Breaking Down or Getting Worse

In spite of your best efforts, your symptoms may progress to the point where they are very uncomfortable, serious, and even dangerous, but you are still able to take some action on your behalf. This is a very important time—you'll need to take immediate action to prevent a crisis.

Label the next tab When Things Are Breaking Down, then make a list of the symptoms that, for you, mean that things have worsened and are close to the crisis stage. Here are examples:

- feeling very oversensitive and fragile,
- irrational responses to events and the actions of others,
- feeling very needy,
- unable to sleep for (specify how long),
- sleeping all the time,
- wanting to be totally alone,
- racing thoughts,
- risk-taking behaviors,
- thoughts of self-harm,
- obsessed with negative thoughts,
- bizarre behaviors
- dissociation (blacking out, spacing out, losing time),
- seeing things that aren't there,
- suicidal thoughts, and/or
- paranoia.

On the next page, write a When Things Are Breaking Down Action Plan to use if early warning signs come up. This plan should help reduce your symptoms when they have progressed to this point. The plan now needs to be very direct, with fewer choices and very clear instructions. Here is a sample plan:

If these symptoms come up I need to do all of the following:

- *Call my doctor or other health care professional and ask for and follow their instructions.*
- *Call and talk as long as I need to one of my supporters.*
- *Arrange for someone to stay with me around the clock until my symptoms subside.*
- *Take action so I cannot hurt myself if my symptoms get worse—for example, give my medications, check book, credit cards, and car keys to my son for safekeeping.*
- *Make sure I am doing everything on my daily check list.*
- *Arrange and take at least three days off from any responsibilities.*
- *Have at least two peer counseling sessions daily.*
- *Do three deep-breathing relaxation exercises.*
- *Do two focusing exercises.*
- *Write in my journal for at least one half hour.*

Other choices for the day might include:

- *Engage in creative activities, and/or*

- *Engage in vigorous exercise.*

Personal Crisis Plan

In spite of your best planning and assertive action, you may find yourself in a crisis situation in which others will need to take over responsibility for your care. You may feel totally out of control. Writing a crisis plan when you are well, to instruct others about how to care for you when you are not well, keeps you in control even when it seems as though things are out of control. Others will know what to do, saving everyone time and frustration and also insuring that your needs will be met.

Label the fifth and final tab Personal Crisis Plan. There are nine parts to this plan. You'll probably remember this from topic 18, where complete instructions are included for filling out each of the nine parts. Hopefully, you already completed most of this exercise in that topic. If not, review that topic and look over the information required for each of the nine parts right now, and develop this plan slowly, over time, when you are feeling well. You'll need to give this serious thought, and you'll probably want to discuss the issue with the people whom you'll be listing in parts 3 and 8. After you've worked your Personal Crisis Plan out to your satisfaction, add the information to the final section of your binder.

Note that you can help assure that your crisis plan will be followed by signing it in the presence of two witnesses. You will further increase its potential for use if you appoint and name a durable attorney. Because the legality of these documents varies from state to state, you cannot be absolutely sure the plan will be followed. However, it is your best assurance that your wishes will be honored.

Personal Crisis Plan

Date:

Part 1: What I'm Like when I'm Feeling Well

_____

_____

_____

_____

_____

_____

_____

Part 2: Symptoms

If I have several of the following signs and/or symptoms, my supporters, named below, need to take over responsibility for my care and make decisions in my behalf based on the information in this plan.

_____

_____

_____

_____

_____

_____

_____

_____

Part 3: Supporters

If this plan needs to be activated, I want the following people to take over for me.

Name: _____

Connection/role: _____

Phone number: _____

Specific tasks for this person:

_____

_____

_____

Name: _____

Connection/role: _____

Phone number: _____

Specific tasks for this person:

_____

_____

_____

Name: _____

Connection/role: _____

Phone number: _____

Specific tasks for this person:

_____

_____

_____

Name: _____

Connection/role: _____

Phone number: _____

Specific tasks for this person:

_____

_____

_____

Name: _____

Connection/role: _____

Phone number: _____

Specific tasks for this person:

_____

_____

_____

Name: _____

Connection/role: _____

Phone number: _____

Specific tasks for this person:

_____

_____

_____

I do _not_ want the following people involved in any way in my care or treatment:

Name: _____

I don't want them involved because: (optional)

_____

_____

_____

Name: _____

I don't want them involved because: (optional)

_____

_____

_____

Name: _____

I don't want them involved because: (optional)

_____

_____

_____

If my supporters disagree on a course of action to be followed, I would like the dispute to be settled in the following way:

_____

_____

_____

_____

Part 4: Medication

Physician: _____

Psychiatrist: _____

Other health care providers:

_____

_____

_____

Pharmacy: _____

Pharmacist: _____

Allergies: _____

Medication or health care preparations I am using (dosage and purpose):

_____

_____

_____

_____

_____

_____

_____

_____

Medications and health care preparations to avoid, and why:

_____

_____

_____

_____

Part 5: Treatments
Treatment:

_____

_____

_____

When and how to use this treatment:

_____

_____

_____

Treatment:

_____

_____

_____

When and how to use this treatment:

_____

_____

_____

Treatment:

_____

_____

_____

When and how to use this treatment:

_____

_____

_____

Treatment:

_____

_____

_____

When and how to use this treatment:

_____

_____

_____

Treatment:

_____

_____

_____

When and how to use this treatment:

_____

_____

_____

Treatments to avoid, and why:

_____

_____

_____

_____

Part 6: Home/Community Care/Respite Center
If possible, follow the following care plan:

_____

_____

_____

_____

_____

_____

_____

_____

_____

Part 7: Treatment Facilities

If I need hospitalization or treatment in a facility, I prefer the following facilities (in order of preference):

Name: _____

Contact person: _____

Phone number: _____

I prefer this facility because:

_____

_____

_____

Name: _____

Contact person: _____

Phone number: _____

I prefer this facility because:

_____

_____

_____

Name: _____

Contact person: _____

Phone number: _____

I prefer this facility because:

_____

_____

_____

Avoid using the following hospital or treatment facilities:

_____

_____

_____

_____

Part 8: Help from Others

Please do the following things that would help reduce my symptoms, make me more comfortable, and keep me safe:

_____

_____

_____

_____

_____

_____

_____

_____

I need (name the person): _____

to (name the task): _____

I need (name the person): _____

to (name the task): _____

I need (name the person): _____

to (name the task): _____

I need (name the person): _____

to (name the task): _____

I need (name the person): _____

to (name the task): _____

I need (name the person): _____

to (name the task): _____

Do not do the following. It won't help and may even make things worse.

_____

_____

_____

_____

_____

Part 9: Inactivating the Plan

The following signs, lack of symptoms, or actions indicate that my supporters no longer need to use this plan.

_____

_____

_____

_____

_____

_____

_____

Signed: _____

Date: _____

Witness: _____

Date: _____

Witness: _____

Date: _____

Attorney: _____

Date: _____

Durable power of attorney: _____

Substitute for durable power of attorney _____:

Any Personal Crisis Plan developed on a date after the dates listed above takes precedence over this document.

You have now completed your Wellness Recovery Action Plan. Update it whenever you learn new information or change your mind about anything. Also, be sure to give your supporters new copies of your Personal Crisis Plan each time you revise it.

Resources

Addictions

Birkedahl, N. *The Habit Control Workbook*. Oakland, Calif.: New Harbinger Publications, 1990.

Catalano, E., and N. Sonenberg. *Consuming Passions: Help for Compulsive Shoppers*. Oakland, Calif.: New Harbinger Publications, 1993.

Fanning, P., and J. O'Neill. *The Addiction Workbook: A Step-by-Step Guide to Quitting Alcohol and Drugs*. Oakland, Calif.: New Harbinger Publications, 1996.

Kinney, J., and G. Leaton. *Loosening the Grip: A Handbook of Alcohol Information*. New York: McGraw-Hill, 1994.

Roth, G. *When Food Is Love: Exploring the Relationship between Eating and Intimacy*. New York: NAL-Dutton, 1992.

Sokolowski, ed. *Loosening the Grip*. St. Louis: Mosby, 1991.

Stevic-Rust, L., and A. Maxmin. *The Stop Smoking Workbook: Your Guide to Healthy Quitting*. Oakland, Calif.: New Harbinger Publications, 1996.

Changing Negative Thoughts to Positive Ones

Burns, D. *Feeling Good*. New York: Morrow, 1980.

———. *The Feeling Good Handbook*. New York: Plume, 1990.

Copeland, M. E. *The Depression Workbook: A Guide to Living with Depression and Manic Depression*. Oakland, Calif.: New Harbinger Publications, 1992.

Fanning, P., and M. McKay. *Prisoners of Belief*. Oakland, Calif.: New Harbinger Publications, 1991.

McKay, M., M. Davis, and P. Fanning. *Thoughts and Feelings*. Oakland, Calif.: New Harbinger Publications, 1997.

Savage, E. *Don't Take It Personally! The Art of Dealing with Rejection*. Oakland, Calif.: New Harbinger, 1997.

Exercise Programs

Anderson, B. *Stretching*. Bolinas, Calif.: Shelter Publications, 1980.

Nelson, M. *Strong Women Stay Young*. New York: Bantam, 1998.

Schatz, M., and W. Conner. *Back Care Basics: A Doctor's Gentle Yoga Program for Back and Neck Pain Relief*. Berkeley, Calif.: Rodmell Press, 1992.

Tobias, M., and J. Sullivan. *Complete Stretching: A New Exercise Program for Health and Vitality*. New York: Alfred A. Knopf, 1992.

Focusing

Copeland, M. E. *Living without Depression and Manic Depression*. Oakland, Calif.: New Harbinger Publications, 1994.

———. *The Worry Control Workbook*. Oakland, Calif.: New Harbinger Publications, 1999.

———. *Winning Against Relapse*. Oakland, Calif.: New Harbinger Publications, 1999.

Cornell, A. *The Power of Focusing*. Oakland, Calif.: New Harbinger Publications, 1996.

Gendlin, E. *Focusing*. New York: Bantam Books, 1981.

Guided Visualization

Fanning, P. *Visualization for Change*. Oakland, Calif.: New Harbinger Publications, 1994.

McKay, M., M. Davis, and P. Fanning. *Thoughts and Feelings*. Oakland, Calif.: New Harbinger Publications, 1997.

———. *Relaxation and Stress Reduction Workbook*. Oakland, Calif.: New Harbinger Publications, 1997.

Healing from Abuse

Adams, C., and J. Fay. *Free of the Shadows: Recovering from Sexual Violence*. Oakland, Calif.: New Harbinger Publications, 1989.

Matsakis, A. *When the Bough Breaks: A Helping Guide for Parents of Sexually Abused Children*. Oakland, Calif.: New Harbinger Publications, 1991.

———. *I Can't Get Over It: A Handbook for Trauma Survivors*. Oakland, Calif.: New Harbinger Publications, 1992.

———. *Trust after Trauma: A Guide to Relationships for Survivors and Those Who Love Them*. Oakland, Calif.: New Harbinger Publications, 1998.

Journaling

Cameron, J., and M. Bryan. *The Artist's Way: A Spiritual Path to Higher Creativity*. New York: Putnam, 1995.

Progoff, I. *At a Journal Workshop: Writing to Access the Power of the Unconscious and Evoke Creative Ability*. New York: Putnam, 1992.

Life Skills

Kahn, M. *The Tao of Conversation*. Oakland, Calif.: New Harbinger, 1995.

Potter-Efron, R. *Being, Belonging, Doing: Balancing Your Three Greatest Needs*. Oakland, Calif.: New Harbinger Publishing, 1998.

Roberts, S. *Living without Procrastination*. Oakland, Calif.: New Harbinger, 1995.

Peer Counseling

Copeland, M. E. *Living without Depression and Manic Depression: A Workbook for Maintaining Mood Stability*. Oakland, Calif.: New Harbinger Publications, 1994.

———. *The Depression Workbook: A Guide for Living with Depression and Manic Depression*. Oakland, Calif.: New Harbinger Publications, 1992.

———. *WRAP: Wellness Recovery Action Plan*. Brattleboro, Vt.: Peach Press, 1997.

———. *The Worry Control Workbook*. Oakland, Calif.: New Harbinger Publications, 1999.

———. *Winning against Relapse*. Oakland, Calif.: New Harbinger Publications, 1999.

Relationship Issues

Brinegar, J. *Breaking Free from Domestic Violence*. Minneapolis, Minn.: CompCare Publishers, 1992.

Enns, G., and J. Black. *It's Not Okay Anymore: Your Personal Guide to Ending Abuse, Taking Charge, and Loving Yourself*. Oakland, Calif.: New Harbinger Publications, 1997.

Evans, P. *The Verbally Abusive Relationship: How to Recognize It and How to Respond*. Holbrook, Mass.: Bob Adams, Inc., 1992.

Kinghma, D. *Coming Apart: Why Relationships End and How to Love through the Ending of Yours*. Oakland, Calif.: New Harbinger Publications, 1987.

Lerner, H. *The Dance of Anger: A Woman's Guide to Changing the Patterns of Intimate Relationships*. New York: HarperCollins, 1985.

Savage, E. *Don't Take It Personally! The Art of Dealing with Rejection*. Oakland, Calif.: New Harbinger Publications, 1997.

Schneider, J. *The Enabler: When Helping Harms the Ones You Love*. Oakland, Calif.: New Harbinger Publications, 1988.

Scott, G. *Resolving Conflict with Others and within Yourself*. Oakland, Calif.: New Harbinger Publications, 1990.

Woodhouse, V., and V. Collins with M. Blakeman. *Divorce and Money: How to Make the Best Financial Decisions during Divorce*. Berkeley, Calif.: Nolo Press, 1995.

Relaxation and Stress Reduction

Davis, M., E. Eschelman, and M. McKay. *The Relaxation and Stress Reduction Workbook*. Oakland, Calif.: New Harbinger Publications, 1995.

McKay, M., and P. Fanning. *The Daily Relaxer*. Oakland, Calif.: New Harbinger Publications, 1997.

O'Hara, V. *Five Weeks to Healing Stress: The Wellness Option*. Oakland, Calif.: New Harbinger Publications, 1996.

Self-Image

Cash, T. *The Body Image Workbook: An 8-Step Program for Learning to Like Your Looks*. Oakland, Calif.: New Harbinger Publications, 1997.

McKay, M. *Self-Esteem*. Oakland, Calif.: New Harbinger Publications, 1993.

Women's Health

Boston Women's Health Collective. *Our Bodies, Ourselves for the New Century*. New York: Simon and Schuster, 1998.

Doress-Worters, P., and D. Siegal. *The New Ourselves Growing Older: Women Aging with Knowledge and Power*. New York: Peter Smith Press, 1996.

Huston, J., and L. Lanka. *Perimenopause: Changes in Women's Health after 35*. Oakland, Calif.: New Harbinger Publications, 1997.

Love, S., with K. Lindsay. *Dr. Susan Love's Breast Book*. New York: Addison-Wesley, 1995.

Nelson, M. *Strong Women Stay Young*. New York: Bantam Books, 1998.

Women's Lives

Fields, J. *A Life of One's Own*. New York: Putnam Books, 1981.

Gordon, B. *I'm Dancing as Fast as I Can: The Classic Personal Story of Overcoming a Drug-Induced Breakdown*. New York: HarperCollins, 1989.

Johnson, P. *Profiles Encourage: Conversations with 20 Women*. Austin, Tex.: Edward-William Publishing Co, 1988.

Kingston, M. *The Woman Warrior*. New York: Random House, 1989.

Koller, A. *An Unknown Woman*. New York: Bantam Books, 1991.

Liebow, E. *Tell Them Who I Am: The Lives of Homeless Women*. New York: Penguin Books, 1993.

Macdonald, B., with C. Rich. *Look Me in the Eye Old Women: Aging and Ageism*. Minneapolis, Minn.: Spinster Ink, 1983.

Marks, M., ed. *Nice Jewish Girls Growing up in America: Stories, Poems and Memoirs*. New York: Penguin Books, 1996.

Martz, S. *At Our Core: Women Writing about Power*. Watsonville, Calif.: Papier-Mache Press, 1998.

McEwen, C., ed. *Jo's Girls: Tomboy Tales of High Adventure, True Grit, and Real Life*. Boston: Beacon Press, 1997.

Miedzian, M., and A. Malinovich. *Generations: A Century of Women Speak about Their Lives*. New York: Bantam Doubleday Dell, 1997.

Miller, D. *Independent Women Creating Our Lives, Living Our Visions*. Berkeley, Calif.: Wildcat Canyon Press, 1998.

Underhill, D. *Every Woman Has a Story: Many Voices, Many Lessons, Many Lives*. New York: Warner Books, 1998.

More New Harbinger Self-Help Titles

I CAN'T GET OVER IT

The second edition of Dr. Matsakis' groundbreaking work guides readers through the healing process of recovering from PTSD one step at a time.

Item OVER Paperback $16.95

THE SCARRED SOUL

The first book written for the victims of self-inflicted violence helps readers explore the reasons behind the impulse to hurt themselves and take steps to overcome the psychological traps that lead to self-inflicted pain.

Item SOUL Paperback, $15.95

SURVIVOR GUILT
A Self-Help Guide

This breakthrough book helps counsel survivors to come to term with feelings of guilt and cope with how they affect their personal functioning and relationships.

Item SG Paperback, $14.95

WHEN ANGER HURTS

A complete guide to changing habitual anger-generating thoughts while developing healthier, more effective ways of getting your needs met.

Item ANG Paperback, $16.95

CHOOSING TO LIVE

A step-by-step program for those who are considering suicide helps readers replace negative beliefs, feel better through coping, and develop alternative problem-solving skills.

Item CHO Paperback, $19.95

Call **toll-free 1-800-748-6273** to order. Have your Visa or Mastercard number ready. Or send a check for the titles you want to New Harbinger Publications, 5674 Shattuck Avenue, Oakland, CA 94609. Include $4.50 for the first book and 754 for each additional book to cover shipping and handling. (California residents please include appropriate sales tax.) Allow four to six weeks for delivery.

Prices subject to change without notice.

Some Other
New Harbinger Titles

Your Surviving Spirit, Item 3570 $18.95

Coping with Anxiety, Item 3201 $10.95

The Agoraphobia Workbook, Item 3236 $19.95

Loving the Self-Absorbed, Item 3546 $14.95

Transforming Anger, Item 352X $10.95

Don't Let Your Emotions Run Your Life, Item 3090 $17.95

Why Can't I Ever Be Good Enough, Item 3147 $13.95

Your Depression Map, Item 3007 $19.95

Successful Problem Solving, Item 3023 $17.95

Working with the Self-Absorbed, Item 2922 $14.95

The Procrastination Workbook, Item 2957 $17.95

Coping with Uncertainty, Item 2965 $11.95

The BDD Workbook, Item 2930 $18.95

You, Your Relationship, and Your ADD, Item 299X $17.95

The Stop Walking on Eggshells Workbook, Item 2760 $18.95

Conquer Your Critical Inner Voice, Item 2876 $15.95

The PTSD Workbook, Item 2825 $17.95

Hypnotize Yourself Out of Pain Now!, Item 2809 $14.95

The Depression Workbook, 2nd edition, Item 268X $19.95

Beating the Senior Blues, Item 2728 $17.95

Shared Confinement, Item 2663 $15.95

Handbook of Clinical Psychopharmacology for Therpists, 3rd edition, Item 2698 $55.95

Getting Your Life Back Together When You Have Schizophrenia, Item 2736 $14.95

Do-It-Yourself Eye Movement Technique for Emotional Healing, Item 2566 $13.95

Stop the Anger Now, Item 2574 $17.95

The Self-Esteem Workbook, Item 2523 $18.95

The Habit Change Workbook, Item 2639 $19.95

The Memory Workbook, Item 2582 $18.95

Call **toll free, 1-800-748-6273,** or log on to our online bookstore at **www.newharbinger.com** to order. Have your Visa or Mastercard number ready. Or send a check for the titles you want to New Harbinger Publications, Inc., 5674 Shattuck Ave., Oakland, CA 94609. Include $4.50 for the first book and 75¢ for each additional book, to cover shipping and handling. (California residents please include appropriate sales tax.) Allow two to five weeks for delivery.

Prices subject to change without notice.